Paths toward Democracy

*The Working Class and Elites
in Western Europe and South America*

The question of whether democratic institutions are introduced through an elite-led strategy from above or a popular triumph from below continues to be a matter of scholarly contention. Examining the experiences of countries that have provided the main empirical base for recent theorizing, namely, Western Europe and South America in the nineteenth and early twentieth centuries and again in the 1970s and 1980s, this book delineates a more complex and varied set of patterns, which for both periods integrates class and political-strategic perspectives. Professor Collier explores the politics of democratization through a comparative analysis of twenty-one countries, examining the role of labor in relation to elite strategies and challenging conventional understandings of both contemporary and historical periods. The analysis recaptures a neglected role for unions and labor-based parties in most recent cases, and for both historical periods it suggests an institutional explanation of labor's role, focused on the way actors' resources and strategies were shaped by prior experiences with democratic regimes and the immediately antecedent, pre-reform regime.

Ruth Berins Collier is Professor of Political Science at the University of California, Berkeley. Professor Collier is the author of *Regimes in Tropical Africa: Changing Forms of Supremacy, 1945–1975* (University of California Press, 1982) and *The Contradictory Alliance: State-Labor Relations and Regime Change in Mexico* (International and Area Studies, University of California, 1992), which was awarded the Hubert Herring Prize of the Pacific Coast Council on Latin American Studies. Professor Collier is also coauthor of *Shaping the Political Arena: Critical Junctures, the Labor Movement, and Regime Dynamics in Latin America* (Princeton University Press, 1991), which in 1993 was awarded the prize for Best Book by the Comparative Politics Section of the American Political Science Association.

D0061330

CAMBRIDGE STUDIES IN COMPARATIVE POLITICS

General Editor
PETER LANGE   Duke University

Associate Editors
ROBERT H. BATES   Harvard University
ELLEN COMISSO   University of California, San Diego
PETER HALL   Harvard University
JOEL S. MIGDAL   University of Washington
HELEN MILNER   Columbia University
RONALD ROGOWSKI   University of California, Los Angeles
SIDNEY TARROW   Cornell University

OTHER BOOKS IN THE SERIES
Carles Boix, *Political Parties, Growth and Equality: Conservative and Social Democratic Economic Strategies in the World Economy*
Catherine Boone, *Merchant Capital and the Roots of State Power in Senegal, 1930–1985*
Michael Bratton and Nicolas Van De Walle, *Democratic Experiments in Africa: Regime Transitions in Comparative Perspective*
Valerie Bunce, *Leaving Socialism and Leaving the State: The End of Yugoslavia, the Soviet Union, and Czechoslovakia*
Donatella Della Porta, *Social Movements, Political Violence, and the State*
Gerald Easter, *Reconstructing the State: Personal Networks and Elite Identity*
Roberto Franzosi, *The Puzzle of Strikes: Class and State Strategies in Postwar Italy*
Geoffrey Garrett, *Partisan Politics in the Global Economy*
Miriam Golden, *Heroic Defeats: The Politics of Job Loss*
Frances Hagopian, *Traditional Politics and Regime Change in Brazil*
J. Rogers Hollingsworth and Robert Boyer, eds., *Contemporary Capitalism: The Embeddedness of Institutions*
Ellen Immergut, *Health Politics: Interests and Institutions in Western Europe*
Torben Iversen, *Contested Economic Institutions*
Thomas Janoski and Alexander M. Hicks, eds., *The Comparative Political Economy of the Welfare State*
Robert O. Keohane and Helen B. Milner, eds., *Internationalization and Domestic Politics*
Herbert Kitschelt, *The Transformation of European Social Democracy*
Herbert Kitschelt, Peter Lange, Gary Marks, and John D. Stephens, eds., *Continuity and Change in Contemporary Capitalism*

Series list continues on the page following the Index.

PATHS TOWARD DEMOCRACY

*The Working Class and Elites in
Western Europe and South America*

RUTH BERINS COLLIER
University of California, Berkeley

PUBLISHED BY THE PRESS SYNDICATE OF THE UNIVERSITY OF CAMBRIDGE
The Pitt Building, Trumpington Street, Cambridge, United Kingdom

CAMBRIDGE UNIVERSITY PRESS
The Edinburgh Building, Cambridge CB2 2RU, UK   http://www.cup.cam.ac.uk
40 West 20th Street, New York, NY 10011-4211, USA   http://www.cup.org
10 Stamford Road, Oakleigh, Melbourne 3166, Australia
Ruiz de Alarcón 13, 28014 Madrid, Spain

© Ruth Berins Collier 1999

This book is in copyright. Subject to statutory exception
and to the provisions of relevant collective licensing agreements,
no reproduction of any part may take place without
the written permission of Cambridge University Press.

First published 1999

Printed in the United States of America

Typeface Garamond no. 3, 11/13 pt.   *System* Penta [BV]

A catalog record for this book is available from the British Library.

Library of Congress Cataloging in Publication data
Collier, Ruth Berins.
Paths toward democracy : the working class and elites in Western
Europe and South America / Ruth Berins Collier.
p.   cm. – (Cambridge studies in comparative politics)
Includes bibliographical references.
ISBN 0-521-64369-4 hb. – ISBN 0-521-64382-1 pb
1. Democracy – Europe, Western.   2. Elite (Social sciences) –
Europe, Western – Political activity.   3. Working class – Europe,
Western – Political activity.   4. Democracy – South America.   5. Elite
(Social sciences) – Political activity.   6. Working
class – South America – Political activity.   I. Title.   II. Series.
JN94.A91C62   1999
320.9182'1 – dc21   99 – 12564
                                                              CIP

ISBN 0 521 64369 4 hardback
ISBN 0 521 64382 1 paperback

To my mother,

Esther Meyers Berins,

for her sustaining love, her generous spirit,
and the music which has so enriched my life

CONTENTS

FIGURES AND TABLES

FIGURES

TABLES

ACKNOWLEDGMENTS

I want to express my appreciation to many people who have contributed to and supported this research. First and foremost, I benefited from the talents, energy, and intelligence of a number of graduate students who were research assistants on this project. James Mahoney's contribution in the early phases was such that he became the coauthor of a working paper, which was the first written product of this research, as well as a subsequent article, "Adding Collective Actors to Collective Outcomes: Labor and Recent Democratization in South America and Southern Europe," *Comparative Politics* 23 (spring 1997). When Jim left to embark on his dissertation research, I was fortunate to have the skillful assistance of Pierre Ostiguy, Jeffrey Sluyter-Beltrão, and Craig Parsons. I am also grateful for the valuable help provided by Benjamin Goldfrank and Susan Grubb as well as the contributions of Benjamin Lazier, Michael Pretes, Gregory Greenway, Marta Assumpção-Rodríguez, Stalbek Mishakov, Nikiforos Biziouras, Marcus Kurtz, and Carol Medlin.

In taking on so many country cases, I relied on the willingness of a number of specialists with country expertise to vet the individual case analyses. In this regard I am grateful to colleagues and friends on whom I imposed the relevant sections of the manuscript: Alan Angell, Nancy Bermeo, Maxwell Cameron, Michael Coppedge, Nikiforos Diamandouros, James Dunkerley, Gerald Feldman, Robert Fishman, Joel Horowitz, Gabriela Ippólito, Jonah Levy, Arendt Lijphart, Scott Mainwaring, Guillermo O'Donnell, Susan Pedersen, Maria Helena de Castro Santos, Seraphim Seferiades, and Laurence Whitehead. Andrew Gould was particularly generous in his willingness to guide me through the analysis of Switzerland.

Others read the entire manuscript and provided valuable feedback: Giuseppi Di Palma, Paul Drake, Thomas Ertman, Sergio Fabrini, Evelyne Huber, Robert Kaufman, Leonardo Morlino, Peter Lange, Jesper Sigurdsson, and Sidney Tarrow, as well as Gerardo Munck, who had the graciousness and collegiality to respond to a request for a second reading of parts of the manuscript on a moment's notice.

I also want to acknowledge the indispensable contributions of Sally Roever, who produced the computer graphics for the cubes, and Jennifer Robin Collier, who assisted throughout the publication process. Robert Fishman supplied the cover photo of the Spanish worker demonstration, which he acquired from the CCOO archive in Barcelona. The other picture, *Den grundlovgivende Rigsforsamling, 1848–49*, painted by Constantin Hansen, depicts the Constitutional Assembly in Denmark. It is used with the permission of Det Nationalhistoriske Museum på Frederiksborg, Hillerød, Denmark. I am grateful to Jesper Sigurdsson for his help in leading me to it.

I was fortunate in having the financial support and remarkable institutional support of the Center for Advanced Studies in the Behavioral Sciences and the Kellogg Institute at Notre Dame University. Both provided ideal settings for concentrated research and writing. While I was a Fellow at the Center for Advanced Studies, financial support was provided by National Science Foundation Grant no. SBR-9022192. At Berkeley, the Institute of Industrial Relations has greatly facilitated my work with financial and institutional support. The University of California Center for German and European Studies also provided assistance, and publication was assisted by the Abigail Reynolds Hodgen Publication Fund.

Given the stages Jennifer Robin and Stephen have reached in their lives, I no longer feel obliged to ask forgiveness for the way my research imposes on them. However I want to express my continual appreciation of the way they enrich my life with their warmth, humor, and support, their wide-ranging interests, and their intellectual liveliness. David, on the other hand, continues to bear the brunt of my research and writing activities, as he also continues to provide emotional and intellectual support. He is truly remarkable in his cheerful willingness to drag draft chapters to Yosemite. Oh, that my gratitude for his feedback were expressed as enthusiastically! Finally, I thank my mother, Esther Meyers Berins, to whom this book is dedicated.

INTRODUCTION: ELITE CONQUEST OR WORKING-CLASS TRIUMPH?

The role of the working class in democracy and democratization is a classic and contested question. Earlier formulations centered around the historical experiences of the nineteenth century and the opening years of the twentieth, particularly in Western Europe. With the renewed interest in democracy stimulated by the "new" democracies of the 1970s and 1980s, this question has been revived in more recent literature and has become contested once again. This book revisits the working-class role in democratization on the basis of a comparative analysis of these historical and contemporary episodes of democratization in Western Europe and South America.

The question of the working-class role in democratization is part of a long-standing debate concerning liberal democracy, understood as a particular set of institutions. Is a democratic regime a result of a victory from below, in which subordinate or excluded groups wrest power from a reluctant elite, or a conquest from above, in which those in power or rising economic groups not holding power pursue their own political agendas and seek to strengthen their political positions? That question is closely related to another concerning the nature of liberal democracy: what is the relationship between liberal democracy and authentic rule by the people, or popular sovereignty, however that may be understood. In the Marxist tradition, of course, the issue was framed in class terms, and the debate centered around democracy as either a mechanism of capitalist rule or a triumph of the working class. As other traditions have emphasized, the working class is not the only subordinate class, politically excluded group, or mass actor that has fought for democracy. Nevertheless, the preponderance of theorizing about democratic pressures from below has focused on the working class.

The emergence of mass democracy as a type of broadly inclusionary, electoral regime based on mass participation often coincided historically with industrialization, the formation of a proletariat, and its organization into parties and unions on a national level. In this context, the historical cases quite naturally drew attention to the possibility that democracy emerged as a concession extracted by working-class pressure. Recent regime change also raises the question of the relationship between the working class and democratization. In southern Europe and South America, the outgoing authoritarian regimes had typically been founded as anti-labor forms of government that organized labor would have a particular reason to oppose. On the other hand, the current "wave" of democratization broadly coincides with another major macrosocial change occurring at the end of the twentieth century, the global reorganization of capital, which has put organized labor on the defensive. If earlier democratization corresponded to the emergence of the working class and a new labor movement organized at the national level as a political and sectoral actor, economic forces of internationalization and marketization at the time of the recent round of democratization have produced pressures for the fragmentation of the working class and the weakening and disarticulation of its organization at a national level. Should these democracies be understood not so much as a popular victory but rather as a product of the strategies of certain elite groups? Indeed, elite strategies have been at the core of the most influential analytical framework concerning late twentieth-century transitions. Is the recent process of democratization in this sense substantially different from that in the second half of the nineteenth century and the beginning of the twentieth century, a period of democratization often analyzed in terms of the demands of the working class?

The focus of the present inquiry is the role of the working class in the process of democratization. What is being undertaken is not an overall conceptualization of the democratization process or even an effort to determine with any precision the relative weight of labor organizations compared with the panoply of other groups and actors. Rather, the objective is a more specific and limited inquiry into the role of the working class, as well as the interaction between working-class pressure and elite choice. In this way, the present study evaluates the two perspectives that have framed the debate about democratization – one focused on class analysis and the other on elite strategies – through a comparative analysis of Western European and South American countries, which have been the main empirical base for theorizing on democratization. Specifically, it analyzes the experiences of seventeen historical cases and ten contemporary cases and seeks to move beyond these alternative frameworks toward a more integrated framework that combines class, political inclusion, and arena of action.

These questions about democratization have a substantial intellectual pedigree and have been contested within both Marxist and non-Marxist traditions. The Marxist debate hinged around not only the empirical question but also the prescriptive one – that is, around whether the working class should fight for democracy. The position taken was related to the assessment of how a democracy functioned. The term "bourgeois democracy" expresses one side of the issue, referring to the notion that liberal democracy, which has emerged in capitalist market economies, necessarily involves the rule of capital, whether it be through an instrumentalist, structuralist, or Gramscian logic or through the atomization and embourgoisement of working-class organizations – parties and unions – as they participated in electoral politics. The idea stems perhaps most strongly from Lenin, who suggested that democracy was the "best possible political shell" for bourgeois rule.[1] Other Marxists and many post-Marxists have seen liberal democracy as "indeterminate" (Jessop 1980) with respect to its class orientation. For them, liberal democracy could be used to advance working-class interests – it could have sufficient representative potential to allow the many to use the vote against capitalism or at least to protect themselves through public policy.[2] Such an assessment has been the basis for the view that workers should be active participants in the fight for democracy.

Among non-Marxists pluralists have emphasized the demands articulated by societal groups and have been inclined toward the assumption that the extension of democracy represents a victory of the outs, of those making a new claim on power. Other scholars have interpreted the electoral inclusion of the lower classes as part of an elite strategy for other ends, such as state building or political entrepreneurship.[3] For example, as Rokkan observed for Western Europe, "The decision to extend the vote was not uniformly a response to pressures from below; it was as often the result of contests for influence at the top and of deliberate moves to broaden bases for an integrated national power structure." Rokkan (1970:31) went

---

1 See the discussion in Jessop 1978.
2 See the contributions in Hunt 1980 and Bobbio 1984.
3 This argument is often made with respect to the extension of the suffrage rather than democratization. The two should not be confused, since two of the important cases for some of these analysts are the manhood suffrage reforms of Bismarck and Napoleon III, hardly a democratic context.

on to note that elites often held the "belief that the entry of the working class into the electorate would strengthen the unity and stability of the nation-state." Bendix (1964:97) suggested that in Europe it was often conservatives who advocated an extension of the franchise, while liberals opposed it: "[L]iberals favored the *régime censitaire* and feared the possibilities of electoral manipulation inherent in the extension of the suffrage to the economically dependent. Conservatives, once they recognized the importance of the vote as a basis of local power, tended to favor the enfranchisement of the 'lower orders.' " Finally, E. E. Schattschneider (1942:48) made a similar argument for the United States, suggesting that important expansions in the electorate occurred when a political party sought support from the masses, rather than as a response to demands from below.

More recently, questions of democracy and who brings it about have again become a major focus of concern. Implicitly or explicitly, the question of the working-class role has reappeared as an axis of contention in the literature. While few perhaps would argue that the working class plays no part, there is substantial disagreement over its importance. Some analysts understand the working class as the most important democratic force and believe that its role is of fundamental importance to the emergence of democratic regimes. For these scholars, understanding the relative strength and organization of the working class is crucial for explaining how democratic regimes are established.[4] Others argue that processes of democratization are best analyzed in terms of political behavior at the elite level, as the outcome of strategic choices made by political elites, thereby at least implicitly relegating the role of the working class to one of minor importance.[5]

CONTRASTING IMAGES OF DEMOCRATIZATION

Two recent approaches have framed current analyses of democratization and in substantial measure have run parallel to the debate about democratization as a process from above or from below. The two perspectives come from distinct analytic traditions. The first is a strategic interaction approach, focusing on the negotiating or bargaining role of leaders or elites.

---

4 The strongest statement of this position is found in Rueschemeyer, Stephens, and Stephens 1992. Similar viewpoints are presented in de Schweinitz 1964 and Therborn 1977.

5 This position is associated most commonly with O'Donnell and Schmitter 1986. The comparative-theoretical statements and chapters contained in following works also deemphasize the role of the working class and tend to stress elite choice: Malloy and Seligson 1987; Baloyra 1987; Di Palma 1990; and Higley and Gunther 1992.

The second continues a long line of class analysis that has its roots not only in Marxist analysis but also in historical sociology.

Much of the literature on recent democratization emphasizes elite strategic choice, downplaying or ignoring the role of labor in democratization. The "transitions literature," as this current work has come to be known, has as its best representative the founding essay by O'Donnell and Schmitter (1986), which established a framework that is implicitly or explicitly followed in most other contributions. Without denying differences and subtleties, one could say that certain emphases within O'Donnell and Schmitter's essay have been selected and elaborated by other authors so that it is possible to aggregate various contributions and in broad strokes map out a basic characterization and set of claims in this literature as a whole.

Aside from cases in which the authoritarian regime is said to suffer an internal collapse or breakdown, the transitions literature has tended to conceive of the democratization process in terms of three stages. The first stage is marked by an internal split among authoritarian incumbents, who divide into factions over questions of how to achieve legitimation and the general problem of how to consolidate or institutionalize the authoritarian regime.[6]

In a second step, a liberalization process is initiated by incumbents, occurring at the point when the relevant faction proposing such a solution to the legitimatization-consolidation problem gains the upper hand. While this liberalization process is understood as a loosening or partial lifting of repression, and not an actual project for democracy, it puts the regime on a kind of slippery slope, starting a process that opens up some space for the opposition and for a dynamic that pushes political change further than the incumbents had originally intended. Liberalization is seen as presenting some opportunities for social movements to get (re)activated. Though the labor movement has certain special advantages, it is seen as only one of many nonelite actors that may engage in protest at this time, and one that arrives fairly late on the scene. Mass protest by the working class or other popular groups in the transition process is typically seen as a relatively brief phase, quickly superseded by the next step.

This final stage is the elite strategic game in which authoritarian incumbents "negotiate" or "bargain" formally or informally with moderate

6 O'Donnell and Schmitter (1986:19–20) recognize that in some cases this "initial" split among authoritarian incumbents may be a reaction to opposition protest. Yet they treat this opposition as prior to the sequence of events they define as initiating the transition, and hence as exogenous to their model and excluded from their analysis. This is an important point of contrast with the present analysis.

opposition party leaders. In this game of interacting strategies, mass action (including labor protest) is generally considered insofar as it affects the political resources and strategies of the individual leaders who actually play the elite bargaining game. Specifically, demonstrations may strengthen the hand of opposition moderates by signaling that the cost of retreating from a broadening reform trajectory may be substantial and even unacceptable repression. Alternatively these demonstrations may signal to hard-line incumbents that the limited process of liberalization within the context of strengthening the authoritarian regime is getting out of control and they had better crack down again. The emphasis from this perspective is thus on the process by which soft-line incumbents and moderate opposition party leaders reach some implicit or explicit agreement on a transition from an authoritarian to a democratic regime. To a substantial extent, this is a model of democratization in which collective actors, mass mobilization, and protest are largely exogenous.

At the risk of caricature, three related points about the transitions literature can be made. First, born under a normative imperative of possibilism and an escape from what seemed like an overdetermined structuralism that had pessimistic implications for democracy, this literature has often emphasized the role of leadership and crafting, thus signaling the importance of individuals, rather than collective actors. Departing from arguments about social requisites or economic determinants that had earlier dominated theorizing about regime outcomes, the new perspective had a different focus. How can actors make choices to establish a democratic regime? Under what impetus will authoritarian leaders within the state move in a pro-democratic direction? And how can opposition leaders strategize to encourage them to do so?

Articulating a perspective that has been generally accepted, O'Donnell and Schmitter (1986:3–5) argue that transitions are periods of high indeterminacy, characterized by the distinctive importance of individual choice and leadership talent. In their view, "elite dispositions, calculations, and pacts . . . largely determine whether or not an opening will occur at all," and "the catalyst" for any ensuing social mobilization "comes first from gestures by exemplary individuals, who begin testing the boundaries of behavior initially imposed by the incumbent regime" (O'Donnell and Schmitter 1986:48–49). The essay by Giuseppe Di Palma (1990:8) likewise argues that "democratization is ultimately a matter of political crafting," and urges scholars to focus on the role of "innovative political actions." In another volume focused on elites and democracy, Burton, Gunther, and Higley (1992a:342) write that "in the final analysis . . . a central conclusion of these studies is the great responsibility of national elites for achieving, or failing to achieve, the degree of consensus and unity necessary for the establishment and consolidation of democracy."

A second point about the transitions literature is that actors tend to be defined strategically with respect to the position they adopt in the "transition game," thus sidelining questions about class-defined actors. With this strategic understanding of actors, the categories of analysis have changed. Whereas democratization in the historical period has typically been analyzed in terms of class-based actors, in analyses of the 1970s and 1980s the categories of upper class and lower class, or bourgeoisie and working class, have tended to be replaced by the categories of incumbents and opposition, hard-liners and soft-liners, maximalists and moderates.

Third, despite an emphasis on formal or informal "negotiations" between government and opposition, the transitions literature has at the same time tended to be state-centric, subordinating societal actors. The privileged role of state actors can be seen in the conceptualization of the transition as beginning with splits among the authoritarian incumbents. This "internalist" account (Fishman 1990b) emphasizes the deficiencies and problems that arise *ex natura* within authoritarian regimes. Divisions arise among incumbents of the state over solutions to problems inherent to authoritarianism.[7] This conceptualization makes questions about the origins of these divisions exogenous.

The state-centric leaning also appears in the typologies of "modes of transitions" found in the literature. Juan Linz's (1978:35) initial typology distinguished between transition by *reforma* and transition by *ruptura*. Transitions by *reforma* are initiated by incumbents and to one degree or another controlled by them. Subsequent typological modifications have distinguished the degree to which the rules of the authoritarian incumbents are followed or, conversely, the degree to which incumbents must "negotiate" the content of the transition.[8] Transitions by *ruptura* come

7 Such an internalist approach was usefully developed in earlier work of both O'Donnell (1979: see esp. 287ff.) and Schmitter (1975: see esp. 20–21) as they, respectively, analyzed authoritarianism in Latin America and Portugal and pointed to the lack of "mediations" in many of these authoritarian regimes and the contradictions related to the forms in which state power is organized and transferred in authoritarian regimes.
8 See, respectively, Valenzuela 1992, and Share and Mainwaring 1986. Huntington (1991: 114) is one of the few who use a typology with a category that explicitly includes a role for the opposition that is nonresidual, making room for the possibility that the opposition may initiate the transition. Yet, interestingly he suggests that his typology is the same as that of Share and Mainwaring, failing to realize that his category of "transplacement" is definitionally more opposition-centered than any category of Share and Mainwaring. Karl (1990:8) more explicitly develops a typology that includes a role for mass actors. See also Karl and Schmitter 1991:275–76.

about when the authoritarian regime collapses. Although such transitions completely escape incumbent control, even this breakdown of the authoritarian regime has been seen in terms of a state-centric image of implosion (associated with coups and/or defeats in foreign wars) and rarely connected to societal mobilization or labor opposition.

The dominant framework used in theoretical and comparative accounts, then, has not only adopted an actor-based rather than a structural perspective, but it has tended to privilege certain kinds of actors: individual elites rather than *collective* actors, strategically defined actors rather than *class*-defined actors, and state actors more than *societal* actors. As a framework, it almost precludes the problematization of the role of working-class and mass action. Indeed, in most theoretical and comparative accounts, the working class and its organizations receive relatively little (if any) attention. O'Donnell and Schmitter (1986:52, 55) see the working class as one layer of a broad, multiclass upsurge that, during a delimited period, can exploit political openings, but only once they are initiated by authoritarian incumbents. They do suggest that at a particular point "the greatest challenge to the transitional regime is likely to come from the new or revived identities and capacity for collective action of the working class." However, subsequent comparative analyses and theoretical accounts have not picked up on or elaborated this original suggestion, and O'Donnell and Schmitter themselves emphasize the "ephemeral" nature of the "popular upsurge" and the subsequent "decline of the people."

Like all approaches, the transitions framework evolved around a specific set of substantive concerns and questions, for which it may have been an appropriate model. But the initial concern regarding how leaders can strategize to bring about democratic regimes hardly exhausts the questions one might want to ask about democratization, and the framework does not easily accommodate other questions. With respect to the current question, it obscures as much as it illuminates. In light of the longer tradition of approaches to democratization, it is interesting the extent to which subsequent comparative and theoretical statements continued to reflect this framework. When this framework became hegemonic, it became not just a framework for posing a particular question, but implicitly, at least, a kind of substantive assertion that sees democratization in terms of the dominant role of elite strategic action. The literature has tended to converge on a view of transitions as occurring either because the authoritarian regime collapses or as a result of the strategic interaction, sometimes even a more formal negotiation or bargain, between a soft-line faction among the authoritarian incumbents and moderate party leaders in the opposition. The latter are willing to come to some understanding with the authoritarians and engineer a transition to democracy on mutually acceptable terms – an understanding that, analysts often assert, involves compromising the interests of labor. The convergence on this account is rather perplexing in light of the fact that monographic accounts often could not tell the story of particular cases without substantial reference to the working class, or mass action or protest.

Within this transitions literature, J. Samuel Valenzuela (1989:449, 447, 450) presents one of the few broadly comparative analyses of the labor movement during recent democratization. He nicely summarizes the "special place" labor occupies "among the forces of civil society," such that it "should not be discussed simply on the same plane with other segments of society." The sources of its unique position particularly within an authoritarian context lie in its unusual capacity for mobilization, its existing organizational network, the commonality of interests and collective identity shared by members, and the relationship between labor demands and activity on the one hand and production and macroeconomic performance and policy on the other. Valenzuela's analysis, however, generally accepts the overall, largely state-centric framework of this larger literature, in which changes within the state (either a crisis or an incumbent decision to liberalize, if not actually democratize) create new opportunities for the labor movement to become activated. Further, if Valenzuela's analysis departs empirically from describing the labor role as an ephemeral upsurge, it prescriptively advocates this pattern as an "ideal mix" or sequence of well-timed mobilization followed by restraint as the path to a smoother and more successful democratic transition.

Interestingly, at early stages of the recent transitions, analysts were struck with the "resurrection of civil society," and events and developments in these countries have given rise to a substantial literature on social movements. Yet, in terms of systematic comparison or theoretical understanding of democratization, this literature has proposed little beyond the initial formulations. As Foweraker (1994:218–19) notes, though a newer literature focuses on popular movements, it

> still stops short of a systematic inquiry into the political principles of popular organization and strategic choice, and so fails to pursue the connections between popular politics and processes of institutional change within political regimes. . . . There is a "top-down" and a "bottom-up" approach, but "ne'er the twain do meet" because they do not explore and explain the linkages between popular political actors and the changing institutions. . . . Little is really known about the popular contribution to making democracy.

Furthermore, given the frequent attention to "new" social movements (and sometimes nongovernmental organizations, or NGOs), the labor movement is often excluded from these analyses. A more integrated approach to regime change and democratization, then, is still beginning to take shape, as in the work of Foweraker (1994) and Tarrow (1995).

In sharp contrast to analyses that see democratization as an outcome of elite bargaining, a second perspective has emphasized the importance of working-class pressures. This account has been associated with the work of Therborn (1977, 1979) and Rueschemeyer, Stephens, and Stephens (1992). Like the transitions literature, these analyses are primarily rooted in the empirical experiences of Western Europe and South America, though over a longer historical time span.[9]

Adopting a class account of democratization in the tradition of Barrington Moore, Rueschemeyer et al. reject his specific argument that associates democracy with the bourgeoisie and argue instead that the working class is the primary carrier of democracy, playing a decisive role in forging democratic regimes. Unlike the transitions approach, which presents an actor-based framework, these authors start from a more structural perspective, whose "core . . . is a 'relative class power' model of democratization" (1992:47). Nevertheless, actors inevitably become important, and at many points the argument emphasizes working-class agency in bringing about democratic change. They see the working class as the most consistent prodemocratic class, the landed classes as the most hostile to democracy, and the bourgeoisie or middle classes as inconsistent or ambiguous. Democracy is an outcome of the struggle between the dominant and subordinate classes and hence an outcome of the balance of class power. Democratization occurs when the democracy-demanding classes, above all the working class, are stronger than the democracy-resisting classes, who reject the demands and pressures of the former, though there is also room in this account for democratic initiatives by other classes as a co-optive response to a working-class threat.

This analysis has much in common with and in many ways reiterates the earlier assertion of Göran Therborn (1979:80), who stressed the "determinant influence of the working class," which "demand[s] democracy" from the bourgeoisie, which, in turn, "first resist[s] then decid[es] when and how to concede." Rueschemeyer et al. (1992:47) identify with Therborn in the way he "recovered this insight of Marx about the central role of the working class in the process of democratization." They thus argue that "the most consistently prodemocratic force" was the working class,

---

9 Though the regions that are the subject of analysis are roughly the same, the cases are not identical, only in part because of the different time horizons. Therborn and Rueschemeyer et al. also include the British settler colonies, Central America, and the Caribbean. On the other hand, Therborn does not include any of the recent cases, and Rueschemeyer et al. do not include the recent European cases.

which "pushed forward" and "fought for" democracy against the resistance of other class actors, often playing "a decisively prodemocratic role." "It was the subordinated classes that fought for democracy. . . . Fundamentally, democracy was achieved by those who were excluded from rule" (8, 46, 59). To the extent other classes were also excluded, they are seen as fighting only for their own inclusion and not for a more universalistic mass democracy – which ultimately depends on working-class demands.

On the one hand Rueschemeyer et al. draw quite sweeping conclusions about the nearly universal salience of the working-class role in democratization, arguing that "the organized working class appeared as a key actor in the development of full democracy almost everywhere . . . [and] in most cases organized workers played an important role in the development of restricted democracy as well" (Rueschemeyer et al. 1992:270). On the other hand, they argue that in Latin America, "compared to Europe the urban working class played less of a leading role as a prodemocratic force. . . . The driving force behind the initial establishment of democracy [in Latin America], then, was the middle class. . . . In a somewhat crude generalization we could say that in Europe the working class in most cases needed the middle classes as allies to be successful in its push for democracy, whereas in Latin America it was the other way round" (182, 185). Similarly, Therborn (1979:85) argues that "the democratic thrust of the labour movement in Latin America has in most cases been more indirect than in Western Europe."

In explaining these differences, Rueschemeyer et al. reject the tendency to read interests off of class position. Rather, they emphasize that class interests are historically constructed, with organizational and party factors playing "crucial role[s] as mediators" (1992:7, 9). Further, their explanation rests on a model of power that has three components: not only the balance of power among different classes, but also the autonomous power of the state (and hence the nature of state-society relations) and transnational power relations. In this way, they move analytically in an extraordinarily broad multivariate space. Nevertheless, the thrust of the argument is to advance the working-class account and to use these other factors in more ad hoc fashion in order to accommodate exceptions to or "modify" (63) their primary model of class balance and their assertion about the centrality of the working class.

These two analytic frameworks, a class approach and an elite-choice approach, present two quite different images. The first sees democratization primarily as a product of the pressure and demands of excluded groups and of subordinate classes; the second, as the outcome of the strategic interactions of those in power and elites in the democratic opposition. The one sees democratization as a popular, especially working-class, triumph, often extracted through mass mobilization and protest; the other, as an outcome of negotiating leaders, whose relative resources may be affected by labor mobilization. We have, on the one hand, the proposition that the working class was the primary carrier of democracy, playing a decisive role in its achievement; and, on the other hand, the proposition that it was at most a marginal or secondary actor in the process of democratization, which is better seen in terms of elite strategies and intraelite negotiations.

The contrasting accounts of democratization derive from analyses of both Western Europe and Latin America. Yet, the two distinct images of democratization partly correspond to different historical epochs and to different antecedent regimes. Thus, these competing understandings of the role of the working class in democratization are to some degree grounded in different empirical and historical realities. In general, the hypothesis concerning elite strategies and intraelite political bargaining, which downplays the working-class role, has been a prominent feature of studies that focus on the recent transitions in Latin America and Europe in the 1970s and 1980s. By contrast, analyses that emphasize the importance of the working class have focused attention on earlier episodes of democratization. Therborn, who wrote before the later transitions, necessarily focuses on earlier time periods. Rueschemeyer et al. make the strongest case for an important working-class role for the nineteenth- and early twentieth-century democratic transitions in Europe. They do not include the recent European cases of the 1970s and devote only three pages to Latin American transitions in this latest period, in an analysis that largely accepts the dominant account of the "transitions literature," modifying it in only a couple of cases.

This difference in the strongest empirical base of the two types of arguments suggests the hypothesis that the working class played a key role in earlier democratization, whereas it played a marginal role in the current episodes. Historical period is correlated with different antecedent regimes and distinct processes of democratization. These contrasting experiences across the two periods make it seem plausible that the historical cases may be closer to working-class triumphs while the recent cases may be more like elite affairs. The earlier democratizations are typically seen as gradual processes, with different "components" of a democratic regime instituted incrementally; the "final" step in the process is frequently the introduction of full or mass suffrage, the last missing component of a democratic regime. Thus, early processes of democratization have often been seen as a move from a restricted democracy to a full one; they represent the politics of incremental inclusion – the achievement of political rights stepwise down the social hierarchy. To the extent that the other components of a democratic regime were already in place, to inquire about the role of the working class in these cases of democratization is to ask about the role of the working class in obtaining its own political inclusion.

Indeed, Rueschemeyer et al. suggest such a process in presenting an image in which each class fights for its own inclusion, but not that of classes "below" or those that come after. In their analysis of Europe they emphasize what they call the "final push" for democracy, which they identify as manhood suffrage. The picture they paint is one in which the bourgeoisie fought for a restricted democracy that would stop short of mass enfranchisement, and they align themselves with Marx in "consider[ing] the achievement of universal suffrage the historical task of the working class" (Rueschemeyer et al. 1992:47). To a substantial extent, then, and with some obvious exceptions, the final step in the historical processes of democratization is typically thought of in terms of enfranchisement of the working class itself, so that it looks like a class process and even a particularistic benefit to the working class.

The process of democratization in the 1970s and 1980s was quite different in this respect. These were processes of *re*democratization. In most of the earlier cases, the principle of democratic rule was first being established in connection with institutional innovation and experimentation. In the later cases, the principle of democracy, along with universal suffrage as a sine qua non, had long since been established and the repertoire of democratic institutions was quite clear (though some democratic *restrictions* were still being invented).[10] Furthermore, in these cases, the antecedent regimes were not restricted democracies but outright authoritarian regimes or autocracies. With virtually all the components of a democratic regime lacking, democratization and the recovery of political rights affected virtually all groups in civil society, including rival elites and opposition party leaders. Hence, later democratization did not single out the working class as a beneficiary and looks less like a class-based process.

To these political distinctions between the historical and recent cases, we can add a socio-economic distinction. In the earlier period, workers constituted an emerging, rapidly growing class, organizing in parties and unions and fighting for basic rights in the context of a newly developing industrial society particularly in the advanced capitalist societies, the pri-

10 The emergence of an international consensus on democratic institutions is discussed by Markoff (1995).

mary locus of most early democratization. In the later period in the 1970s and 1980s, the working class was decidedly on the defensive in the face of economic recession, the uncertainty of the oil shocks, the debt crisis, and the reorganization of production at the firm, national, and global levels. By the 1970s, the age of national industrialism, with its material and political base for class compromise, was drawing to a close. The "post-industrial," socio-technological revolution, and global reorganization of capital brought a relative decline in the size of the working class, put unions on the defensive, and presented challenges to working-class parties and to the political clout of workers, particularly in middle-income countries, which were the locus of late twentieth-century democratization.

It thus makes some sense to hypothesize that the working class played a key role in earlier democratization, whereas it played a marginal role in the current episodes. This is, in a sense, the received wisdom, which this book critically explores. It will suggest that the role of the working class has generally been overstated and misspecified for the historical cases and underemphasized in the contemporary cases. In understanding the participation of the working class in democratization, it argues that the type of antecedent regime is indeed important, but in ways not anticipated on the basis of the literature. The analysis reveals the way the prior regime can affect the resources and perceived interests of different actors and therefore their choice to pursue the goal of democratic reform.

IDENTIFYING THE ACTORS

The issue of democratization from above or from below is here treated in terms of which actors had explicit democratic agendas and played a central role in achieving democratic reform. It is an agential question about the goals and effectiveness of actors concerned with the installation of democratic institutions. The present analysis distinguishes patterns of democratization according to which actors pushed for regime change or democratic reform and furthermore were effective or consequential in the politics of democratization. As indicated earlier, the analysis focuses specifically on the role in democratization of the working class and that of elites.

THE WORKING CLASS AND DEMOCRATIZATION

In this analysis, what is meant by "the role of the working class" in democratization? There are two elements here: the working class and the role. As the very term suggests, "working class," or "labor," is a collective concept and is not equivalent to an aggregation of workers. What is at stake is not participation by atomized individual workers, but rather action in which some sense of solidarity or identity and collective purpose must be involved. This notion of class solidarity or identity can take the form of a common construction of meaning in the participatory act, as in the understanding of democratization as a workers' issue, as a benefit to workers as a collectivity. Usually (but not always) it is expressed organizationally. Hence, in *most* cases we are talking about the organized working class and pro-democratic action led or undertaken by *unions* and labor-affiliated or *labor-based parties*.

Since the organized working class is numerically only a part of the working class, this point raises another: in analyzing the role of the working class I obviously do not require, nor do I want to imply, that all or even most workers must be involved – either actively or even in terms of lending assent. Just as most peasants or workers did not participate in the Chinese and Russian revolutions and yet analysts refer to these as peasants' and workers' revolutions respectively (and not because of their subsequent "pro-peasant" or "pro-worker" policies or claims), so in the present study it is hardly appropriate to insist that a working-class role in democratization requires the participation of some minimum percentage of the workers, who may be – and, in fact, often were – divided over the issue of democracy. Rather, the issue is whether a group of workers became part of the democratization process as a self-conscious collectivity and played an active role that affected the democratic outcome.

Another point about the conception of working class employed here is that it does not single out proletarian wage earners or factory workers as distinct from artisans. While it is certainly the case that in many ways artisans occupy an ambiguous class position, given the timing of democratization we typically encounter them in the following histories at a point when there is evidence of their collective identity as workers – at a point in the nineteenth or early twentieth century when, as Michael Mann (1993: 517) put it, they also "felt entrepreneurial pressure" and were being displaced by the rapid growth of factory production and the process of proletarianization. Recent scholarship has emphasized the way in which the transformation of labor processes in nineteenth-century industrialization created working-class consciousness not only among the rising group of proletarians and factory workers, who would confront employers, but also among declining artisans, who were retreating with the penetration of factory production. As Mann suggests, it may be artificial and inappropriate, for present purposes, to draw a fine distinction among different categories of workers (artisan, proletarian, factory worker), since the spread of entrepreneurial capitalism helped to forge a kind of class identity across very different labor processes and homogenized workers "in a distinctive, underappreciated way."[11] Indeed, the origins of working-class consciousness and worker protest can often be traced to the defensive reaction of artisans rather than the later mobilization of proletarians. As Sewell (1986: 52) suggested with reference to France, economic change transformed artisan production, reorganizing it and increasing the level of exploitation, so that artisans developed class consciousness and "had as much reason to protest as factory workers"; or, as Katznelson (1986:23) put it more generally, "artisans played the key role in developing a response to proletarianization." Thus, the present conception of working class includes workers on both sides of the transition from skilled artisan production to proletarianized wage labor, who, in response, developed collective identity and understanding. It also includes proletarianized agricultural workers but not peasants.

We come, then, to a consideration of what is meant by the working class playing a "role" in the democratic process. First of all, in attributing a role to the working class I am interested in those cases in which the working class (or the relevant part of it) took a *pro-democratic* position. I do not here include an "indirect" role in which the working class presented an apparent threat to the existing political or economic system that was met with a reform response by those in power. That is, for present purposes it is insufficient if labor protest centered around economic or workplace demands or nondemocratic revolutionary goals, which may have been seen as a threat to capitalism or destabilized authoritarianism by threatening the government's capacity to maintain order but did not constitute a demand for democracy. In such a situation democratization would be better analyzed in terms of an elite strategy to pursue a particular goal than a working-class strategy. In "scoring" the cases, then, the labor movement is considered to have contributed to democratization only if it engaged in activity that was pro-democratic, that is, if it had a democratic agenda.

This point merits some emphasis because it may diverge from some structural accounts of democratization. There is no question that the presence of a working class (especially a strong and organized one) may have altered the strategic calculations of many actors, posing challenges or even

11 Mann 1993:518–19. The important role of artisans in the early history of working-class protest is evident in many of the countries analyzed here. See, for example, Sewell 1986.

threats in a host of ways. As we shall see, working-class action may provoke co-optive or support mobilizational responses as well as repressive ones. But this, of course, is quite a different matter from asserting that the working class favors or acts to promote democracy. It is this latter issue that is of present concern.

Second, the present inquiry concerns a *consequential* role in democratic reform. That is, for the working class, or important parts of it, to have been pro-democratic is not sufficient. Rather the criterion concerns direct activity and participation in the events that constitute the democratization process. The distinction here is between two separate questions: was the working class pro-democratic, and did working-class action and agitation for democracy have an important effect in promoting or advancing episodes of democratic reform or the adoption of democratic institutions? The criterion, in other words, can be stated by asking the counterfactual question: would the democratization process have been quite different if the pro-democratic activities of the working class had not occurred? The focus is on the politics of regime change rather than on working-class activity per se: the issue is less whether the working class was pro-democratic than whether democratic reform was at least in part an outcome of pro-democratic labor action.

ELITES AND DEMOCRATIZATION

Although the central inquiry of this study concerns the working class, its role in the process of democratization is explored in juxtaposition to that of "elites." It is certainly possible, and no doubt relevant, to inquire about other actors, but this juxtaposition frames the present discussion, given the centrality of elite strategy in the current literature. The present analysis of the working class and elites in democratization sets up a number of polarities, which reflect different conceptions of "elite." In this regard, a three-way distinction may be made. One conception of elite is social and two are political.

The first is a class conception. It distinguishes the working class from classes "above" it in the social hierarchy. The elite strata may consist of the more traditional landed classes or the "middle classes" or "middle sectors" – a heterogeneous category of mostly urban social sectors (including bourgeois, professional, petit-bourgeois, managerial, and white-collar groups) spawned by the spread of industrialization, commercialization, and capitalist growth. Here the question becomes democratization as a product of working-class action, as opposed to the action of elite strata.

Second, the term elite may refer to those with political power, that is, to incumbents (including those participating in government but forming the opposition). In this sense, to ask about democratization as an elite strategy is to ask about the strategy of the "ins" or those already included by the regime, as opposed to the role of the "outs," or groups excluded by the rules of the regime, without political rights or accepted institutional avenues of participation.

A third conception of elite is again political and essentially refers to leaders. Much of the transitions literature emphasizes this notion of elite. In a more explicit but quite typical approach, Burton et al. (1992b:8) define elites as "persons who are able, by virtue of their strategic positions in powerful organizations, to affect national political outcomes regularly and substantially. Elites are the principal decision makers in the largest or most resource-rich . . . organizations and movements in a society." This conception of elite emphasizes the role of individuals more than mass protest or demonstrations. As in most of the transitions literature, their emphasis is on negotiation, bargaining, and "agreements that can be struck" (Burton et al. 1992b:10).

Although this conception theoretically includes union leaders (and perhaps even leaders of mass protest more generally), these are not the particular leaders generally singled out in the literature. Rather, the elites in these frameworks tend to overlap with the other two conceptions of elite. Thus, most accounts of the recent transitions focus particularly on two sets of leaders: the incumbents or the "ins," whose authoritarian projects were centrally anti-popular and especially anti-labor; and, among the "outs," the "moderate" party or political leaders in the opposition – not labor leaders but those willing precisely to reach agreements and give assurances about any potential working-class "threat," that is, assurances not only regarding amnesty to the military itself against human rights abuses but also regarding the protection of the original class-related goals of the regime. Although labor leaders are largely ignored in the theoretical literature, this leader conception of elite nevertheless invites an inquiry into the role of leaders of unions and of labor-affiliated parties not only in leading and coordinating mass protest but also in negotiating and reaching agreements.

The present analysis seeks to disentangle these various conceptions of elite. In doing so, it looks explicitly at the process of democratization in terms of the role of the working class as opposed to the middle and upper classes; those included as well as those excluded by the antecedent regime; and the negotiating role of leaders, including union leaders and leaders of labor-based parties as well as government incumbents and leaders of other parties.

DIMENSIONS AND PATTERNS OF DEMOCRATIZATION

In order to establish an alternative framework, this analysis focuses on three dimensions that follow from the foregoing. These dimensions are *class*, *prior inclusion*, and *arena of action*. Patterns of democratization are distinguished in terms of the role of actors located at the intersections of these dimensions.

Figure 1.1 gives an overview of these three dimensions. The first is social class, with the central concern for present purposes to distinguish the working class from elite strata, that is, from the more traditional upper classes as well the middle classes or sectors, which in analytic traditions of both Europe and South America are considered elite strata. The second dimension is inclusion or exclusion under the prior regime. It distinguishes

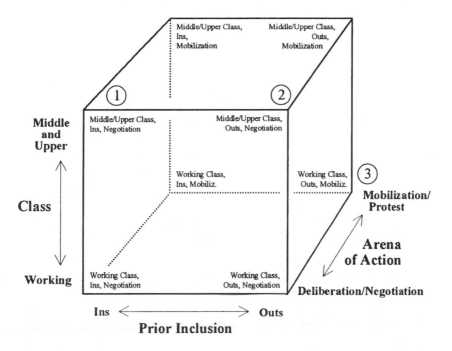

Figure 1.1. Dimensions of democratization: Class, inclusion, and arena of action

what we may refer to as the "ins" and the "outs." Finally, the third dimension concerns the arena of action. It distinguishes a mobilization/ protest arena of collective action from a deliberation/negotiation arena of authoritative decision making. The contrast is between, on the one hand, collective action, mobilization, or protest in the streets and, on the other hand, the activities of individual leaders, as they negotiate, legislate, and adopt policies or positions, in some face-to-face forum (e.g., legislature, meeting). The one arena employs expressive or coercive action, ranging from strikes to rebellions; the other, decisions, deliberation, and/or bargaining. This dimension, of course, differs from the others in that a given actor, identified in terms of its positions on *one* end of each of the other two dimensions, can potentially be located at *both* ends of this dimension. For example, leaders of mass protests may also act in the deliberation/ negotiation arena.

The contrasting images of democratization as a process from above or from below – as the outcome of elite strategies or working-class action – implicitly combine these dimensions. In stylized fashion and with some ambiguities and simplifications, one may suggest that these two images of democratization have tended to encompass the following constellations. The account from above emphasizes the role of leaders of the elite "ins" pursuing calculated strategies and often "bargaining" with pro-democratic reformists excluded from power, with both generally representing middle- and upper-class interests (corners 1 and 2 of Figure 1.1). The account from below emphasizes the role of the excluded lower classes engaging in mass action and protest to demand democracy and extract concessions (corner 3).

The following analysis demonstrates that neither of these images provides an adequate general description of the process of democratization. Nor is it appropriate to suggest that one fits the historical cases whereas the other adequately describes the later cases. The two approaches are complementary; each captures a meaningful aspect of the process of democratization. It is important to understand democratization in terms of both class and strategic perspectives – by the way it is "pushed forward by class interests" (Rueschemeyer et al. 1992:46) and also motivated by political strategies. In most cases the politics of democratization is a combination of processes from above and below, involving combinations of class interests, strategic actors, and forms, sites, or arenas of action.

The analysis, then, recovers a role for strategizing political leaders in the historical cases – including those cases in which the working-class role was most prominent. By the same token, the analysis recovers a role for the working class in the recent cases. This certainly is not to say that the working class single-handedly brought about democratic transitions or that other actors were not essential, but rather that the story should not be told without the working-class contribution, which is often neglected, especially in more comparative, theoretical accounts. Congruent with many country monographs where the point has not been missed, comparative theorizing about these transitions should include a more central place for working-class action.

Beyond that, however, the insights of the two approaches or frameworks of democratization should be combined and integrated in another way – not only in that most cases involve both working-class protest and elite strategic action or, as Markoff (1996) has suggested, a dialogue between reforming elite insiders or powerholders on the one hand and challenging, mass-based social movements in the opposition on the other. The degree to which the three dimensions of analysis appear in different constellations should also be recognized. That is, while these stylized images of democratization tend to locate the action at two or three corners of the cube in Figure 1.1, more corners in fact come into play. For instance, democratization should sometimes be understood in terms of the actions of excluded middle-class groups acting in the mobilization/protest arena; the working class could sometimes be counted among the "ins"; and leaders of labor organizations sometimes participated in negotiations.

The goal of comparative analysis is not necessarily to uncover a single generalization that encompasses all the cases under study. While there is certainly room for such generalizations where warranted, analysts should proceed as splitters as well as lumpers. A great deal of international diffusion is central to the process of democratization, so that democracies share a ("minimal") set of institutional traits to the point that it is indeed possible to talk of a relatively standardized set of features that constitute a democratic regime. Nevertheless, this institutional commonality does not mean that the process of institutional adoption proceeds according to the same pattern. As Rustow (1970:345) cautioned years ago, there are many roads to democracy, reflecting the outcome of a wide variety of social conflicts and political contexts. Different groups push for regime change or reform, often with quite different goals and motivations, and employing different arenas of action. The two epochs represent disparate patterns of democratization, and furthermore each embraces within it substantial variability. Within this diversity, however, distinct patterns can be discerned.

In analyzing cases of democratization, I delineate the various patterns as different constellations of the three dimensions – different combinations of corners in Figure 1.1. These patterns are laid out as analytical constructs, with many cases having elements of another pattern though predominantly fitting one. Chapter 2 presents the historical cases in which democratization occurred primarily as a result of the action or initiative of the middle and upper classes. Either the working class did not pursue democratization as a goal or democratic institutions were adopted prior to the emergence of a working class or any significant process of proletarianization. These cases indicate that working-class pressure is not necessary (no less sufficient) in either agential or structural terms. A strong working class is not necessary as a pro-democratic actor or as a threat that provokes a co-optive (democratizing) response. Rather, these cases are analyzed as two patterns – Middle-Sector Democratization and Electoral Support Mobilization – which represent different constellations of the dimensions under consideration but both of which involve the initiatives of middle and upper classes.

If working-class action does not always figure in, it does in most cases. Chapter 3 presents the Joint Projects pattern among the historical cases, which is analyzed in terms of the interacting strategies of both working-class organizations and parties with middle- and upper-class constituencies. Chapter 4 distinguishes four patterns of democratization among the recent cases, three of which involve the participation of labor unions and/or labor-based parties. In Destabilization/Extrication, Transition Game, and Parallel Tracks, labor unions and/or labor-based parties participated in the process in different ways and with varying impact. In the Interelite Game, the one recent pattern without labor participation, the military failed to win the support of the political right, and democratization proceeded largely in terms of the resulting conflict between those two groups.

Patterns of democratization with a labor component thus occur in both the historical and recent periods. Indeed, when these two sets of cases are considered in comparative perspective, it is difficult to say the labor role was more significant in one group as opposed to the other. In both sets of cases many class actors participated in the democratization process, and both protest and negotiation arenas came into play. In addition, both "ins" and "outs" were centrally involved; in the historical cases, however, the working class was more likely to be an "in" actor by the time it got involved, whereas in the recent cases it remained an excluded actor under the authoritarian regime. Yet both periods had cases in which labor organizations undertook a kind of dual militance, participating in negotiations, particularly through labor-based parties, and organizing mass protests, particularly through union activity.

The final chapter draws comparisons across the patterns in the different time periods. Seeking to go beyond economic and social structural explanations of the patterns, it suggests an institutional and path-dependent explanation of labor participation in democratization, one that views actors' strategies in the context of prior experience with democratic regimes and the type of antecedent regime.

Table 1.1. *Cases of democratization*

Historical		Recent	
Switzerland	1848	Greece	1974
Denmark	1849, 1915	Portugal	1976
France	1848, 1875–77	Spain	1977
Greece	1864	Ecuador	1979
Chile	1874/91	Peru	1980
Great Britain	1884, 1918	Bolivia	(1979, 1980),
Norway	1898		1982
Finland	(1906), 1919	Argentina	1983
Sweden	1907/9, 1918/20	Uruguay	1985
Portugal	1911, 1918	Brazil	1985
Argentina	1912	Chile	1990
Italy	1912, (1919)		
Netherlands	1917		
Belgium	1918		
Germany	1918–19		
Uruguay	1918		
Spain	1868, 1890, 1931		

IDENTIFYING EPISODES OF DEMOCRATIZATION

The unit of analysis in this study is the episode of democratic reform, with special emphasis on that specific transition which can be said to put a country across a threshold consistent with conceptualizing the political regime as democratic. Although I discuss earlier reforms that occurred prior to this transition, they are not given equal weight for two reasons. First, in some cases, especially in the 1970s and 1980s, they are more appropriately considered part of a single reform process. Where they are not, especially in the historical cases, one should not adopt a teleological position regarding these earlier episodes and the democratic trajectory which, in retrospect, they appear to have been following.[12] Treating these episodes of democratization as separate would increase the number of episodes in the earlier period with no working-class role, thus making labor appear far less important than in the recent cases. Table 1.1 presents the countries and the main episodes of democratization considered in the present analysis.

12 See the interesting discussion of Markoff (1995: esp. 33).

The definition of democracy one chooses determines the choice of episodes to be analyzed. I follow the bulk of social science writing on democratization and use the term democracy to refer to liberal democracy as a set of institutions. Democracy, as a regime type, may be defined in terms of three components: constitutional, electoral, and legislative. As such it includes the following attributes: (1) liberal *constitutional rule*, underwritten by an independent judiciary, in which government leaders and state actors, including the military, are constrained from arbitrary action by the rule of law; (2) *classical elections;*[13] and (3) a *legislative assembly* that is popularly elected and has substantial autonomy from the executive power. As Markoff (1995) has usefully emphasized, the very meaning and institutions of democracy have themselves been the object of political struggle, and these have changed substantially over the historical sweep currently under consideration. Historical comparisons must come to grips with these difficulties. The episodes used here to mark democratization correspond to those widely accepted in the literature. Yet some complicated issues arise, and the criteria employed should be made explicit.

If democracy is here understood as a particular set of institutions, democratization, in turn, is understood as the introduction, adoption, or installation of those institutions, or the events and politics that lead to the introduction or adoption of the institutions that constitute a democratic regime. That is, the present study is concerned with *democratization*, as the politics of introducing democratic institutions, not *democracy* – as a type of rule.[14] The criteria employed for identifying a democratic transition do not

13 Following Hermet 1978:3, classical elections are those in which a mass electorate at regular intervals chooses among alternatives to select leading government decision makers. Such elections are relatively unrestricted in terms of "contestation" (the extent to which elections are open to competing contenders, fair and relatively free of fraud in conduct, and supported by a guaranteed array of basic freedoms such as association and expression) and inclusion (the extent of the suffrage or who may vote). See Dahl 1971.

14 Two conceptions of democracy have implicitly or explicitly dominated the current literature: democracy as a type of sovereignty (rule by the people) and democracy as a type of regime (as defined in the text). The former has been the stuff of political theory and philosophy since ancient times. It is normatively important and motivates much interest in studying democracy and democratization. Yet this is a difficult concept for the comparative analyst doing empirical work. One must first determine who the people are and what it means for them to rule (see Held 1996:1–3). At this point, of course, we are back to theoretical or conceptual analysis.

In general, recent analysts have been careful to set out an institutional definition of democracy of the sort adopted here. Nevertheless, there has been a tendency to slip to a conceptualization of democracy as rule by the people. That is, the domain of democracy as a concept has often proved slippery and has changed from democracy as a type of regime to democracy as a type of sovereignty. Partly this slippage is a result of the difficulty of sticking with a "neutral" definition of a word so politically and normatively charged. The current literature has generated a remarkable number of

require that a democratic regime is subsequently consolidated or that all these components of democracy are firmly in place. Like Elster (1996:95) in his approach to constitution making, I am concerned with the politics of decisions regarding the regime – with reforms or the introduction of institutions that are presumably intended to matter and to endure, but not with whether they actually matter or endure. I agree with Rustow (1970) and Przeworksi and Limongi (1997) that the analysis and explanation of democratic genesis or transition are quite different from those of democratic persistence or functioning. The emphasis is thus on policy making and institutional adoption – on the politics of collective decision making regarding institutional or regime change, but not necessarily on effective implementation or post-adoption practice.

This decisional approach involves a rather formal, legal-constitutional conception that includes cases where democracy was not in fact subsequently consolidated, where it may have been quite fleeting or its implementation effectively undermined by informal practices. Many analyses of democratization in the nineteenth and early twentieth centuries have tended to focus primarily on episodes in northern European countries, where the process was more unidirectional, and to ignore cases in both southern Europe and South America, where the introduction of democratic institutions turned out to be a shakier, less durable enterprise. Either the democratic constitutions were reversed outright, or they were undermined by informal practice as the political implications of the new institutions were worked out. It is important, however, to recall that these countries were often the early pioneers of democratic institutions. Although one can give a democratizing account of most northern European countries and an unstable and/or authoritarian account of most southern countries, this

---

definitions and subtypes of democracy (Collier and Levitsky 1997), in part as analysts have tried to make their institutional definitions compatible with some notion of popular sovereignty.

Beyond that, however, the problem almost inevitably arises because the analyst must make decisions about what to include in an institutional definition. This is obviously a tricky issue that may blur the line between democracy as a set of institutions and democracy as a type of sovereignty. To what extent, for instance, should one include institutions (such as registration or oversight procedures) that have eventually been widely adopted to ensure a certain kind of democratic functioning or a "fair" democratic order or that rule out the informal ways in which it may be undermined? If we insist on these, are we justified in the typical choices commonly made, such as including the United States as democratic even during the heyday of the electoral machine? Or excluding as democratic requirements other widely adopted institutional arrangements, such as proportional representation systems, which minimize the distortion in party representation and achieve a more equal weighting of votes? Or excluding, hardly even mentioning, the weak but not completely powerless British or Canadian upper house except in terms of its symbolic, social (or financial) context but not in terms of democracy?

should not preclude analysis of these often earlier, unsuccessful episodes of decisions to introduce democratic institutions, just as recent democratic transitions are included even if they may have been undermined by informal practice or, as in Peru, even reversed.

It might be noted that with this emphasis on democratization understood in terms of the politics of democratic reform, institutional change, or democratic transition rather than consolidation, the present analysis is not strictly comparable to those concerned with a democratic "path" or the emergence of democracy as an ongoing pattern of rule. For instance, the present analysis treats the reforms that led to the Weimar Republic as a case of democratization, whereas analyses such as those by Moore (1966), Luebbert (1991), and Ertman (1998), with rather different foci and analytical puzzles, consider Germany in terms of a fascist path. The strict differentiation between installation and consolidation means that certain episodes included here as cases of democratic installation are sometimes treated by other authors in terms of democratic failure.

While this emphasis on the politics of institutional adoption can be justified theoretically, it is also helpful in terms of the practical difficulties of establishing consistent criteria for choosing episodes that will be considered cases of democratization. For instance, it alleviates the problem of finding systematic comparative data on a range of informal practices or legal measures for addressing them that were invented only gradually over the two centuries of innovation in democratic institutions (Markoff 1997). At issue here are such things as actual (versus de jure) legislative autonomy, military influence and prerogatives, judicial independence, and "notable liberalism," which may depend on certain types of patronage politics, "semicoercive" voting, or the electoral politics of deference (Mann 1995: 26–27). However, other scoring difficulties remain. Assembling systematic comparative data on several arrangements crucial for holding free and fair elections is extremely difficult. This information particularly concerns issues such as registration procedures, secret voting, and the oversight of elections. Because these issues cannot be handled systematically across all cases, they have not been considered in the present dating of the cases, except where country specialists have indicated that these are a particular problem (e.g., the 1912 reform in Argentina, which addresses such problems, is universally treated as a democratizing episode).

Even beyond these considerations, establishing the institutional criteria for democracy and hence the choice of episodes for analysis remains difficult in a few cases. A particularly thorny issue for the earlier period concerns the extent of inclusion or enfranchisement required. On one level, of course, one would like to say that nothing short of universal suffrage can pass as democratic, but this criterion would exclude virtually the entire experience of Europe in the nineteenth century, the locus classicus of debates on the working class and democracy. Typically in analyses of historical processes of democratization, manhood suffrage is substituted for universal suffrage, and I have followed this research tradition. However, the conceptual issues are complex. Once the requirement of universality is loosened, what is the theoretical basis on which a decision regarding inclusion should be made? Does it make theoretical sense to overlook the exclusion only of women? Is the idea rather that of *popular* elections based on a *mass* electorate? If so, what kind of decision rule emerges for establishing an appropriate criterion?

As a practical matter of scoring, these issues do not usually arise. In the recent cases, the new democracies all have universal suffrage. As can be seen in Table 1.2, in some of the historical cases the episode that is of most concern here was preceded by an earlier reform that introduced a very broad suffrage or even full manhood suffrage.[15] In others, this episode itself constituted such a reform. In either situation, at the time of the episode chosen to mark a democratic transition, regimes were characterized by a massive expansion of the suffrage, encompassing about three-quarters or more of males above legal voting age. Thus, if the analyst is willing to stop short of women's suffrage, only a few cases are problematic. For cases that are, two key questions then arise: does the extent of enfranchisement reach at least most of the working class (a central question for the present inquiry), and what percentage of the potential electorate remain excluded?

Great Britain, as always, is a difficult case. While some scholars point to the reform laws of 1867 and 1884 as the introduction of a mass franchise, others use the 1918 reform as the threshold. According to the estimate of Flora et al., the 1884 reform enfranchised nearly two-thirds of the male population above the legal voting age;[16] the 1918 law, nearly 90 percent. Apparently most of the working class was enfranchised by 1884; indeed, there is evidence that this was accomplished by the 1867 law and

15 An unrestricted suffrage, of course, does not exist, insofar as, at minimum, citizenship and age qualifications exist everywhere, and other "minor" qualifications are typically ignored by analysts.

16 Flora et al. 1983: 1:184. While this is the figure typically given in most sources, it might be noted that Mackie and Rose assert that "by 1911 [that is, still under the same legal framework of the 1884 reform] only 12 per cent of the adult male population was not able to claim a vote but stringent registration procedures reduced the proportion *actually registered* to 65 per cent of adult men" (emphasis added). Mackie and Rose 1991:438.

Table 1.2. *Effect of democratizing reform on enfranchisement*
(percent enfranchised, of those meeting age and gender restrictions)

Country	Year of reform	Pre-reform: Percent enfranchised	Post-reform: Percent enfranchised
Argentina	1912	Manhood	Manhood
Belgium	1918	92	93
Chile	1874/91	n/a	n/a[a]
Denmark	1849	3[b]	73
	1915	88	92
Finland	1906	9[c]	87
France	1848	3	91
	1875–77	Manhood	87
Germany	1918–19	94	98
Greece	1864	Manhood	Manhood
Great Britain	1884	36	64
	1918	64	89
Italy	1912	32	90
	1919	90	103[d]
Netherlands	1917	69[e]	95
Norway	1898	43	90
Portugal	1911	Near manhood	Near manhood[f]
	1918	Near manhood[g]	Manhood
Spain	1868, 1890	11, 17	Manhood
	1931	Dictatorship	Manhood
Sweden	1907/9	34	78
	1918/20	78	96
Switzerland	1848	Varies by canton	Manhood
Uruguay	1918	63[b]	Manhood

[a] Data are not available, but nationally, the number of registered voters increased threefold between 1872 and 1878, presumably as a result of the reform (J.S. Valenzuela 1996:234). Census data indicate that remaining literacy requirements in the 1874 reform in Chile may have restricted the vote to about 35 percent of adult males. According to the 1875 census, about a third of males above the age of seven were literate at that time. While data for adult males are not available, subsequent censuses indicate that the figures are only a couple of percentage points higher for that group. They also indicate an increase in literacy of about ten percentage points each decade from 1875 to 1930, when three-quarters of males over the age of twenty were literate.

[b] Andren 1964:32.

[c] According to Andren (1981:47), the 1906 reform in Finland increased the electorate tenfold.

[d] Figure is more than 100 percent because it represents the percentage of people enfranchised within age and gender restrictions, plus a few categories of men

that the greater impact of the 1884 law was in the countryside (see Chapter. 2). A further complication is that during this whole period, plural voting continued, and it is noteworthy that even the 1918 reform reduced but did not abolish it.[17] The subsequent discussion considers both the 1884 and 1918 reforms.

The case of Chile is complicated by a literacy requirement, which persisted until 1970. While to some extent, as Therborn (1979:78) argues, "the long democratic record of Chile" is therefore a "myth," there is no question that during the twentieth century Chile had a mass electorate and a large part of the working class was enfranchised and electorally powerful, traits of Chilean politics that have led country specialists to characterize Chile as a long-standing democracy despite the ongoing literacy requirement. The impact of the literacy requirement obviously lessened as the Chilean population became more literate over the course of the century in which it was in effect; and calculations indicate that a mass electorate could be said to date from about 1920. Therefore Chile is included here as a case of early democratization based on the enabling reforms of 1874–91. If the 1970 date is used, Chile would drop out of the analysis of the earlier period.

Another issue concerns the existence of a nondemocratic upper house. In terms of comparability, it should be remembered that to this day

17 After the reform, university graduates, comprising .3 percent of the electorate elected twelve MPs, and businessmen, comprising 1.1 percent of the electorate, were given two votes, one in the constituency where the business was located in addition to one in the constituency of their residence. Mackie and Rose 1991:438–39.

Notes to Table 1.2

below the normal voting age who were nevertheless enfranchised (e.g., those who had completed military services [Rokkan and Meyriat 1969:208–9]).
*e*Flora et al. (1983: vol. 1) estimate that the 1896 reform in the Netherlands enfranchised 51 percent of the male population over twenty-five years of age, but by 1917 those meeting the same restriction had risen to 69 percent.
*f*See text.
*g*Suffrage somewhat restricted in 1913. See text.
*h*Before the 1915 reform, the Uruguayan franchise was limited by literacy requirements. This figure was calculated using information from the 1908 census, which indicates that 63 percent of males over the age of nineteen were literate.
Sources: Flora et al. 1983 unless otherwise indicated. Greece: Campbell and Sherrard 1968; Spain: Cuadrado 1969. Figures for Uruguay and Chile are calculated from census data.

Table 1.3. *Timing of democratization: Historical cases*

Country	Reform	Next election/new government
Argentina	1912	1912
Belgium	1918	1919
Chile	1874/91	1891
Denmark	1849	1849 (Parliamentary)
	1915	1918
Finland	1906, 1919	1907, 1919
France	1848	1848 (CA, presidential)
		1849 (Parliamentary)
	1875–77	1877
Germany	1918–19	1919
Greece	1864	1865
Great Britain	1884	1885
	1918	1918
Italy	1912	1913
	1919	1919
Netherlands	1917	1918
Norway	1898	1900
Portugal	1911	1911
	1918	1918
Spain	1868, 1890	1869, 1891
	1931	1931 (Municipal, CA)
		1933
Sweden	1907/9	1911
	1918/20	1921
Switzerland	1848	1848
Uruguay	1918	1919

Note: CA = Constituent Assembly.

Canada and the United Kingdom retain nonelected upper houses, which are weak but not powerless, the former with veto power and the latter with delaying (or revising) power; yet these regimes are widely considered democratic. It is difficult to specify when a nonelected upper house is sufficiently weak so as not to disqualify the regime as democratic, or what kinds, if any, of alternative forms of representation in part of one branch of government are compatible with a democratic regime. In the present analysis, the question arises with respect to Britain prior to 1911 when the House of Lords lost its veto power. Similarly, in Italy, the king continued to nominate the Senate until the 1948 republican constitution, though the Senate had been declining in power and importance since 1882. In Spain

Table 1.4. *Timing of democratization: 1970s and 1980s*

Country	Decision to transfer power	Election	New government
Argentina	1982 (ES)	1983	1983
Bolivia	—	1979, 1980	1979, 1980, 1982
Brazil	Incremental process	1985	1985
Chile	1988[a]	1989	1990
Ecuador	1976	1979[b]	1979
Greece	—	1974	1974
Peru	1977 (ES: CA)	1978 (CA) 1980	1980
Portugal	1974	1975 (CA) 1976	1976
Spain	1976 (ES)	1977	1977
Uruguay	1984	1984	1985

Notes: ES = election scheduled; CA = Constituent Assembly.
[a] Result of outcome of 1988 plebiscite as per 1980 constitution.
[b] First round of presidential election in 1978.

in the post-1890 period, the upper house comprised a combination of appointed and corporately elected members, and some senators chosen by corporate groups have been a consequential feature in Chile since 1990. In Denmark the full manhood franchise for both houses introduced in 1849 was restricted in 1866 for the upper house, and in Sweden manhood suffrage was introduced in the lower house in the 1907/9 reform, but a property requirement remained for the upper house until the 1918/20 reform. Finally, the French constitution of 1875 provided for an indirectly elected Senate, with one-quarter of that first Senate receiving a life term.

To the extent that this study considers all major episodes of democratizing reform, these issues present little problem. To the extent special weight is given to episodes that cross some democratic threshold and concluding generalizations are drawn from comparisons of those specific cases, these issues become more important. Yet, rather than make a hard-and-fast "scoring" decision, I have adopted an inclusive approach to the analysis of democratic episodes. France in 1875–77, Italy in 1912, Spain in 1890, and Chile in 1990 are included in the analysis, as are both the 1884 and 1918 episodes in Britain. The 1915 and 1918/20 reforms in Denmark and Sweden respectively are included in the analysis, although relaxing the upper-house criterion would eliminate these episodes. The dissenting reader is invited to exclude these or other episodes as deemed appropriate.

Finally, although democratization must be seen as incomplete until the transfer of power to an elected government, the present emphasis on the events concerning the politics of reform and the decision to introduce democratic institutions invite two further comments. First, in the more recent cases, the focus is particularly on the point when authoritarian incumbents took the steps that indicated their decision to eventually step down and yield to a democratic regime. This event, which is typically quite proximate to the election that implements the new democracy, represents a concrete decision to abandon authoritarianism and to relinquish power in a relatively short period of time. Usually the decision is to convoke a constituent assembly, thereby handing to the democratic opposition the authority to determine the rules of the new regime, or to hold relatively free elections, thereby ceding government power to party or political leaders.[18] The emphasis on this decision often places the focus of analysis on a point prior to the negotiations and decisions about the final details of the new regime. Although the details of institutional design at this point remain unclear, the issue of democracy is settled and an effective transfer of power to democratic forces is made. Tables 1.3 and 1.4 present the dates of the democratizing reform and the election that inaugurated the democratic government in the historical and recent cases respectively.

The second point concerns the dates that are used to refer to or label these episodes. In the literature, the historical cases are usually designated by the date when the democratic reforms or constitutional changes were passed; the recent cases, by contrast, are typically designated by the date of implementation of the new order – specifically the installation of the government elected under the new democratic rules. As mentioned, the primary emphasis of the present analysis is on the politics of decision making and hence on the earlier of these dates. Nevertheless, I follow conventional usage in labeling the recent transitions with reference to the change of government. Somewhat asymmetrically, I also follow conventional practice in dating the historical cases with the adoption of the reforms. The reader in search of consistent dates across the two epochs should consult Tables 1.3 and 1.4.

---

18 Thus in most cases the analysis emphasizes the politics of the period prior to the inauguration of what Shain and Linz (1995) call interim or caretaker government.

2

ELITE-LED REFORM IN
EARLY DEMOCRATIZATION

Among the historical cases, two of the patterns of democratization were shaped by the goals and strategies of elite strata, that is, middle- and upper-class groups. The popular classes in general and the working class in particular had little or no effective role. In Middle-Sector Democratization, reform occurred when the "outs" demanded political inclusion, but these petitioners were middle-sector groups, not the working class. The working class came to be included essentially by default. The second pattern, Electoral Support Mobilization, occurred as a result of incumbent projects: democratization was not a result of the "outs" trying to get in, but the outcome of strategies of those already in. Electoral Support Mobilization was a strategy pursued by political parties and groups with the goal of partisan mobilization in the context of electoral competition or support mobilization around a "national" question.

What was the position of the working class in these patterns? In some cases, these events occurred at a very early stage of industrialization, prior to the emergence of class-conscious workers acting as a group, articulating working-class grievances, and advancing working-class demands in a fight for democracy. This factor of timing, examined at greater length in Chapter 5, is important; however, artisans did play a key role in France in 1848, suggesting that working-class participation does not necessarily depend on a greater development of the proletariat or more modern forms of unionization.

Elsewhere, democratization occurred in a context in which the working-class had already emerged as a class-conscious actor, articulate and often organized, but, particularly in Latin countries, labor groups rejected

participation in bourgeois or liberal politics and did not constitute a force
for democracy. While individual workers may have been pro-democratic and
may have participated in liberal or republican movements, workers as a group
and working-class organizations were not oriented toward a democratic project, but rather conceived of their interests differently and were aware of the
co-optive potential of these projects from above. Consequently, there was
little working-class presence as such in these cases of democratization. At
most, on the level of sentiment and attitude, the working class was divided.
On the level of collective action or strategy, little happened. The partial exceptions in this regard are Norway, where the still tiny Labor Party favored the
1898 reform, and Britain, where Chartism had earlier put democratic
reform on the working-class agenda and where working-class groups participated in some mobilization around democratic reform. In both cases,
labor activity served primarily to demonstrate workers' availability as a
potential support base, but did not produce sufficient pressure that the
reforms should be viewed as responses or concessions rather than as the
strategies and initiatives of the competing parties to mobilize support.

The historical cases comprise three patterns of democratization. A
third, Joint Projects, describes those cases with significant working-class
participation and is discussed in the following chapter. Table 2.1 outlines
the three stylized patterns of democratization among the historical cases.

MIDDLE-SECTOR DEMOCRATIZATION: LIBERAL AND REPUBLICAN PROJECTS

The first pattern of democratization consists of liberal, sometimes republican, projects that were typically pursued by middle-sector groups. Excluded from political participation, these groups adopted a liberal agenda
in their fight to gain their own political inclusion and to oppose the
hegemony and dominance of the politically privileged traditional elite and/
or corporate groups. This liberal agenda often included the notion of full
manhood suffrage. When democratization occurred before the emergence
of a class-conscious or organized working class, the commitment to these
principles was not challenged by this type of class conflict. Elsewhere,
liberals were often divided and ambivalent about the strategy of enfranchising the working class. Nevertheless, sometimes those favoring manhood suffrage succeeded without working-class allies or support. In these
cases, the working class was included willy-nilly. The cases considered
in this pattern are Denmark (1849), Greece (1864), France (1848, 1875–
77), Portugal (1911, 1918), and Spain (1868, 1890, 1931). In Argentina

Table 2.1. *Patterns of democratization: Historical cases*

	Middle-Sector Democratization	Electoral Support Mobilization	Joint Project
From above	Liberal/Republican movements Labor included by default	Generation of political support	Mobilization and coalition strategies Accommodation to labor pressure
Labor role	None Mostly hostile or indifferent	None At most divided over response to elite project	Pro-democratic parliamentary labor-based parties and unions
Cases	*Denmark 1849* *Greece 1864* *France 1848,[a]* *1875–77* *Argentina 1912* *Portugal 1911,* *1918* *Spain 1868, 1890,* *1931*	*Switzerland 1848* *Chile 1874/91* *Britain[b] (1867),* *1884* *Norway[b] 1898* *Italy 1912* *Uruguay 1918*	*Denmark 1915* *Finland 1906,* *1919* *Sweden 1907/9,* *1918/20* *Netherlands 1917* *Belgium 1918* *Germany 1918–19* *Britain 1918*

[a] Substantial working-class protest and demonstrations.
[b] Some working-class participation.

manhood suffrage had long since been introduced, but the exclusionary regime was sustained through a pattern of electoral corruption that the 1912 reforms sought to address.

The episodes of democratization in this pattern are not chronologically concentrated, but rather stretch out from the earliest to the latest among the historical cases. The relationship of the working class to these middle-sector democratic movements varied accordingly, but nevertheless, these are generally cases in which the working class did not push for democracy. In Denmark in 1849 and Greece in 1864, there is only a very limited sense in which a working class could be said to have existed. In the other cases, a group of class-conscious workers did exist but played little part in pressing for democratic inclusion. The Argentine working class, largely belonging to the anarchosyndicalist current, was skeptical about the merits of "bourgeois democracy." In Spain, the working class was divided, with one current similarly influenced by anarchosyndicalism and much of the socialist current allied with the authoritarian regime until the final moment of the transition to democracy. France is analyzed at two points, 1848 and the mid 1870s. Of the cases considered in this pattern, France in 1848 represents the only one in which the working class played a strong pro-democratic role.

In cases that follow this pattern, then, democratization was largely a product of the efforts of middle-sector groups, which explicitly demanded and led the struggle for a competitive and inclusive regime. This was not a "popular" process of democratization in that the protagonist was an ascendant elite group, but it often took place in the mobilization/protest arena: sometimes the middle sectors operated in the negotiation arena to bring about political reform, but often they exerted pressure through mobilizations that backed demands with the use or threat of coercive action, involving the emergence of dissident allies within the army, coup rumors or attempts, and successful coups and citizen rebellions.

DENMARK

In Denmark, democratization was primarily pushed forward by a bourgeois-rural coalition that demanded the replacement of an absolute monarchy with a constitutional form of government.[1] The reforms of 1849 went very far in introducing a democratic regime, though the upper house was indirectly elected and the secret ballot was not introduced until 1901. In 1866, a partial democratic reversal took place with changes in the upper house. We return to Denmark's subsequent steps in the democratization process in Chapter 3.

The reform movement in Denmark represented a confluence of three currents that grew in strength particularly after 1830. A nationalist movement grew increasingly concerned with retaining the duchy of Schleswig in the face of the rising oppositionist and separatist demands of the German-speaking minority there and in Holstein. Rising German nationalism in the two duchies provoked a reformist response on the part of the Danish king, so that one factor in institutional change was the national interest of the monarchy itself, in addition to the middle-class nationalists. Second, a middle-sector liberal movement seeking political and economic reforms gathered momentum following the July Revolution in France in 1830. The movement started among students, whose organization in Copenhagen became a center of liberal thought, and developed into a constitutional movement in close association with the bourgeoisie, particularly

1 This discussion draws on Miller 1968:29–34; Fitzmaurice 1981:12–15; Oakley 1972: ch. 13; Jones 1986: ch. 2; and Luebbert 1991:73–75.

in the Wholesale Association (Hovde 1943:511). The final current comprised the middle peasantry or farmers – a rural middle class of, according to Hovde (1943:520–21), "independent owners of moderately sized farms," who had also become "small capitalist traders" with the growth of the commercialization of agriculture. The middle peasants mobilized to ensure that the decline of tenancy and the privatization of land would occur in a way that would allow them to benefit rather than redound to the advantage of the large landlords.[2] "The so-called 'peasant-movement' . . . was essentially a conflict of the rural middle class against the great proprietors" (Hovde 1943:545). This movement favored freedom of occupation, local self-government, and "adequate national parliaments" (Hovde 1943:521). In the mid-1840s, the national liberal and peasant movements allied when Anton Tscherning led the former in founding the Society of the Friends of the Peasants, championing constitutional and social reforms.

The first significant reform of absolutism came in 1834, when Frederick IV, in response both to the nationalist demands in Schleswig-Holstein and to liberal pressures in Denmark, established four consultative provincial assemblies, one in each of the two duchies and two in Denmark itself. Members of the assemblies were voted into power by an electorate that included "owners of city property, rural estates, and small farms, including tenants with seven acres of land; the lowest rural and urban classes were excluded" (Miller 1968:31). While the assemblies had no formal law-making power, the king was required to consult them on ordinary legislation, and their existence spurred on a broader democratic reform movement among urban liberals (merchants, provincial leaders, and students) and their rural allies within the assemblies.

The pace of democratization accelerated with the ascendance in December 1839 of Christian VIII, who had identified as a liberal in his youth (Seymour and Frary 1918: 2:176) and promised significant reforms. This change in the throne and the suggestion of political transformation galvanized opposition groups, leading them to join together as the Friends of the Peasant Association in 1846 and to step up their demands for popular government. These pressures reached a peak in 1847, when Christian VIII finally yielded and directed the preparation of a constitution.

This task was completed under Frederick VII in 1848, a year of nationalist ferment and revolution throughout Europe, when the question of political reform became particularly intertwined with the issue of nationalism (Fitzmaurice 1981:12–13). In January the king proposed a new constitution, which "was far too moderate to satisfy the democrats and

2 See Christensen 1983:21–54 for a summary of agricultural reforms of the period.

conceded too much to German nationalism" (Hovde 1943:549) in providing for a common Schleswig-Holstein government. In March, the
Schleswig and Holstein assemblies met together and voted for a common
constitution and incorporation into the German Confederation. The National Liberals reacted immediately and sent a delegation to the king
demanding a popular constitution that incorporated Schleswig. He agreed
and called for a constituent assembly elected under a full manhood suffrage. The Assembly did its work in the context of the war which broke
out with Holstein. It promulgated a new constitution the following year.
The new provisions retained manhood suffrage for elections to the new
bicameral Parliament (the upper house was indirectly elected) and required
that all laws be passed by Parliament, although the king retained executive
power, including the power to appoint his ministers (Svensson 1993:178–
79). Democratization in Denmark thus took place as a middle-sector movement without working-class participation, and Christiansen notes that it
was only after this constitution was instituted "that political movements
of any importance could be observed among the urban workers" (Christiansen 1988:14–15).

GREECE

Modern Greek democracy is generally dated from the 1860s, even though
the power of local political bosses and electoral irregularities affected its
subsequent practice. That episode can be classified as Middle-Sector Democratization. It had its origins in the Greek war of independence, which
was molded by Westernized modernizers (intellectuals, teachers, profes-
sionals, and bourgeois groups), and in the ensuing civil war, after which
these middle-sector groups, supported by the Great Powers dominating
the region (Russia, France, and Britain), "managed to impose their views
on the *form* at least that the future political institutions of modern Greece
would take."[3] If peasants and artisans participated in the early, nationalist
phase of the fighting against Turkey, they were quickly marginalized and
played no role in the ensuing politics of institutional change and democratization (Mouzelis 1978:13).

   In 1833, following the end of the war, Greece established a monarchy
under King Otto of Bavaria, thereby, in a certain sense, failing to make
good its newly won independence. Not only had Otto been offered the

3 Mouzelis 1978:13. See also Diamandouros 1983; Campbell and Sherrard 1968; Augustinos 1977; Young 1969; Woodhouse 1968; Carey and Carey 1968.

Greek crown by Russia, France, and Britain, Greece's "protecting powers," but Otto ruled by decree, through a large number of top officials and administrators imported from Bavaria. The resulting exclusion of Greeks from power fostered within Greek society a substantial consensus against both Bavarianism and absolutism and in favor of liberal democracy as a channel for capturing the state (Diamandouros 1983:48). Even members of the political elite came to see a parliamentary regime as an instrument for undermining the monarchy and establishing their own political auton-omy and means to rule, given their potential influence over the local vote. Thus, the ensuing episodes of democratization "cannot be seen as popular victories" (Mouzelis 1978:16); rather they should be seen primarily in terms of substantial upper- and middle-class consensus.

Although scholars occasionally refer to the establishment of democratic institutions at this time in terms of the prominent role of "oligarchic" or "notable" families, it should be kept in mind that this group was more similar to what elsewhere has been called "middle sectors" than to the traditional landed, upper classes usually connoted by those terms. Greece had an unusual social structure based predominantly on a pattern of small holding, bequeathed by Ottoman rule, and on early urbanization, commer-cialization, and the growth of a very large state. The result was an unusu-ally large urban group of civil servants and an "extraordinary development" of a merchant class. These groups, who were also the transmitters of Western ideas, played a leading role in nationalist and independence move-ments. The more traditional social elite was ambivalent about indepen-dence, leaving "the field open for the mercantile bourgeoisie to set the new values and standards, and so almost from the beginning to shape the major institutions of Greek society along liberal-bourgeois lines" (Mouzelis 1986: 41; see also 10–11, 39–40).

The first step was the 1843 coup by military officers from the war of independence, backed by disaffected politicians. Reflecting a more general antipathy to the Bavarianization of the country (also seen in Otto's loyalty to Roman Catholicism), these officers' discontent was particularly related to the unemployment and humiliation that attended the monarchy's re-placement of the Greek irregular forces with Bavarian troops (Campbell and Sherrard 1968:85–86). The coup forced the king to call a National Assembly and accept a new constitution which he negotiated with it. The constitution established a bicameral legislature, with a lower house elected on the basis of manhood suffrage but with an upper house appointed by the king. Other provisions, as well as opportunities for controlling deputies through corruption or even coercion meant that the king emerged with much of his power intact (Campbell and Sherrard 1968:86–92). With this change, as Augustinos (1977:12) put it, Greece passed from an autocracy to a semiconstitutional monarchy.

In 1862 a broad-based revolt deposed Otto. A number of forces had converged: students, who were influenced by the French Revolution and developments in Italy and who had attempted to assassinate the queen the previous year; a new generation of pro-Western politicians; and junior army officers, who were likewise influenced by the new ideas as well as desires for promotion (and some of whom, in the beginning of the same year, had attempted a military revolt). Local notables joined the uprising, but, with the first signs of worker action and organization still about twenty years away, no class-conscious group of artisans or workers was represented. The following year, a new king was recruited, this time from Denmark. In 1864 the Assembly wrote a new constitution, which has been characterized as "the most democratic in Europe" (cited in Noutsos 1990: 440); it limited the power of the monarchy and established the sovereignty of a new unicameral Parliament, elected by universal manhood suffrage.

FRANCE

From the time of the French Revolution, the course of democratic reform in France followed a series of initiatives and reversals. Following the Convention, which was elected by universal manhood suffrage but never implemented the constitution it wrote in 1793, an era of continuing institutional change ensued, characterized by a shifting trade-off between greater parliamentary sovereignty and full male suffrage, the latter a prominent feature of the two Napoleonic empires when it was married with restricted competition and an impotent legislature. The two democratic components coexisted in the Second and Third Republics, briefly in the former and more durably in the latter. These episodes of 1849 and 1877 are explored here.

Although the working class is more present in French democratization than in other cases in this pattern, these reforms are analyzed herein as projects of the middle and upper classes. Whatever democratic impulses had been involved in the 1871 uprising of the Paris Commune, that movement had been crushed and workers were not a pro-democratic force in the following years. The establishment of the Second Republic in 1848 can also largely be seen as Middle-Sector Democratization, with the big difference that the working class played an important pro-democratic role in addition. Virtually stillborn, the establishment of the Second Republic was a kind of "joint project" (see Chapter 3), but it differs from those other cases in the Joint-Project category in that middle-sector "outs" rather than parliamentary parties (including working-class parties) played the dominant role.[4]

The unusually early role of the working class in France grew out of the historical experience of the French Revolution, which "fundamentally altered the ways workers conceived and talked of class [and] created new categories of citizen and rights" (Katznelson 1986:34). The working class emerged as a class-conscious actor, "utilizing a radical republican discourse fused to the language of socialism" (Katznelson 1986:25). As a result of the combination of the revolutionary abolition of guilds and, a more common factor, the transformation of handicraft production, it was discontented artisans, rather than factory workers, who were still very small in numbers, who dominated the working-class movement. As Sewell (1986: 53) has argued, "Class consciousness emerged in France as a transformation of the artisans' corporate understanding of labor under the twin impact of capitalist development and revolutionary politics." Particularly important in these developments were the politics of the early 1830s: workers participated in the liberal July revolution of 1830, but the new, more liberal Orleanist monarchy rejected their demands (Sewell 1986:59–60).

The Second Republic reintroduced manhood suffrage for the Constituent Assembly elections of April 1848 and reaffirmed it in the resulting constitution. These provisions were implemented only for the presidential elections of December 1848 and the parliamentary elections of May 1849, after which the good showing of the democratic-socialist alliance led conservatives to roll back the suffrage and fostered rightist support for Louis Napoleon's coup of December 1851.

The context of the 1848 reforms was the Republican challenge to the monarchists. At the core of Republican movement was a broad range of middle-sector groups (Aminzade 1993:35) that championed representative government and an extension of the suffrage. The class-conscious workers largely supported the Republican movement and also put a number of working-class issues on the agenda. The 1847 campaign for broadening the suffrage was radicalized in the beginning of 1848, culminating in the February insurrection. The Republicans, who seized power and set up a provisional government, were socially conservative. Nevertheless, the workers' movement forced the government to introduce a number of measures including manhood suffrage and a number of social reforms of particular interest to the working class, such as a reduced work day and national

4 In this respect it is similar to the 1906 reforms in Finland, although those failed to achieve parliamentary sovereignty, which was not attained until 1918.

workshops as a vehicle for a guaranteed right to work (Price 1975:28). Indeed, elaborating a socialist rather than a liberal form of democracy, workers were able to establish the Luxembourg Commission, which was to formulate labor legislation and which was based on representatives of workers' corporate trade associations. The latter, in turn "were to become the constituent units of a new 'democratic and social republic' based on the sovereignty of labor" (Sewell 1986:66–67).

This democratic experiment rapidly led to polarization. The April 1848 elections created a Constituent Assembly "that was dominated by Conservatives, whether Republican or Monarchist" (Price 1975:31) The Assembly replaced the provisional government with a conservative executive commission, arousing the suspicion and dissatisfaction of the workers. When the government limited access to the national workshops, the working class responded with a second insurrection in June. Though the insurrection was defeated, it left a legacy of polarization and antagonism. Fearing continued working-class revolt and anarchy, conservatives carried out increasing levels of repression over the next two years (Price 1975:42). In 1850, France reverted to a restricted democracy when conservatives introduced a new electoral law that disenfranchised 2.8 million men, mostly workers, excluding 62 percent of the electorate in Paris and 40 to 50 percent in other relatively industrialized areas (Price 1975:44).

The 1848 events in France constituted the rare case in which a middle-sector project combined with working-class pressure and demands to institute democratic reforms. Indeed, workers were instrumental in bringing about the Republican victory in addition to affecting the institutions of the Second Republic. As Aminzade (1993:35, 20) has stated, "French workers, mainly artisans, constituted the revolutionary force that put the Republican party in power in February 1848 . . . and working-class pressure from the streets of Paris forced liberal Republican leaders . . . to reluctantly concede universal male suffrage."

The transition to democracy in 1877 had as its historical backdrop the authoritarian regime of Louis Napoleon Bonaparte (1851–70). Under Louis Napoleon, elections with manhood suffrage were regularly held, but most forms of political contestation and organization were limited by law or harshly repressed in practice. Thus, unlike many pre-democratic regimes among the historical cases, this regime was nondemocratic because it lacked basic contestation rights, rather than broad political inclusion. In the 1860s, due to economic hard times and a series of diplomatic setbacks, Louis Napoleon liberalized the regime as a means of mobilizing domestic support (Rueschemeyer et al. 1992:90). The revival of Republican and working-class opposition may have also contributed to his decision to liberalize in order to gain popularity (Aminzade 1993:211). Although this move was conservative in its intentions and by no means brought France to the point of a democracy, it did serve to open up some political space for domestic opposition and helped trigger renewed calls for the formation of a Republican government. This political opposition formed the basis for the Republican movement, which would champion the struggle for democracy in the 1870s.

The key event that brought about the fall of the old regime was France's defeat in the Franco-Prussian War and Napoleon's capture at Sedan, which created a political vacuum in Paris. The Third Republic was established in September 1870, under a provisional leadership (ironically, mostly monarchical elites) until elections for a National Assembly the following February. The Assembly was given a mandate to determine the form of a new national political regime within a four-year period. The victory of conservatives in the February elections and the anti-worker policies of the new government triggered a major working-class uprising and the attempt by the Commune to orchestrate a revolutionary seizure of power. In May 1871 Versailles troops successfully pacified the Commune, killing some twenty thousand people in a one-week period.[5]

Against this background, the democratic constitution of 1875 and the resolution of the deadlock in 1877 can be understood in terms of both divisions within the governing monarchical elites and the rapid political recovery of the Republican movement. Although monarchists won nearly two-thirds of National Assembly seats in the elections of February 1871,[6] their Legitimist and Orleanist factions were unable to implement an agreement that would have restored a constitutional monarchy. A Republican resurgence in July 1871 by-elections gradually induced a convergence of forces at the political center, effectively marginalizing "ultra" Legitimists on the extreme right as well as the most radical Republicans on the left. This centrist compromise produced the ambiguous 1875 "constitution" — three basic, institution-defining laws that included both a "presidency designed for easy conversion into kingship" (Wright 1995:217) and a republican label that would attract the support respectively of moderate monarchists and also Republicans, who anticipated further institutional change in a more radical democratic direction. The problem posed by these

5 Anderson 1977:8. The question arises concerning the degree to which the Commune may have had some effect on the decision to introduce manhood suffrage four years later. Rueschemeyer et al. (1992), who make the strongest argument about a working-class role in democratization, apparently give it no weight.

6 An overview of the elitist parliamentary politics leading up to the 1875 constitution can be found in Thomson 1964: esp. 75–91 and Wright 1995:212–18.

ambiguities soon came to a head when a political stalemate followed the solid Republican victory in the 1876 elections, leading to a constitutional crisis in May 1877. When monarchist president MacMahon dissolved the Chamber of Deputies over the choice of premier and called new elections, the Republicans successfully defined them as a plebiscite over presidential prerogatives and thereby over the nature of the republic itself. The 1877 elections produced another clear victory for the Republicans and democratic institutions based on parliamentary supremacy.

This episode of democratic reform, then, was led by the Republican movement, which was "a broad national coalition of capitalists, petty producers, and peasants" (Elwitt 1975:21). Although the Republicans sometimes collaborated with the working class, this was a tactical alliance, and labor was not an important element in the Republican coalition (Elwitt 1975:42). For its part, the working class did not prominently support the Republican cause. As Elwitt writes, "Many among the dispersed working class found radical democracy attractive. Others saw in Napoleon III's social projects equal promise for the future" (Elwitt 1975: 44). The real push for democratic reform came from the middle sectors.

ARGENTINA

Argentina was a case of very early adoption of a democratic constitution and manhood suffrage. The 1853 constitution of the unified nation was modeled on that of the United States, and in 1856 the Congress adopted an unrestricted suffrage for males over seventeen years of age. Nevertheless, turnout remained very low until the electoral reform of 1912, and the political system is usually described as a highly restrictive one, dominated by personalistic circles of conservative oligarchs who competed for control of the country's only major political party, openly rigged elections, and generally made decisions through informal agreements. Thus, despite the provisions for manhood suffrage and regularly held elections, the political system provided no effective channels for popular demands. In this context, the transition to democracy is generally considered to have come about as a result of the electoral reform of 1912 (the Sáenz Peña Law), which established the secret ballot and compulsory voting and provided for mechanisms that would correct fraudulent registration and electoral practices. It indeed resulted in the first electoral defeat of the landed oligarchy.[7] In none of these developments, including the

7 Smith 1978:9–11. See also Remmer 1984: ch.4; Rock 1975: ch. 2; Smith 1974; Alonso 1996.

1912 reform, was the working class an effective advocate of democratic reform.

The push for the 1912 reform came from the politically moderate Radical Civic Union (UCR), which had its origins in a series of divisions within the dominant classes in the last decade of the nineteenth century. In 1890, groups opposing the government formed the Civic Union, which in the same year staged protests involving some thirty thousand demonstrators and, with military support, carried out a revolt against the government. The Civic Union was internally divided over the issue of popular democracy, and the following year those who favored reform to address the corruption, manipulation, and oligarchic control that characterized the Argentine political system left the Civic Union and founded the UCR (Rock 1985:159–60, 184–85).

Continuing the path initiated by the Civic Union's 1890 revolt, the new UCR "pledged itself to . . . insurrection to implant popular democracy," carrying out a number of uprisings in 1893 (Rock 1985:183). In 1898, the UCR began to boycott the fraudulent elections and renewed its commitment to revolution as its historic mission ("La Causa") (Rock 1985:185). Another uprising in 1905 had the effect of attracting support within the army as well as increasing Radical appeal among the urban middle classes, which soon came to lead the movement. The threat posed by the UCR grabbed the attention of a worried ruling class, with one faction increasingly seeing electoral reform as a necessary response for maintaining stability.

Working-class militancy also challenged the social order. During these same decades at the turn of the century anarchism took root among workers, as new labor confederations were founded and the general strike was adopted as a primary weapon. In contrast to the constant demands for political inclusion by the middle sectors, the labor movement was generally indifferent or even hostile to democracy, often viewing it as a means of elite co-optation. Although the Socialist Party, founded in 1894, had a pro-democratic agenda, at this point its appeals found very little receptivity among the blue-collar workers, who embraced anarchosyndicalist tactics of direct action, which the Socialists opposed (Rock 1985:188).

Although during the early twentieth century significant labor protest did occur, it was centered around class-based social issues rather than political reform. Massive demonstrations were met with states of siege, restrictive legislation, vigilante action, and police repression (Rock 1985:187). By 1910 severe repression and restrictions had served to marginalize organized labor and limit its capacity to mobilize. Differing views about how best to respond to labor militancy had divided the oligarchy, but at the time of the electoral reform, labor was on the defensive.

Thus, mobilization and protest of both the middle and working classes seemed to threaten the old order, although only the middle-class movement was pro-democratic and the working-class movement was already in retreat when the government responded in 1911. In that year, the government introduced into the legislature the Sáenz Peña Law of electoral reform. The conservative elites who promoted the reform of 1912 did so in reaction to the demands of the emergent middle sectors, but with the calculation that the political status quo would be maintained and power would not pass to the lower classes. Smith (1978:11–12) describes the general feeling among conservative power holders as follows:

> Whereas power had previously been parceled out to competing factions within the landed aristocracy, it would now be shared between the aristocracy and rising middle-class groups (to the virtual exclusion of the lower classes). . . . There would be no class warfare: disagreements under the new system ought to be muted, controlled, undemagogic, settled gracefully by "gentlemen." And the retention of Conservative majorities would ensure that the socioeconomic elite would continue to run the political system. All the rules would stay intact.

Rock further points out that while Sáenz Peña (the reform bill's sponsor) believed that the Radicals might succeed in taking power through a revolt, they would not be able to win an election. Thus, the overall effect of the legislation would be to undercut the revolutionary tendencies of the UCR (Rock 1975:34–35). In fact, it was believed that the 1912 reform would divide the middle and lower classes and in the process pacify both groups. In short, the establishment of democracy in Argentina was a response to middle-class pressures and was carried out by elites who believed that democratic reform would not threaten their hold on power.

PORTUGAL

Although at most only fleetingly implemented, a democratic constitution was introduced in Portugal with the Republican Revolution of 1910, after nearly a century of partial (and vacillating) steps toward more democratic structures. The earlier nineteenth-century reforms, the outcome of liberals' attempt to replace absolutism with a constitutional monarchy, occurred in two phases. The first consisted of two episodes when parliamentary sovereignty was introduced but the electoral principle remained limited. In the second, the limitations were reversed: electoral institutions were reformed but parliamentary sovereignty remained limited. In the twentieth century, the Republican Revolution precipitated a new ebb and flow of constitutional forms. The new Republican constitution of 1911 soon met a democratic setback with new suffrage restrictions, although full manhood suffrage was introduced in 1918, again in the context of regime instability. The working class played little role in any of these reforms, which rather were taken above all at the initiative of middle-sector liberals and their military allies.

The struggle against absolutism, marked by rebellions, coups, and civil war, began in the third decade of the nineteenth century. Two episodes of democratic reform, in the 1820s and 1830s, provided for parliamentary sovereignty. A military revolt led to the adoption in 1822 of a liberal constitution that dramatically limited the powers of the king. It also enfranchised most literate males, but only one of two chambers in the legislative Cortes was elected. Although this was in principle quite a progressive franchise, a very high illiteracy rate (still three-quarters of the population in 1911 [Robinson 1979:361]) in fact disqualified the overwhelming majority. Within two years absolutism was restored. In 1836 another military rebellion briefly reinstated the 1822 constitution, but a new one was immediately promulgated and reintroduced income restrictions for the suffrage, as Septembrism (as the rebel movement came to be called) became less and less radical. The experiment came to a more definitive end with the restoration in 1842 of the 1826 Charter, which again gave the king extensive power and further restricted the franchise.

The last half of the century saw a series of reforms that significantly expanded the electoral principle, but the degree of royal power contradicted effective parliamentary sovereignty. Another rebellion in 1851 introduced a long period of relative stability under a constitutional monarchy, during which a number of reforms were introduced. In 1852 direct elections were restored, and in 1885 the hereditary Chamber of Peers was again reformed.[8] For the lower house, the 1878 reform expanded the suffrage substantially to encompass 68.2 percent of adult males (Tavares de Almeida 1991:216), excluding those who fell outside the three categories of enfranchised voters: those who could read and write, were heads of families, or had a minimum income. In 1895, however, a further change marked a retreat from this broad suffrage.[9] A major limitation on democratic reform remained the power of the king,

8 With the rather frequent change of constitutions during the nineteenth century, there was considerable alternation between direct and indirect elections to the lower chamber and change in the composition of the upper chamber.
9 The changes halved the minimum income requirement but eliminated enfranchisement of heads of families (Tavares de Almeida 1991:214).

who dissolved Parliament an average of once every year and eight months (Marques 1972:44–49).

Working-class demands were not a part of any of these developments. Rather, the reforms were the result of new currents that took hold among sectors in the military, the bureaucracy, and the liberal elite. Freemasonry was important in the 1822 reform movement, and the 1836 rebellion has been seen as "a reaction of the urban industrial bourgeoisie allied to middle-class traders" (Marques 1972:42, 65). The second half of the century saw the emergence of two political foci, with the conservative Regenadores opposed by the more liberal Historicos (later the Progressives). The reforms of 1852, 1878, and 1895 were undertaken because of the pressures or efforts of these liberals. However, some dynamic of competitive bidding for popular support began to enter the picture with the appearance and growth of the Republican movement during this period (Livermore 1976: 298).

The next period of democratic reform occurred during the very unstable Republican period. Like the previous reforms, these too were the product of military rebellions supported by reformist societal groups, this time the Republican movement, which had organized in the Portuguese Republican Party (PRP) in the last decades of the nineteenth century. Republicanism was primarily an urban middle-class and lower-middle-class movement, with important support among the middle bourgeoisie, civil servants, students, journalists, and military officers, as well as an appeal to the urban lower classes (Marques 1972:50, 74, 140, 174; Pinto 1995:87). As in Argentina, a restricted franchise was less the problem than informal practices that maintained the political exclusion of these groups. Two episodes of democratic reform are of interest here: the Republican Revolution of 1910 and the New Republic of 1918. Though the young and growing labor movement was beginning to flex its muscles during this period, it did not assume a pro-democratic position. Reform is thus analyzed as middle-sector democratization.

The Republican Revolution of 1910 occurred as a result of a navy rebellion, with the support of street demonstrations led by Republican leaders. The core of the Republican movement was its opposition to the throne, the church, and the nobility, all three of which the ensuing Republican government attacked or eliminated (Livermore 1976:319; Marques 1972:131). With an eye to defending bourgeois interests, the Republicans viewed the democratic franchise in instrumental terms. Indeed, the Constituent Assembly that met in 1911 established parliamentary sovereignty and expanded the suffrage, reintroducing the enfranchisement of heads of families, although the potential electorate continued to fall short of that from 1878 to 1895. Nevertheless, the restriction (those who were neither literate nor a family head) was apparently small, and we may see the Constituent Assembly as having taken the decision to introduce a democratic regime.

The working class was not an important part of the Republican movement or of the democratic reforms of the Republican period. Individual workers participated in the street demonstrations of 1910 and favored Republicanism, but the mobilization of class identity was not a feature of these events. Indeed, since the 1870s the working-class movement had taken an increasingly "apolitical" turn in opposition to Republicanism, which was seen as limited in its purview to only institutional forms and unconcerned with larger social issues and the question of socialism. From 1872 labor leaders "opposed the essentially political claim of emerging Republicanism," arguing that it would fail to unleash the social goals and transformations they favored. With the divisions in international socialism, the workers' movement became aligned with the anarchist position of Bakunin and Kropotkin (Serrao 1982:338). Supplanting socialism, the anarchosyndicalist current became predominant within the labor confederations and adopted a clear anti-politics strategy. The 1890s launched a period of substantial ideologizing and strike activity. The strike wave was still rising at the time of the Revolution and continued to shake the country in the following months, with the offensives of 1909 and 1910–12. Anarchosyndicalism and its predominant influence within the labor movement, then, was a "central element of the anti-system role played by the Unions from the turn of the century and, above all, during the Republican period" (Pinto 1995:94).

Some analysts have argued that Republicans came to understand that striking workers were an important political resource, and that "the opening to the 'rabble' was . . . necessary" to the movement's success (Serrão 1982:366). Thus, the Republicans may have appealed for popular support, and some analysts have seen the immediate legalization of the right to strike as recognition of the support the lower classes lent to the Republican movement (Robinson 1979:37). But, though strikes were on the rise, the labor movement had not mobilized for democratic reforms or political goals, and pro-democratic pressures from below were virtually nonexistent given the "anti-politics" strategy of the anarchosyndicalists (Marques 1972:135–36; Pinto 1995:97). Any initial sympathy soon turned to mutual opposition. In the period from 1913, in response to a new and militant labor movement that was beginning to take advantage of its new rights, the Republicans clearly put a higher priority on control than on support mobilization. In 1913, in reaction to growing labor strength and protest and the creation of a new labor central, the government moved to curb labor's power, both by repressing strikes and reinstating restrictions on the franchise. Even at a time when the government passed into the hands of the Republican faction (now a separate party) that had been more sympathetic to the working class, the enfranchisement of family heads was eliminated, leaving a restrictive literacy requirement that nearly halved the number enfranchised (Marques 1972:160). The brief introduction of democratic institutions following the 1910 Revolution can thus be seen as a middle-sector movement.

Another largely unimplemented move toward democratic forms occurred following the garrison revolt led by Major Sidonio Pais at the end of 1917. As in 1910, the rebellion took place against a backdrop of mounting working-class protest and a new wave of strikes, including a general strike in Lisbon, that led to open fighting, arrests, and persecution. Although the unrest expressed the unpopularity of the government as it oversaw growing wartime shortages and plummeting real wages, the labor movement did not support Sidonio Pais. Rather, the UON, a new national labor confederation founded in 1914, adopted a position of "benevolent neutrality" toward the new government, and the confrontations, strikes, and violence continued (Robinson 1979:37). The working class did not press for democratic or electoral reform, which came in 1918 when Sidonio Pais introduced a presidential constitution with full manhood suffrage and declared a New Republic.

If the New Republic with full manhood suffrage included a Bonapartist bid for popular support, it was not successful – or at least not for long. Sidonio won the 1918 elections under the new constitution, but with the Republican boycott of the elections, he increasingly relied on monarchists, clericals, and the upper bourgeoisie (Marques 1972:169). As repression continued or even increased, Sidonio Pais quickly lost whatever popularity he may have had and was assassinated just a year after his revolt. That event brought an end to the New Republic, and the political system reverted to the prior constitutional framework and a period of political crisis.

Thus, though essentially stillborn, twice during the Republican period decisions were taken to introduce a democratic regime with full or nearly full manhood suffrage. Working-class demands for democratic reform were absent from these events, although the 1910 Revolution and the 1917 rebellion undoubtedly found some initial popularity among individual workers. Both took place against a backdrop of rising labor agitation, but this was primarily anarchist and/or economist rather than pro-democratic in orientation.

SPAIN

The Spanish history of attempts to introduce democratic institutions began early and included many episodes that failed to produce stable democratic regimes. None of these episodes involved the working class. Rather, the nineteenth century was marked by conflicts between the forces of absolutism and liberalism, with democratic reforms occurring during periods of liberal ascendancy and reversals taking place when conservative forces gained the upper hand. The reintroduction of democratic institutions in 1890 was not so quickly reversed, remaining in place until the 1923 coup, although informal practices undermined democratic functioning. In 1931, middle-sector opposition groups – under the banner of a democratic republican movement – forced a defensive extrication on the part of the Primo de Rivera military dictatorship and prevented a subsequent stabilization of a new nondemocratic order by monarchist forces. The divided labor movement played little role in this democratization process, with the Socialists collaborating with Primo de Rivera's government until the middle-class Republican opposition had already largely succeeded, and anarchosyndicalists remaining indifferent to the struggle for "bourgeois" democracy.

The prolonged period of instability and attempted democratic reform in the nineteenth century can be divided into three phases,[10] each of which was characterized by an innovation and each of which contained cycles of reversals. The first began very early, as Spain quickly felt the influence of the French Revolution. In 1812 Spain adopted a constitution, modeled on the French charter of 1791, that provided for parliamentary government and manhood suffrage in the context of indirect elections. It was at the time, according to two constitutional historians, "Europe's most influential constitution. . . . [Written as a] weapon against France and Napoleon . . . , it was also an effort to establish revolutionary principles, and to bring new individualistic and egalitarian concepts to the traditional society" (Blaustein and Sigler 1988:114). Brief intervals of liberal rule, then, occurred in 1812–14, when upper- and middle-class liberals seized an opportunity that came with the Napoleonic invasion and abdication of Ferdinand VII, and again in 1820–23, when a military revolt forced Ferdinand, who had returned from exile and reestablished absolutist rule, to submit to the 1812 constitution until French troops again invaded, this time under Louis XVIII, and again reinstated absolutism.

10 Cuadrado 1969:39ff. On the historical process of democratization in Spain, see also Carr 1980; and Kern 1974: ch. 1.

The second period was inaugurated with the 1837 constitution, which introduced direct elections, but greatly restricted the suffrage (during this period the percentage of the population enfranchised varied from less than .2 to about 2 [Mackie and Rose 1991:385]). This innovation took place in the context of the Carlista War in the seven years following Ferdinand's death in 1832. The war, which saw tremendous constitutional instability, ended with the ascendancy of the liberals, but they immediately split into conflicting Moderate and Progressive factions, continuing the pattern of frequent constitutional change.

The third period began with the "glorious revolution" of 1868, a military revolt that led to the constitution of 1869, which reintroduced manhood suffrage, this time along with direct elections. However, instability soon followed until informal practices were developed to allow for the formal political inclusion of the lower classes on terms that would not fundamentally threaten the balance of power. Thus, the attempt to establish a republic in 1868 yielded to the Restoration regime in 1875, which initially reintroduced restrictions limiting the suffrage to only about 5 percent of the population (Mackie and Rose 1991:385). At the same time, an arrangement known as El Turno was instituted in which Spain's two main political parties – the Liberals and Conservatives – simply alternated in power at each election. Furthermore, elections and voting were so thoroughly controlled by local political bosses (caciques) that electoral contests were negotiated before elections, with the press often publishing the results before polls were opened.[11] Under these conditions the Liberal Party restored full manhood suffrage in 1890.

During this period working-class organizations were still incipient and did not figure into the politics for democratic reform. The previous decade had seen the emergence of socialist groups and working-class organizations: the Socialist Party (PSOE) was founded in Madrid in 1879 and nationally in 1888 when the General Workers Union (UGT) was also founded. Social unrest and a number of important conflicts put the social question on the agenda. In the following years UGT membership grew steadily, and anarchist groups formed as well (Castillo 1990:216–17, 235–39; Cuadrado 1969: 536). Nevertheless, the Restoration regime achieved some stability until 1923, "based on moderate elite liberalism" and oligarchic competition, with the military retaining a privileged position that included seats in the appointive Senate (Payne 1993:6–7; Bertelsen Repetto 1974:450–53), and the PSOE never managed to win more than a handful of parliamentary seats.

The coup of Primo de Rivera in September 1923 put an end to this long tradition of semicompetitive politics in Spain. Of the historical set of

---

11 On the Restoration regime, see Carr 1980: ch. 1; and Gómez 1976.

cases discussed in this chapter and the next, the Primo de Rivera dictatorship most closely resembles the pre-democratic regimes typically found in
the 1970s and 1980s: a military regime based on an alliance between top
generals and technocratic sectors oriented toward economic growth (though
Primo de Rivera also drew support from the crown).

At the time of the 1923 coup, the bulk of the labor movement was
divided between the Socialists and the anarchists of the anarchosyndicalist
union (CNT). The latter was founded in 1911, after the violent repression
of the *semana trágica* of 1909, which had the effect of radicalizing the
working class and favoring the "apolitical," anarchist faction (Castillo
1990:238). The CNT quickly emerged as the dominant labor central. In
1920, UGT membership reached about 211,000, while that of the CNT
was about 700,000 (Meaker 1974:235, 273; Payne 1993:27). Neither the
socialist nor anarchist faction constituted a pro-democratic opposition during the dictatorship. The anarchists were committed to revolution, often
favoring terrorist tactics, and rejected political democracy; under Primo de
Rivera this group would bear the brunt of the state's repressive activities
(Carr 1980:103; Meaker 1976:29–72). The Socialists, by contrast, initially
accepted and collaborated with the military government, forming an im-
portant pillar of support for Primo de Rivera as he stabilized his rule.[12]
They had been passive in the face of the 1923 coup, and, once in power,
Primo de Rivera quickly succeeded in co-opting both the PSOE and the
UGT. While some PSOE leaders were leery of working with Primo de
Rivera, the majority adopted a collaborationist stance, best represented by
Julian Besteiro. Besteiro, head of both the PSOE and the UGT, felt that
collaboration with the regime would strengthen the Socialist Party and the
labor confederation, and that it was the role of the bourgeoisie, not the
working class, to establish political democracy (Preston 1978:13–14).
Taken together, as Carr notes, repression against the anarchists and the
acceptance of the dictatorship by the PSOE can explain why the working class was "so docile" during the Primo de Rivera years (Carr 1980:
103).

It follows that democratic opposition to the Primo de Rivera dictatorship had to come from outside of the labor movement. The first important
opposition came from traditional politicians and intellectuals, then spread
to university students. In the mid-1920s, a full-blown Republican movement blossomed, with broad support from the middle sectors, at the same
time that discontent within the army mounted over declining military
autonomy and prestige. In 1926 army officers failed in their attempt to

12 On the Socialists' collaboration with the Primo de Rivera dictatorship, see Preston
   1978: ch. 1.

overthrow the government in a coup which had the support of Republicans. By 1928 this opposition movement and the general withdrawal of support by the right discredited the Primo de Rivera regime. The following year saw further anti-government protest with the eruption of student demonstrations and strikes along with Republican meetings and public denunciations of Primo and his attempt to write a new constitution. The Socialists, meanwhile, "were gradually being isolated as the dictator's only supporters outside his own Union Patriótica" (Preston 1978:12). The PSOE distanced itself from the destabilized regime only as localized labor militancy and the growing internal weight of the party's anti-collaborationist wing challenged Besteiro's cooperative line, but it never actively contested Primo's rule (Preston 1978:10–15). In January 1930, facing widespread societal opposition and lacking previously reliable bases of support in the army, church, and key sectors of the economic elite, Primo de Rivera resigned. In the subsequent events leading up to the establishment of a democratic regime, the PSOE, UGT, and CNT participated in the opposition, but the middle-sector Republican movement maintained its leading role, preventing the creation of a new nondemocratic regime by monarchist elites and pushing the king to permit democratic municipal elections in April 1931 (Ben-Ami 1978:38–44).

In this way, working-class organizations played little role in the democratic transition from the Primo de Rivera dictatorship. The PSOE was a reluctant pro-democratic organization, joining the Republican forces at the last moment before the April elections. As late as the beginning of 1930, it was the assessment of the Spanish police that the Socialists constituted a force for stability rather than opposition (Payne 1993:27). Thus, although the Socialists emerged as one of the main beneficiaries of democracy with the 1931 elections to the Constituent Assembly, they had little role in the pro-democratic opposition to the authoritarian regime. Among working-class organizations, the CNT remained dominant. During the 1920s the UGT had seen only marginal membership gains despite its collaboration with the dictatorship, while the CNT membership grew very rapidly once it was relegalized in 1930 (Payne 1993:27–28). In accordance with its anarchosyndicalist orientation, the CNT concentrated on direct action and played a decidedly subordinate role in these events.

ELECTORAL SUPPORT MOBILIZATION

In a second pattern, Electoral Support Mobilization, the enfranchisement of the working class can be understood as a strategy of political entrepreneurship. The goal was to gain political advantage by mobilizing a large support base often in a context of partisan competition. Here, in contrast to the first pattern, democratization was a project of those in power. In common with that pattern, the working class was not the initiator of democratic reform or, generally, even an important pro-democratic actor; it was, however, the recipient or target of an expanded suffrage. Incumbents extended the suffrage to the working class much less in response to lower-class pressures than in response to their own political needs as they jockeyed for political support.

The countries following this pattern of democratization are Switzerland (1848), Chile (1874/91), Britain (1884), Norway (1898), Italy (1912), and Uruguay (1918). Switzerland and Chile experienced democratization at a very early stage in the development of a working class, and the attempts to mobilize support were not targeted at the working class as such. Elsewhere, the suffrage extension was more explicitly targeted at the working class, which by then had a clearer identity.

The leaders who carried out the reforms calculated that a suffrage extension would play into their party's hands in the electoral arena and that it would help them with their political agenda. In addition to partisan considerations, other goals were sometimes part of the support-mobilizing agenda, such as Norwegian independence and Batlle's "model country."

In sharp contrast to the notion that the working class led the process of democratization, labor in these cases was divided over how to respond to elite political mobilization. Labor leaders in Britain, Italy, and Uruguay were by no means blind to these moves from above. Rather, in each case, some leaders spoke out against political inclusion, arguing precisely that it was electoral support mobilization geared toward elite politicians' interests. At the very least, a significant segment of the working class was opposed to political incorporation under elite tutelage, viewing the status of junior partner or electoral support base as contrary to the interests of the working class.

SWITZERLAND

The achievement of a democratic regime at the national level in Switzerland can be dated with the constitution of 1848.[13] Swiss democratization

13 Analysts such as Therborn choose a later date to mark the introduction of democracy. After 1848 the liberals were threatened by reversals, which did succeed at the subfederal level in some cantons, and at the federal level "the system" operated in a way that limited popular influence in the face of the power of the "federal magnates," thus provoking a reform movement for forms of direct democracy. These met widespread success at the cantonal level in the 1860s and at the federal level with the constitutional revision of 1874. Although restrictions remained in some of the cantonal governments,

took place at two levels. At the cantonal level, democratic reform had met with substantial success in the 1830s. These changes can be seen primarily in terms of the Middle-Sector Democratization pattern, discussed earlier, in which middle-class "outs" sought reforms that would achieve their political inclusion. Nothing was accomplished at the federal level, however, until 1848. The politics of these changes, also a project of middle-sector liberals, were undertaken by the liberal "ins" and can be seen in terms of a strategy no longer for inclusion but to advance and build support for a national political-economic project, specifically a more secular state and the creation of more centralized federal institutions that would eliminate barriers to the creation of a national market. The democratic form of these institutions would create a political base to support them.[14]

Before 1848 Switzerland was a decentralized confederation composed of sovereign cantons and lacking a central authority (save for a token federal assembly). At the height of the "old regime," during the seventeenth and eighteenth centuries, the cantonal political systems were characterized by competitive oligarchies in which members of a small elite group competed in elections under an extremely narrow suffrage and strong informal pressure in nonsecret voting (Gould forthcoming). The first attempt to transform this system came from Napoleon Bonaparte, who, after invading and occupying Switzerland in 1798, approved the Mediation Act in 1803. This act expanded the number of cantons from thirteen to nineteen and permitted representative government based on near manhood suffrage in the six new cantons. The removal of the French by the allied forces in 1813, however, brought on the abrogation of the Mediation Act and the question of a new constitution emerged. Initially, through the Federal Pact of 1815, the Restoration reestablished the decentralized and oligarchic institutions of the old regime.

Middle-class liberals sought to reform these restoration regimes, from which they were largely excluded. Starting in 1829–30, they met substantial success. Though they began earlier, the July Revolution of 1830 in France gave a further impetus to Swiss liberal movements throughout the country. At the cantonal level the "regeneration" movement reformed political structures particularly in those cantons with elitist patrician or guild governments, though the liberal movement was weak in cantons

---

the 1848 federal institutions of representative democracy met the definitions currently employed. Rueschemeyer et al. also date Swiss democracy from 1848.

14 Accounts of the Swiss democratization process can be found in Gould (forthcoming); Bonjour, Offler, and Potter 1952; Gillard 1955; Rueschemeyer et al. 1992: 85–87; Dändliker 1899; Fahrni 1987; Thürer 1971; McCrackan 1901; Jost 1990; Ertman 1998. I have also relied on several rounds of communication with Andrew Gould.

with assembly traditions, where the political rights of the middle classes had not been restricted as such (Gould forthcoming: ch. 5). The result was the widespread introduction of democratic forms of government at the cantonal level, which had the primary effect of empowering another elite stratum, the urban middle class and their allies of rural notables.[15]

In addition to cantonal political reform, the liberal agenda included economic reform of the guild restrictions and the intercantonal barriers to the free movement of goods and people and the construction of federal institutions, which would centralize certain aspects of economic regulation and constitute Switzerland as an integrated national entity. In this regard, the liberals had made no headway. Twice in the 1830s, they introduced proposals to reform the national constitution, but these failed as they were unable to construct a national coalition at the elite level "and did not yet have the resources to build a mass movement with these objectives" (Gould forthcoming). This was achieved in the following years.

The construction of a mass movement and a process of support mobilization had begun in the pre-1830 political struggles, as the liberal movement sought to advance its goal of stronger national government by creating a feeling of national sentiment among the people. Aspects of this attempt could be seen in the political use of social organizations. A good example was a national shooting society, which was open to all men and, as stated in article 1 of its constitution, sought to foster the feeling of national unity. Its assemblies were political events that shunned conservative speakers as they welcomed liberals and constituted an implicit pro-federalist protest (Gould forthcoming).

After 1830 the process became more pronounced as the federal question continued to be posed at both cantonal and national levels, since reversals as well as new gains occurred for the liberals at the cantonal level. In this context, the conservatives activated a new axis of competition, introducing a cultural cleavage. In Protestant cantons, the conservatives sought to deprive the urban middle-class liberals of their rural supporters by appealing to anti-urban, fundamentalist religious sentiment in the countryside. At the federal level, however, the religious cleavage benefited the liberals (Gould forthcoming). The result was heightened levels of conflict as religious differences came to coincide with the political differences, with liberals favoring a secular federal state and conservatives favoring a decentralized confederation that protected the broad institutional authority of the Catholic Church.

15 As elsewhere, elite politics continued even after the reforms, as the formal political rights of the lower classes were effectively limited by residence and other restrictions for voting and political participation (Gould forthcoming).

Tensions came to a head in 1847, when radicals, having just achieved a majority in the confederal Diet, declared illegal the separatist, defensive league of seven conservative Catholic cantons, which had been formed in 1845. The brief Sonderbund War broke out between the sides, and the victorious centralizing reformers were then able to consolidate a national state through the constitution of 1848, which established democratic institutions at the federal level.

In Switzerland, then, the introduction of democratic institutions in 1848 followed the goals, conflicts, and strategies of groups already included in the political game and engaged in intense conflict as religious and political cleavages came to coincide with and reinforce one another. Furthermore, the sides were quite evenly balanced: before war broke out in 1847 the liberals had *just* achieved a majority in the federal Diet following the liberal victory in one of the cantons. In this context, the constitution, which immediately followed the ensuing civil war and which introduced mass democratic institutions at the federal level, may be seen not only in terms of adopting a familiar institutional model to which liberals had already demonstrated their commitment at the cantonal level or a borrowing of the American model of a new type of federal constitution. In addition, the choice of institutions may be seen in more strategic terms. The victorious middle sectors specifically constructed institutional forms that would promote liberal dominance. The new constitution imposed democratic elections in the still unreformed cantons and thereby broke the power of the elites both in those cantons and in the new federal institutions. In terms of partisan mobilization, democratic institutions channeled support behind the liberals and made it virtually impossible for the conservatives to make a comeback at the national level. In terms of substantive goals, democratic elections, in providing for popular participation and for the representation of individuals in national government for the first time, were a way to generate national sentiment and identity. They were thereby a means to build mass support for and guarantee the ongoing existence of the new central institutions, the goal for which the liberals had fought.

Workers as individuals participated, but as a collectivity they did not figure into these events. Although Switzerland was a very early industrializer, it was unusual in the degree to which urbanization did not accompany industrialization: at midcentury the working class was still primarily composed of part-agriculturalist "rucksack" workers and home industrial workers, widely scattered in rural villages. In the ferment of the 1830s, many new clubs, societies, and associations were formed in which workers participated, and in the 1840s Swiss society became aware of the "social question." Yet the organizational push of the working class occurred in the years after 1848. As Fahrni noted, "It was middle-class progressives who voiced the demands for democratic reform" (Fahrni 1987:56, 62; Jost 1990).

CHILE

The analysis of Chile focuses on the reforms in the decade and a half between 1874 and 1891, which expanded the suffrage and targeted informal practices through which the executive interfered in the electoral process. Despite these important democratic advances, a literacy restriction on the suffrage was retained until 1970. If a "mass" (rather than full manhood) suffrage criterion is adopted, it could be argued that, in a period when literacy rates were rising rapidly, mass enfranchisement was achieved by 1920.[16] The reforms of this period are analyzed in terms of the politics of support mobilization, as parliamentary parties – and particularly the Conservatives – sought to increase their power vis-à-vis the executive. Working-class pressure had no part in these dynamics. As J. Samuel Valenzuela (1985:19–20) has argued, "Chile extended the suffrage gradually, less in response to pressures from below than as a consequence of elite strategies to maximize electoral gain." Even if we examine the period through the opening decades of the twentieth century, when working-class unions and parties were formed, we find little evidence of working-class agitation for further democratic reform. Indeed, for present purposes, what is striking is that even in subsequent decades (the 1930s and 1940s) in a country with the strongest electoral left in Latin America and during one of the world's few episodes when a popular front government came to power – when the labor-affiliated Socialist and Communist parties were part of the majoritarian electoral coalition and, at some points, even joined the cabinet – further reforms were not on the agenda and a full suffrage was not instituted.

Competitive elections were held in Chile as early as the 1830s, although democratic limitations included a suffrage restricted by property and literacy requirements, the absence of the secret vote, and the subordination of the legislature to the executive.[17] Over the next several decades, the legislature gradually pushed through reforms that weakened the power of the chief executive. At the same time, career civil servants became

16 Calculations from the census of that year indicate that two-thirds of adult males were literate, a figure that would produce an enfranchised population roughly equivalent to that following the 1884 reform in England. If the criterion of full manhood suffrage were used, then Chile would no longer constitute a case of democratization in this earlier time period.

17 This discussion of Chile follows J. S. Valenzuela 1979, 1985, 1996; and A. Valenzuela 1977, 1983.

increasingly autonomous within the state. Their growing power and more liberal orientation challenged Conservative landed elites and threatened to upset traditional relations in the countryside by curbing Church privileges. The gradual ascension of the legislature vis-à-vis the executive constituted an institutional base from which the Conservatives could check the power of this group.

Before 1874 property and income qualifications restricted the franchise but did not completely exclude the lower classes. Valenzuela's analysis has shown that already the majority of the electorate comprised "men of middle-lower- to lower-class background," and that the income qualifications "could be met by artisans, most if not all adult male salaried workers and miners, and petty merchants" (J. S. Valenzuela 1996:224). Indeed, the government had sought electoral support among lower-class groups, particularly public employees, including army officers, policemen, and national guard troops (J. S. Valenzuela 1996:228–29), and its reliance on electoral support had led to practices through which the government manipulated the voter registration lists. Therefore, two linked issues were on the reform agenda: the franchise and the impartiality of the two local juntas with responsibility for and oversight of registration lists. The 1874 electoral reform addressed both of these issues. It effectively eliminated all suffrage restrictions other than literacy (J. S. Valenzuela 1996:224, 233) and re-formed the composition of the juntas to increase their independence.

The passage of the 1874 reform was based on Electoral Support Mobilization. The reform was favored by the Radical Party because it drew its support primarily in the newer urban classes. However, the more important force pushing the reform and sponsoring it in the legislature was the Conservative Party, which, in 1872, had abandoned its coalition with the governing Liberals. Now in the opposition, "Conservatives soon realized that they had no choice but to push for an expanded and freer suffrage if they were ever to succeed in capturing the state" (A. Valenzuela 1983:19). In the new reform, the party sought to enfranchise and register its own rural constituency, by expanding the suffrage to all literate males and by eliminating government interference and ongoing discretion in voter registration. Indeed, the effect of the new law was primarily to enfranchise those who listed their occupation as agriculturalists, a group that rose to nearly half the national electorate (J. S. Valenzuela 1996:233).

Despite the 1874 reform and the existence of national political conventions, the government continued to have the informal power to choose "official" candidates (Remmer 1984:19–21). As the practice became increasingly unpopular, the issue was again addressed following the 1891 civil war and the establishment of the "parliamentary republic," which reduced presidential power. In that year, the Law of Municipalities established popularly elected local councils, which were granted autonomy from executive power and were charged with overseeing voter registration and the elections themselves. These reforms broke central government control of the electoral process and reduced oligarchic power, while the role of electoral power brokers recruited from more popular sectors gained in importance. As elsewhere, many informal "undemocratic" practices remained or replaced older forms of control. These included bossism, patron-client relations, vote buying, electoral fraud, and agreements to limit the voter rolls, as well as, in 1914, a law that withdrew responsibility for the administration of the suffrage from the local councils (A. Valenzuela 1977: 193–94, 213–15). Nevertheless, the 1891 electoral reform represented a democratizing change, and the coalitional base and political motivation of this reform remained the same as that of the earlier reforms: "since their fall from power [the Conservatives] suffered from electoral intervention as much as they had formerly profited by it" (Galdames 1941:364). Democratic reform was thus largely an interoligarchic affair – an integral part of partisan competition and the related institutional struggle between the executive and the legislature.

BRITAIN

"The British case is so singular in so many ways, both in terms of the antecedents of democracy and the process of democratization, that it is virtually impossible to decide which factor(s) was (were) the most important on the basis of comparative analysis" (Rueschemeyer et al. 1992:95). Indeed, given the exceptionally incremental nature of the process, there is much scholarly controversy about the point at which Britain crossed the threshold of "democracy," as well as about the interpretation of the politics of reform. If the suffrage criterion is the enfranchisement of much of the working class or a mass electorate, one can argue that those conditions were met, respectively, in the Reform Acts of 1867 and 1884, even though the percentage of adult males enfranchised was somewhat lower than the other cases considered here (see Table 1.2). With the 1884 act, a uniform householder and lodger franchise gave the vote to adult men with a decent settled home (Blackburn 1995:74). In addition, of course, one must remember that this franchise attached only to the House of Commons, and the nonelected House of Lords continued to wield a legislative veto. We consider the 1867 and 1884 reforms here, and the 1918 reform in Chapter 3. The former reforms are commonly understood primarily as a process of competitive support mobilization by Conservatives and Liberals.

Although the democratization process had its beginnings much earlier (e.g., the Reform Act of 1832 and even before), the Reform Acts of 1867 and 1884 were explicitly directed at incorporating the lower classes. The 1867 act, which introduced the household suffrage in the boroughs, enfranchised roughly two-thirds of the male working-class population and made the working class the majority of the electorate in the country at large (Himmelfarb 1966:107). While the 1884 act was primarily directed at the countryside by extending the household suffrage to the counties, it further extended the working-class vote primarily among agricultural workers and miners (Mann 1993:617; Price 1990:8). While the reforms of the 1860s to 1880s were primarily the result of the strategic calculations of the major parties, some working-class protest was also present.

The Reform Act of 1867 must be understood above all in terms of the political competition between Liberal and Conservative parties. The 1832 Reform Act had extended the vote to the middle classes, so that prior to the 1867 reform the working class remained largely disenfranchised. The reform had primarily enfranchised a middle-class constituency that benefited the Liberal Party, leaving the Conservative Party in an increasingly weak position. Since that earlier reform, two alternative strategies had emerged within the latter: the Peelites looked to an alliance with the conservative bourgeoisie, and the Young England Disraelians favored an appeal to the working class on the basis of paternalistic social reform. Neither triumphed. The former were driven from the party in 1846, and the latter languished. In the two decades after 1846, the Conservative Party, having failed to pursue either coalitional strategy, became a permanent minority (Smith 1967:1–24).

Reform was on the agenda, however, of interest particularly to industrial and commercial factions, whose policies were blocked in a Parliament that disproportionately represented landed groups. Two reform issues were salient: the distribution of seats and an extended suffrage, although entrepreneurial groups were divided over this last and the possibilities of enlisting working-class support (Searle 1993:202–13). In 1866, the Liberal Party introduced a moderate reform bill. The defection of the so-called Adullamites not only defeated the reform but brought down the Whig government, ushering in a minority Conservative government. The following year, under Disraeli's leadership, a much broader reform bill was introduced and passed.

Blake (1967:456), a biographer of Disraeli, has stated, "The process whereby the 1867 Reform Bill was launched constitutes one of the oddest histories of confusion, cross-purposes and muddle in British political history." Be that as it may, the bill was passed within the strategic context of the Tories' electoral position. A competitive dynamic surrounding reform with perhaps three components had set in. The first was an electoral appeal to the working class, as groups within both parties saw some possibilities of attracting elements within the working class. As Smith (1967:29) has argued, "No party which aspired to govern could, in the mid-'sixties, altogether ignore the growing social and political force of urban labour . . . If the Conservatives were to re-establish their fortunes on a stable and permanent foundation, it was essential that they should find means of cultivating support among the urban working men." The strategy to enlarge the Conservatives' constituency was based on an expectation about the predisposition of the working class. According to Himmelfarb (1966: 113), the Tories widely held "the belief that the lower classes were not only naturally conservative in temperament but also naturally conservative in politics. . . . The Tories were democratic, one might say, because they assumed the demos was Tory."

Second, and relatedly, once reform had been put on the agenda, the parties competed for the ability to shape it, to cast it in a form to their benefit. With respect to the suffrage itself, a more limited extension was seen as enfranchising that segment of workers more likely to vote Liberal, whereas a broader suffrage was seen as including a constituency more potentially amenable to a Conservative appeal (Smith 1967:1–36, 90; Lee 1994:141). Third, the Tory leaders viewed reform as a way to change the party, from a backward-looking minority party of traditional, landed interests to a more competitive one that was relevant to the new, emerging issues and social forces.

The reform issue, then, had become a focal point of competition in the two-party system, and the passage of the 1867 bill must be seen in that light. The form that it took in Tory hands resulted from the strategic position of the Conservative Party (Lee 1994:140–41). "Only a genuinely large measure could bring them any popularity in the country . . . , put the Reform question to rest, and prevent the Liberals from using it as a recurring device to place themselves in a popular and the Conservative party in an obstructive posture" (Smith 1967:92).

Although this case is seen as deriving its primary impulse from the competitive strategies of those in power, some working-class demands were present in the British history of democratization. Such pressures for democratizing reforms went back to the Chartist movement of 1838–48, though after 1848 the movement had subsided. In the 1860s, however, working-class attention to the issue of political reform and the franchise was revived. Demands for reform first arose from the middle-class liberal Reform Union in the early 1860s, and then from its working-class partner, the Reform League, beginning in 1865. By 1866 the Reform League had enlisted the support of much of the growing trade-union movement (including the London Trades Council, which officially endorsed the Reform League's program in January 1867). In the year following June 1866 – the period between the defeat of the Liberals' moderate reform bill and the passage of the Conservative bill – the Reform League mounted demonstrations of ten to a hundred thousand participants in London and other major cities (Finn 1993:246–48; Biagini 1992:261–62).

The main impact of these demands has been much debated (Lee 1994: 142), but the mobilization of the Reform League was less to force concessions from a reluctant government than it was to draw attention to an issue over which the game of partisan competition between the major parties could be fought. In June 1866, after the defeat of the Liberal bill and the fall of the Liberal government, "middle-class liberals were forced to court the working classes in an effort to wrest the initiative of reform from the Tories. . . . In the process of seeking to mobilize labour in this manner against the Tory government, middle-class liberals engaged in a gradual, public rapprochement" with the working class (Finn 1993:245). With bourgeois radicalism growing in response to working-class agitation, the Tories saw an opportunity to "deprive the Liberal party of the popular benefit of this expanding liberal vision . . . [and] pre-empted the Liberals' claim to constitute the party of parliamentary reform" (Finn 1993:253–54).

The politics of the Reform Act of 1884 continued the pattern of competitive support mobilization, but this time Liberal leader William Gladstone was the chief sponsor. Gladstone pursued this reform in connection with another strategy as well: he saw the reform as a means to address the issue of home rule and the Irish problem (Jones 1972:178). Workers had made their electoral participation felt by helping to bring about a Conservative victory in 1874, and, although the 1871–75 period was probably the only time in which most working-class voters supported the Tories, a substantial minority continued to vote Conservative throughout the nineteenth century (Luebbert 1991:15–16; Hunt 1981:271).

Disraeli's use of a suffrage extension to bring his Conservative Party to power and win a base of working-class supporters offered a model for Gladstone. Just as Disraeli had cut into a natural Liberal constituency, Gladstone saw a suffrage extension to the countryside as a means to increase the Liberals' support base and draw support from a potential Tory sector. As Wright summarizes, "The principle of democracy having been admitted in 1867, the Act of 1884 owed even more to cold political calculation. Liberals had long realized the need to broaden the basis of their support in the countryside, especially since the appearance of new suburban Toryism" (Wright 1970:13; see also Cole 1941).

In addition to calculations regarding partisan advantages, Gladstone saw another benefit in extending the franchise: it would make class politics more politically salient in a way that would not threaten the social order but help strengthen the empire. Specifically, it would diffuse "the growing nationalism in the periphery . . . [and] dilute the forces for Home Rule. . . . For the Liberals the new identities derived from class could be seen as potentially useful" (Wellhofer 1996:46).

Once again, some working-class agitation was a part of the politics of reform, though most of the labor movement, whose urban base had been substantially enfranchised in 1867, remained aloof. Despite the fact that the 1867 reform fell short of full manhood suffrage, the question of its further extension "was no longer of immediate interest" (Biagini 1992: 277) to the Reform League. Indeed, "on the passing of the Reform Act [of 1867], the leaders of the Reform League held that its work was done, and decided to dissolve it" (Cole 1948:191). Its place was in some sense taken by the Labour Representation League, founded in 1869 to promote working-class registration and candidates and to follow the course of legislation of relevance to workers (Humphrey 1912:32–33; Biagini 1992:288).

However, the reform issue was taken up in the 1870s by those workers still excluded after the 1867 reform: miners in the villages and agricultural workers. The movement among the miners was largely limited to the northeast and agitation regarding the franchise ceased after 1874 (Cole 1948:191). The agricultural workers, who composed the main population excluded by the suffrage restrictions, generally found little sympathy or cooperation among the urban workers, some of whom found the former wanting in intelligence, education, and habits (Biagini 1992:291). Indeed, "after the radical triennium of 1872–74, manhood suffrage was relegated to the margins of plebeian politics, having more or less the same position as women's suffrage and a wider lodger franchise, measures which few radicals objected to *in principle*, but which many did their best to obstruct *in practice*" (Biagini 1992:306).

Agricultural workers, however, did demonstrate for the county household franchise and, starting in the 1870s, organized a steady succession of meetings and demonstrations (Biagini 1992:292–93; see also 296). When the Third Reform Bill was introduced on 28 February 1884, rural workers launched an intensive campaign throughout East Anglia and northern England. After the Lords vetoed the bill in July, demonstrations and meetings accelerated (Biagini 1992:298–301; Jones 1972:162–72).

In many ways, the main effect of working-class agitation in favor of political reform was once again to demonstrate the strategic possibilities of seeking labor support. As in the 1860s, the Liberals saw an opportunity in this rural agitation, the effect of which was to "whip up Liberal support for the county franchise" (Biagini 1992:297). The growth of trade unionism also alerted some Liberals to a potential appeal available to the Liberal Party. In the 1870s the Labour Representation League had sought closer ties with the Liberals but had been rebuffed; now, with the ascendancy of Radicals in the Liberal Party, Gladstone was pushed in this direction. Similarly the Amalgamated Labour League representing agricultural workers made overtures and held out the possibility of establishing a Liberal support base during the 1880 election that brought Gladstone's victory (Wellhofer 1996:46). The strategic calculation of the Liberal Party was clear. As Chamberlain noted, the franchise was "the card to play which would give the Liberals a majority at the next elections" (Jones 1972:28). Yet the final passage of the bill came as a result of a compromise, in which the Liberals were forced to yield some of their strategic advantage with the Redistribution Act of 1885, which virtually eliminated the traditional two-member constituencies (Butler 1963:5). Nevertheless, "one immediate result of this was that the agricultural labourers, grateful for the gift of the vote, began to throw themselves wholeheartedly in support of the Liberal Party candidates in the forthcoming general election" (Scotland 1996:162).

In this way, Britain's two political parties carried out back-to-back suffrage extensions as part of a competitive gambit in order to draw support from a constituency normally associated more closely with the opposition. As Judge (1984: 16–17) has suggested, the extension of the suffrage must be seen in terms of the "search for cross-class alliances by competing factions of capital coupled with exigent drives for partisan and personal political advantage within the Commons. . . . [Evident are] the considerable limitations of mass action. . . . Only when [the existing political] order was willing to admit the working class into parliamentary competition on something more like its own terms was the franchise extended."

NORWAY

The establishment of a democratic regime in Norway occurred in the period from 1814 to 1898. The main reforms that constituted the democratization process can be understood in terms of the dynamics of party competition and electoral mobilization, with the working class appearing on the scene in the final step of democratization.

In 1814 Norway, ceded to Sweden by Denmark, gained political autonomy in all but external affairs and adopted a constitution that provided for an indirectly elected parliament, or Storting, and a suffrage that enfranchised about 45 percent of adult males (Terjesen 1990:111). Despite the establishment of the Storting, in practice government at this time was dominated by the Swedish king, who retained the right to dissolve the parliamentary body at will, and a central administrative elite (Rokkan 1966:74–75). In the 1860s, an opposition movement against "the regime of the officials" (Rokkan 1966:75) and in favor of parliamentary sovereignty vis-à-vis the king came together. Based on a weak and fractious coalition of rural populists and liberal urban middle sectors, the movement found temporary unity in its anti-oligarchic, anti-Swedish position. The 1884 reforms took place within this context of political struggle, which led to "unprecedented mobilization of new voters on each side" (Rokkan 1966:75).

Despite some efforts, the "Left opposition," as it became known, was at first only marginally successful at mobilizing the working class, which was quite small and neither organized nor very politicized. From their side, the workers took little initiative in demanding political reform. The first worker associations were not formed until the 1870s, and these were mostly charitable or philanthropic, and were led by other classes. "At most, they served to ventilate the question of extending the franchise" (Derry 1973:134). By the end of the 1870s, however, the left was able to win a majority in the Storting and in 1881 proposed an extension of the suffrage, but an income qualification that was almost twice as high in urban as rural areas was included in the reform. According to Derry, wealthy farmers "would have offered bitter opposition to any more extensive change, and their attitude was not challenged by any vociferous demand among the unenfranchised" (Derry 1973:137).

With the left and the right finally organized into the Venstre and Conservative parties respectively, a new reform was passed in 1884 as a result of fierce struggle that almost erupted in civil war and finally culminated in impeachment proceedings against the King's Council. The new law not only established parliamentary sovereignty, but expanded the franchise, increasing the number of urban voters by 49 percent. This extension of the suffrage, which included many workers and employees, has been interpreted in terms of the Venstre's need for working-class votes (Terjesen 1990:112).

The final step in the democratization process occurred in 1898 with the introduction of manhood suffrage (with minor qualifications), followed in 1905 by the achievement of independence from Sweden and the adoption of direct elections to the Storting. The working class played some role in these developments, beginning to find an independent, pro-democratic voice with the creation of the Labor Party in 1887, though in the first several years the party met with little worker receptivity. An indispensable factor, however, was the political strategy of the Venstre. Almost immediately after the 1884 reform, the coalition that made up the party, always divided by rural-urban and religious cleavages, fell apart, and the moderate wing defected to form a new party (Luebbert 1991:66–68, 121–22). Having difficulty in maintaining control over the Storting, the weakened Venstre championed two issues which helped rebuild electoral support following the party split. The first was the nationalist issue, concerning the demand for autonomy in external relations, which remained at the forefront of Norwegian politics and gained added immediacy within the Venstre at this time as Norway moved to become a major sea power and trading economy.[18] The second was the issue of manhood suffrage, which in turn was also expected to "add weight to nationalist demands" (Derry 1973:155).

The main dynamic of the 1898 reform was thus strategic support mobilization by the Venstre, which faced greater electoral competition after the party split and was increasingly eager to make a credible claim for external autonomy from Sweden. To some extent, however, the party's electoral and political-economic strategy interacted with working-class preferences for an extended franchise. The working-class vote was potentially available to the Venstre as a way to attract support both for the party in elections and for the nationalist cause: even as the party was breaking apart, the working class increasingly offered its support, eventually forming an alliance with a branch of urban radicals. At the same time, the still tiny Labor Party (which won no seats and fewer than one thousand votes, or 0.6 percent, in 1897 [Mackie and Rose 1991:360–61]) supported full manhood suffrage. In presenting an alternative for additional defections from the Venstre, the Labor Party thereby defined a basis on which the Venstre would have to compete for workers' votes. In the end, manhood suffrage was established in 1898 as a result of Venstre strategy supported by labor demands for an extended franchise.

ITALY

The move beyond a restricted parliamentary regime in Italy can be dated with the 1912 reforms, which established manhood suffrage. The initiative

18 Norwegian trade and navigation expanded substantially at the end of the century, far outstripping that of Sweden. See Carstairs 1980:88.

grew out of Giolitti's strategy to broaden the base of his liberal coalition and achieve parliamentary consensus as he pursued expansionist policies abroad. Giolitti vastly extended the suffrage to include nearly all of the working class and peasantry with the hope that the Italian masses would provide patriotic support for himself, his liberal coalition, and his plan to make Italy a major world power. However, the colonial venture itself radicalized workers and the trade-union movement, as in reaction they moved from a reformist, cooperative orientation to overt opposition. Further, a significant part of the Socialist Party recognized the conservative, system-supporting nature of Giolitti's suffrage extension. As a consequence, workers and working-class organizations were at most divided over the merits of Giolitti's reform from above, with many leaders strongly opposed to the reform.

As in Britain, the process of expanding participation of the parliamentary regime followed a series of previous reforms. Inspired by the French republican movement and Napoleonic influence, a liberal movement grew in Italy, reaching a peak in a series of revolutions in the Italian kingdoms in 1848 and the forced flight of the pope from Rome, where, in 1849, a Constituent Assembly elected by universal manhood suffrage proclaimed a Roman Republic. These liberal republican movements were soon defeated, until Piedmont succeeded in uniting most of Italy in the 1860s, completing the process with the annexation of Rome in 1870.

Italy, as a unified entity, was founded as a parliamentary regime with a lower house directly elected on a highly restrictive suffrage, which limited the vote to literate males who paid a set minimum in direct taxation, thereby enfranchising about 2 percent of the population in 1870.[19] The next step occurred following the "parliamentary revolution" of 1876, when the government of the Right fell and the Left came to power on a program of liberal reforms. Quickly, however, the reform program moderated as the Left grew "fat and satisfied in power" (Seton-Watson 1967:51). Nevertheless, in 1882 a new suffrage law extended the franchise to literate males over twenty-one who, in addition, met a lowered property qualification or had a primary education. The working class did not champion the 1882 reform. Following the Paris Commune it had become strongly influenced by Bakunist anarchism and, adopting a revolutionary rather than reformist line, it had attempted two insurrections in 1874 and 1877. The more reformist Socialist Party was not formed until 1892 (Andreucci 1990:192).

19 This discussion of Italy especially draws on Salomone 1945; Seton-Watson 1967; and Webster 1975.

The effects of the new law were minimal for two reasons. First, during the next two decades the liberals consolidated a dominant centrist bloc of the moderate Right and moderate Left to protect themselves against the potential impact of the electoral reform. At its core, Trasformismo, as the pattern of conciliation was called, was a system of political clientelism based on the formation of ad hoc parliamentary groups that monopolized political office by using patronage and fraudulent elections to ensure electoral success. Second, although the broadened suffrage was the project of liberals and continued to exclude most of the lower classes (virtually all the peasantry and the great majority of artisans and workers [Salvemini 1945:xv]), it was viewed as too strongly favoring the Italian Socialists and anarchists, who were gaining considerable organizational strength in the last decades of the nineteenth century, and thus potentially threatening the liberals' political hegemony. In 1884 Crispi's government revised the electoral register, disenfranchising some 874,000 voters, a move adopted in part "for the repression of anarchism" (Seton-Watson 1967:167).

Giolitti's reforms of 1912 established nearly universal manhood suffrage and laid the basis for support mobilization in the elections of 1913.[20] Part of Giolitti's political strategy was to build as large a support base for the liberals as possible, and to that end he attempted to co-opt reformist elements in the Socialist Party and the working class more generally. Giolitti believed that the Socialists and labor leagues could be brought into the liberal coalition as subordinate partners, a strategic alternative to state repression for controlling these groups. According to Webster (1975: 23, 24), "He strove to bring into the ministerial system all the outsiders who could bring votes and influence with them: radicals, republicans, socialists, and Catholics of varying provenance. . . . Only anarchists and syndicalists were permanently frozen out – they explicitly advocated violence." By bringing new groups into the coalition, "the liberal parliamentary oligarchy would go on governing Italy. It would simply assimilate its opponents, co-opting one group after another."

The specific timing of the 1912 reforms was tied to winning support for upcoming elections in the immediate aftermath of Giolitti's decision to wage warfare in Africa. Prior to his decision to invade Libya in 1911, Giolitti had already faced substantial opposition from the far Right, which encouraged him to engage in a much more ambitious war of conquest. The Libyan adventure was now certain to draw criticism from the Left, yet still without mollifying the Right, thus potentially leaving Giolitti and his

20 The 1912 Reform Act raised the voting age to thirty but kept it at twenty-one for men who had served in the armed forces or paid a minimum property tax. This increased the electorate from 3 million to 8.5 million. Salvemini 1945:xv.

liberals isolated for the elections of 1913. Facing cross pressures from the Right and Left, Giolitti extended the suffrage as a means to mobilize the electoral support of Italy's previously disenfranchised sectors, including the working class.

The working-class organizations played little role in these developments. Since the 1880s working-class politics had been marked by considerable tension between workers and intellectuals, a tension that pushed workers toward a syndicalist orientation. In 1882 workers had formed a Labor Party, specifically restricting membership to workers out of disgust with intellectual quibbling (Landauer 1959:385). The two groups united in 1893 to form the Socialist Party, which gained seats in Parliament. Yet divisions remained. Although the left syndicalists did not oppose electoral and parliamentary participation, they emphasized revolutionary action through the general strike. The Left gradually grew, receiving an impetus from the same event that motivated Giolitti's suffrage reform, the Libyan War, which was opposed as a colonial adventure by the General Labor Confederation. "Many workers, who a short time before had supported reformism . . . turned to the radical side because they wanted a complete break with the liberals whom they considered war mongers" (Landauer 1959:389).

The Socialist Party itself was split over the war and divided over how to respond to a suffrage extension initiated by Giolitti. Socialist leaders widely recognized that Giolitti's motives "had a double purpose: to temper, if not actually to tame, the revolutionary tendencies of [the Socialists], and to assure himself the necessary Socialist votes to maintain his parliamentary majorities" (Salomone 1945:58). The famous debate between the Socialists Gaetano Salvemini and Filippo Turati over Giolitti's potential electoral reform illustrates this division even among reformist Socialists. Salvemini held that universal suffrage must be won by the people, rather than bestowed from above by Giolitti, to which Turati replied: "I would accept it not only from Giolitti, but, if necessary, from the pope himself" (Salomone 1945:70). While Turati's resolution was initially approved, he "was to confess in 1911 that Salvemini's prediction in regard to universal suffrage as a mere grant from above was on its way to realization" (Salomone 1945:58). In the end, Giolitti's gamble failed. Through the reform he had hoped to win Socialist support, but in 1912 the revolutionary syndicalist faction won a majority at the party congress. By then, however, Giolitti was committed and could not go back on the reform even though the Socialists had gone into opposition (Landauer 1959:389). The dominant view within the labor movement was expressed by Benito Mussolini, who suggested that Giolitti's grant of manhood suffrage "was merely the oxygen pump administered to the dying parliamentary regime in order to prolong its life a while, but it could not be the instrument for the complete emancipation of the proletariat" (Landauer 1959:77).

With the 1912 reforms, Italy met the institutional criteria employed in the present analysis. Nevertheless, because of the ongoing informal practice of intervention in the electoral process, some analysts have dated the move to a democratic regime with the 1919 reforms, which, in addition to eliminating the remaining restrictions on the suffrage for males between twenty-one and thirty, introduced proportional representation, thereby substantially curbing those practices by giving an advantage to well-organized parties. This reform episode was also concerned with support mobilization as parties already participating in the electoral arena attempted to oppose the Giolittian parties and gain a competitive advantage. Working-class organizations played a minor role in this reform: the Socialist Party was split between the reformists and the revolutionary maximalists inspired by the Russian Revolution, with the former happy to reap the benefits of the reform but the latter in control of the party apparatus. Although reformists were prominent in the Socialist-affiliated unions, the strike wave of 1919, which preceded the reforms, was not oriented toward issues of democratic reforms. Rather than a working-class project, the reforms were a product of the broad consensus that, in the context of deep divisions over the war, the old parliamentary regime had been discredited. The reforms were championed by, perhaps more than any other party, the Popular Party, newly organized out of earlier Catholic groups and intent on mobilizing a broad multiclass support base (Seton-Watson 1967:510–47).

URUGUAY

Uruguayan democracy can be dated to the 1918 constitution.[21] In the nineteenth century the country had been politically unstable, with foreign interventions, military interventions, and dictatorships more characteristic than the restricted democratic rule outlined in the country's founding constitution of 1830. Nevertheless, out of the turmoil emerged two oligarchic parties that became deeply entrenched and well institutionalized and that would continue to dominate Uruguayan politics. It is difficult to assess the period prior to the 1918 constitutional reforms in terms of the

21 It should be noted that different authors refer to different dates for these same reforms, depending on when they were adopted or implemented. The democratic constitution was drafted and approved by plebiscite in 1917, formally became the law in 1918, and was implemented through elections held under the new provisions in 1919.

accountability of the indirectly elected president, the effective power of the legislature, and the impact of the literacy restriction on the franchise. In 1893 and 1898 reforms had increased the suffrage, improved registration procedures, and changed the electoral law, but the literacy qualification and the lack of a provision for the secret ballot continued as important limitations. These were addressed in the 1918 constitution, which according to González (1991:4) brought Uruguay to the point of democracy. The 1918 provisions were brought about as a reform from above and resulted from the changing strategic calculations of Uruguay's two, highly competitive, traditional political parties.

The reforms of 1918, as well as those of the 1890s, must be seen against the background of a long history of both intense partisan conflict and also cooperation among factions of the two opposing parties that had come to dominate politics during the nineteenth century. The last half of the 1880s inaugurated a period of civilian political supremacy based on the dominant political position of a faction of the Colorado Party, a position that electoral fraud helped to perpetuate. In the 1890s two groups engaged in competitive mobilization against the hegemonic Colorado faction: the opposition Blancos and a Colorado faction, the latter led by José Batlle y Ordóñez and representing a new middle-sector constituency (Reyes Abadie and Vázquez Romero n.d.:498, 507). The initiative for the 1898 reform came from the Blancos. In 1897 the opposition Blancos rebelled in favor of clean elections, the secret vote, and minority representation in government. In the pact that brought the Revolution of 1867 to an end, the parties agreed on a plan of coparticipation that turned political control of eight departments over to the Blancos. The pact also committed the parties to reform the electoral laws the following year (Reyes Abadie and Vázquez Romero n.d.:240–48).

The reform initiative subsequently passed to the Batllista faction of the Colorados. In 1903, José Batlle was elected president, and sought to restructure Uruguayan politics. His reform project had three main components. First, he broke the coparticipation pact with the opposition Blancos and proceeded to lay down the conditions and groundwork for party government based on securing the electoral dominance of his Colorado Party. Second, at the same time he sought to establish a collective executive as an institutional avenue through which the opposition party would participate. Third, Batlle sought to establish a "model country" through a set of progressive social and welfare reforms.

Batlle saw the working class as a central part of his project. Workers were in many ways the main beneficiaries of the social reforms, which centered on the regulation of work conditions, the right to organize, and support of strikes, in addition to wide-ranging social reforms, such as education and pensions. An expanded suffrage was a central part of Batlle's vision. These reforms not only benefited the workers in accordance with Batlle's progressive orientation and his vision of the worker as citizen (Nahum 1995:2:36; Vanger 1980:209–11), but they were also intended to win Colorado support among that growing class. That support would be crucial to securing a dominant electoral position for the Colorados over the longer term and in the short run to passing his constitutional reforms, most saliently his extremely controversial proposal for a collective executive. Thus, mobilization of a majoritarian and secure electoral support base was essential to this institution-building and political restructuring project, and "it is clear that Batlle sought worker support, acted and legislated in order to achieve it" (Barrán and Nahum 1982:284).

In 1913 Batlle produced an outline of his constitutional reforms, and in 1915 the Colorado majority in the legislature passed a new electoral law that provided for full manhood suffrage and the secret ballot for elections to a Constituent Assembly the following year. Although those elections came during the time when the Batllistas were most active in passing social reforms, the Colorados did not succeed in winning a majority. Rather, elections, which were hard fought particularly around the controversial executive reform proposal, produced a victory for the conservative forces: the Blancos in combination with a dissident faction of the Colorados.

In the next step, the Blancos resumed the lead. Having benefited from the reform provisions, the Blancos attempted to introduce similar measures for the upcoming legislative elections. For their part, recognizing that the reforms had played into the hands of their political opponents, Batlle supporters in the legislature reversed themselves. They proceeded to block the proposals, rely on old restrictions, and introduce new mechanisms by which they ensured their continued but reduced majority in the legislature.[22]

In the end, the reforms embodied in the 1918 constitution came as a compromise between the parties. Set up for a confrontation between the Blanco-dominated Constituent Assembly and the Colorado-dominated legislature, the parties made a pact and came to an agreement on the new provisions. Fresh from their victory under the reforms that had governed the elections for the Constituent Assembly, it was now the Blancos who championed the introduction of the 1915 legislation into the constitution.

---

22 Reyes Abadie and Vázquez Romero n.d.:214, 225–26; Zubillaga 1985:34; Costa Bonino 1995:103–9.

With the batllistas clearly on the defensive, the electoral reforms came about during a period that has been analyzed as the Conservative Republic or the conservative reaction against the progressive program of Batlle (Caetano 1992; Collier and Collier 1991).

Working-class demands were not part of the reform process. Indeed, workers were not particularly oriented to electoral politics as a vehicle for achieving their collective ends. Anarchism was still influential within the labor movement and in the new FORU, which had been founded as a labor central in 1905. In accordance with this orientation, workers were often encouraged not to take part in electoral politics. With worker demands centered on economic rather than political issues and expressed primarily through strikes rather than the vote, the politics of democratic reform must be seen in terms of the competitive mobilization and strategic interaction of Uruguay's two traditional parties.

CONCLUSION

This chapter has examined two patterns of democratization from above, two patterns that follow the political logic not of popular or lower-class groups and their demands but of an elite stratum of middle- and upper-class groups. In the first pattern, primarily middle-sector groups, sometimes joined by fractions of more traditional upper classes, pursued liberal or republican projects. These groups sought to further their political aims by seeking a new basis of legitimacy and changing state institutions in a way that would give them access to state power. Often the politics of regime change or democratic reform in this pattern took place in the protest arena proceeding through rebellions, revolts, and/or coups, and often including military groups. The two cases without outright rebellions or revolts were Argentina and Denmark. In Argentina, however, the middle sectors in the UCR had already demonstrated a willingness to undertake insurrectionary activities and the government finally followed the prudent course and adopted the reform. The Danish middle sectors exerted pressure primarily through their position in the existing consultative assembly, although the reforms were finally adopted in the context of a war in which the middle sectors of Schleswig and Holstein participated in the 1848 wave of national, liberal uprisings and also demanded secession from Denmark. This pattern, then, primarily consisted of middle-sector "outs" seeking democratic reform in the protest arena.

The other pattern of democratization from above was characterized by initiatives on the part of those in power as they undertook a strategy of

Support Mobilization. These are not cases of "outs" seeking inclusion or access to power, but of those already included as formal powerholders within the regime seeking to solidify their positions or gain the advantage in the context of partisan competition.

In these patterns of democratization from above, the popular classes in general and the working class in particular played little or no role. In neither pattern was it envisioned that power would effectively pass to the majority. This calculation rested either on the anticipation of co-optation or on confidence in the operation of clientelism and "deferential communities" (Mann 1995:26–27). The three cases where the working class participated as a pro-democratic actor are France, Britain, and Norway. Nevertheless, these democratizing episodes are best understood primarily in terms of the goals, strategies, and initiatives of the upper- or middle-class groups.

3

POLITICAL CALCULATIONS
AND SOCIALIST PARTIES

The advent of social democracy brought about a third pattern, Joint
Projects, in which the working class most clearly played an important
role. Although these are the cases most often described as working-class
democratization, a number of features in this depiction lack sufficient
recognition. This pattern combines projects from above and from below in
class terms, in that democratic reform was the outcome of the strategies of
the working class as well as other classes. Also these cases primarily entail
incumbent projects – that is, all the major actors, including the working
class by the time it got involved, had the political status of an "in" group.
A final feature is that both arenas of action came into play – the delibera-
tion/negotiation arena and the protest arena of mass mobilization. In the
pattern of Support Mobilization, analyzed in the preceding chapter, democratic reform was pursued by strategizing elites or political leaders to
build an electoral support base. What has often been overlooked is the
extent to which this strategic dynamic was also part of the cases in the
Joint Projects pattern – and the fact that parliamentary labor-based parties
were players in this game of competitive struggles among parties.

JOINT PROJECTS

The temporal and geographical clustering of the cases characterized by
Joint Projects is striking and reflects important processes of economic
development, political strategizing, and diffusion of political innovations.
We return to this issue in Chapter 5. For now, suffice it to say that these

77

are cases with the strongest, most organized working class and the cases where working-class organization took place in a way that trade unions were "deeply integrated" with the socialist party (Katznelson 1986:27). This of course is not to say that the whole working-class movement was allied with the socialist party; indeed, in Germany, Belgium, Netherlands, and Britain, it was politically divided. Nevertheless, the socialist party and the union movement aligned with it mobilized mass demonstrations and general strikes in pursuit of democratic reform and constituted an important part of the politics of democratization. On the other side, from the point of view of state and capital interests, the emergence of a working class, organized and politically activated, posed the problem of reaching an accommodation with it. Such an accommodation is an issue confronted everywhere in the course of capitalist development. In many of these cases, it achieved greater urgency from World War I, which heightened the need for working-class cooperation with respect to both production and military recruitment.

A further observation may be made about the effect of World War I. The concentration of reforms at the end of the war – even in the single year of 1918 – jumps out. It is commonly asserted that the war had important democratizing influence in the way it strengthened and legitimated the claims and demands of an emboldened working class, whose contribution and suffering in the war effort earned the gratitude of the whole nation. While there is certainly some truth to this account, one should not overstate this explanation, as it may not describe the main dynamic of these democratic reforms. First of all, in some countries the year is an artifact. In the Netherlands, the reform measure was proposed before the war and considered during its course. In Belgium it could be argued that reform occurred in 1918 as a product of war-induced delay rather than precipitation. Second, in some ways the events of that period not only increased the leverage of a democracy-demanding working class, but they also brought other classes to the pro-democratic column. In some cases non-working-class incumbents came to entertain democratic reform more seriously in connection with the necessity to seek the cooperation of labor unions and parties for war mobilization – both for production and conscription. In others the clout of working-class parties was increased from above by the formation of coalition or national unity governments (as in Britain and Germany), again in connection with the conduct of the war, or (in Belgium) by the formation of a unity government in exile. Third, heightened working-class pressure was surely activated as much by the Russian Revolution as by World War I. From the side of the working class, what perhaps changed most was not the greater force of its pro-democratic agitation, but the revolutionary rather than democratic example of the Russian Revolution, and hence the co-optive pro-democratic strategy of other classes and political actors. This tendency was apparent in Germany, Belgium, and Sweden. The revolutionary threat was particularly central in Finland, where the final step of parliamentary sovereignty was taken by conservatives, not as a co-optive response but in a desperate attempt to achieve independence from Bolshevik Russia.

Within the Joint Projects pattern, the balance of forces and the relative weight of different groups varied. At one end of the spectrum, the working class was a relatively minor actor; at the other, we come close to a situation in which the working class could be said to have forced concessions – particularly noteworthy in this respect are Sweden, Belgium, and Germany. Whatever the relative weight, the cases in the Joint Projects pattern are those for which the strongest argument has been made for a key working-class role – and particularly for the importance of working-class protest, as workers engaged in demonstrations that were in some cases very impressive and insistent. Nevertheless, the image presented in some of the literature of an excluded working class demanding participation and inclusion in the political arena, of working-class "outs" trying to get "in" and wresting concessions from an unwilling elite is not apt. As already suggested, it is inappropriate in two ways.

First, to one extent or another the working class was already "in" – and that "in" position was a crucial element of its political strategy to advance reform. That is to say, at the time of the reform, the working class was already at least partly enfranchised (with the exception of Finland 1906), with the result that a labor-based party had already won seats in parliament. Furthermore, that party was sometimes the largest in parliament (Denmark, Sweden in 1918, Germany); it was often in the governing coalition (Denmark, Sweden in 1918, Germany, the Netherlands); and in Germany it even headed the governing coalition. The earlier reforms that enfranchised the working class were typically not the doing of the working class itself but usually belonged to one of the other patterns described in Chapter 2. Sometimes these reforms had resulted from an array of strategies from above – from the earlier liberal project in Denmark in 1849 to the Bismarckian authoritarian project of 1867/71, both of which established universal male suffrage. Sometimes parties had engaged in support mobilization as strategies of partisan competition, as in the Netherlands and Belgium (although in the latter the working class did exert pressure). And sometimes at least partial working-class enfranchisement came through a process that can be called "bracket creep," in which the failure to reform restrictive suffrage requirements based on income or tax payment resulted in a progressively lower barrier as economic and social change proceeded (Sweden, the Netherlands). For all these reasons, then, the working class had already been at least partly included in the formal, constitutional political arena when it became an actor in the politics of democratic reform.

The second point about this pattern is that even though the working class had representatives in parliament where they could champion reforms and furthermore exerted substantial pressure outside of parliament through demonstrations and general strikes, other parties were also involved and not just in terms of making concessions that were in effect forced upon them. Rather, they must be seen as following their own positive strategies, though clearly the very presence of important and growing working-class parties – apart from any substantive demands – had altered their strategic environment. In this respect, the structural argument about the impact of the working class is important. The point is not simply that the working class demanded democratic reform, though this is part of it, at least in the final steps of the democratization process. The point is equally that the presence of a strong working class already admitted to the electoral arena through previous reforms made it necessary for all parties to reassess their strategic situations, choose new options, and strike bargains to maximize their electoral positions and minimize their vulnerabilities. Confronted with this situation, nonlabor party strategies varied and included attempts to mobilize partisan votes of their own, to pursue coalitions with the labor-based party, or to engage in logrolls in which, for instance, declining conservative forces sought to survive through proportional representation schemes.

Two subtypes can be distinguished within this pattern. The first is the joint lib-lab project, in which labor and liberal forces allied to bring about change in the face of conservative resistance (Denmark in 1915, Belgium in 1893, Finland in 1906, Sweden in 1918). The second is the grand compromise, in which a broad consensus, one that also included more conservative forces pursuing their own strategies, was negotiated (the Netherlands in 1917, Germany in 1918–19, Sweden in 1907, Britain in 1918).[1]

Two scoring problems were discussed at the outset (see Chapter 1): the minimal criteria for a democratic suffrage as "mass" rather than manhood or universal enfranchisement, and the criteria regarding the upper house. In this pattern we confront these issues. These scoring decisions affect the democratic status of Britain in 1884, Sweden in 1907/9, and Denmark prior to 1915. Based on a mass suffrage and a less demanding

---

1 The Belgian reform of 1918 is sui generis: a combination of a unity government and a Constituent Assembly elected under reformed rules adopted in response to unusually strong working-class pressure.

criterion for the upper house, an argument could be made that these cases meet the minimal democratic requirements. Because of the way these cases have often been treated in the literature, however, this analysis will include the subsequent reforms in Denmark in 1915, and Britain and Sweden in 1918.

Finland is included in this category despite its somewhat equivocal working-class role in the reforms through which Finland acquired democratic status in 1918. The Finnish Social Democratic Party participated in the politics of reform in 1906. However, the establishment of parliamentary sovereignty in 1918 was primarily a bourgeois project, and many of the working-class organizations had largely abandoned a democratic for a revolutionary path. Divided over the issue, the Social Democrats had lost their parliamentary majority, and the reform to achieve parliamentary sovereignty was carried out by bourgeois groups seeking independence from Bolshevik Russia.

DENMARK

In Denmark, as we saw, pressures for a constitutional democracy were led by a coalition of urban liberals and farmers in the mid-1830s, culminating in the constitution of 1849, which established manhood suffrage. From then until 1864 the National Liberal Party of the urban middle sectors dominated Danish politics in alliance with the peasant-oriented Venstre. In 1866 something of a democratic setback occurred when the franchise was restricted for half of the (indirectly) elected seats in the Landsting (the upper chamber of the bicameral system), and twelve seats (one-sixth the total) became appointed by the king (Rokkan and Meyriat 1969:60). The suffrage requirements for the lower house (the Folketing) remained unchanged. The context for this reversal was the defeat in the Dano-Prussian War of 1864, for which Liberals were held accountable, although rural-urban cleavages had gradually weakened the governing coalition even before this event (Luebbert 1991:75–77).

In the closing three decades of the nineteenth century, two issues became important to reformers: the appointment of ministers from the majority party in the lower, democratic chamber rather than the upper, now nondemocratic chamber, as was the practice; and the restoration of full suffrage for elections to the upper house. The reform movement gathered strength as the growth of a working class and the formation of pro-reform parties to the left of the Venstre changed the party system. One may recall that because the suffrage requirements for the Folketing were unchanged from 1849, "the Danish working class was born largely enfranchised"

(Luebbert 1991:134). Yet the incipient working class overwhelmingly voted for the urban-based Right in the Folketing until the 1880s.[2] In the 1870s workers' organizations were formed, including the Social Democratic Party, which won one to three seats in Folketing elections from 1884 to 1892 and increased that number to twelve by 1898 (Mackie and Rose 1991:88). After the mid-1890s the Social Democrats began to play "a critical role in realigning urban workers from the right to the left," shifting their support from Conservatives to urban liberals as well as Social Democrats, both of which championed the restoration of manhood suffrage in the Landsting (Luebbert 1991:136). The political realignment of the working class was reflected in the party system. In the 1890s, an urban radical wing within the Venstre gained strength, and this "Reform Venstre" formed a coalition with the Social Democrats as the subordinate partner. In 1901, with their Social Democratic partners winning 14 seats and 19 percent of the vote and Conservatives winning just 8 seats out of 102, the Venstre forced the king to cede ministerial responsibility to the Folketing and to accept the formation of the first Venstre government.

The suffrage reform for the upper house occurred in 1915, after political realignment took a further step. In 1905, the Venstre, moving to the political center, split, producing a pro-reform coalition between the new Radical Venstre and the Social Democrats. By 1913 this coalition enjoyed new success, with the Social Democrats becoming the leading party in terms of popular votes and the allied Radicals forming the government. In 1914 the Conservatives lost their Landsting majority to the Venstre, which offered little resistance to reform of the upper chamber, since a suffrage extension stood to broaden its constituency among the rural poor. The following year, a constitutional amendment introduced universal suffrage (male and female) for both chambers (the second chamber remained indirectly elected). The democratic transition in Denmark can thus be seen as the outcome of goals of both the growing Social Democratic Party, with its working-class constituency, and the Radical Venstre, with a base among urban intellectuals, middle-class progressives, and rural smallholders, as well as the electoral strategy of the increasingly conservative Venstre.

2 Luebbert 1991:78, 136; Dybdahl 1969:6–17. The Social Democratic Party was founded in 1871, but it did not gain a seat in the Folketing until 1884 and did not attempt to become a mass party until that victory (Callesen 1990:140–41).

SWEDEN

Swedish democratization followed a process of gradual regime reform, as the franchise was extended through a series of reform acts in 1866, 1909, and 1918 in a manner similar to England's.[3] Although labor played no role in the initial Reform Act of 1866, one can make a case for a significant labor role in the Reform Act of 1907/9, and its role was clearly decisive in the final step of 1918.

The Parliament Reform of 1866 replaced the long-standing four-estates system with a bicameral parliamentary system, but established only limited suffrage. The First Chamber was indirectly elected by taxpayers according to taxable income, with wealthy individuals granted as many as five thousand votes. Property qualifications restricted the electorate for the Second Chamber.[4] The Reform Act was directed primarily at the incipient urban bourgeoisie and the middle peasantry, which were now incorporated into the Second Chamber, and was enacted before the historical appearance of a significant Swedish working class. Although the reform was sponsored by a moderate liberal, Louis de Geer, opposition to the bill was not very great, and the legislation "is best viewed as a shrewd conservative accommodation" that would not change the existing socio-economic order, and that indeed initially changed very little in terms of the composition of the Riksdag (Tilton 1974:567). In fact, for many conservatives, "control of one house out of two was in some ways better than one Estate out of four" (Verney 1957:89).

The reform of 1907/9 represented what has been called "a great compromise" (Rustow 1971:20).[5] In the 1890s the suffrage became a major issue, pushed especially by the creation of suffrage associations, two "Peoples' Parliaments," and the Liberal and Social Democratic parties, whose lower-middle- and working-class constituencies, respectively, were affected by the suffrage restrictions. Though they disagreed over tactics, with the Liberals rejecting the use of the political strike favored by the Social Democrats, the two parties cooperated on the suffrage issue. Popular pressure and labor agitation thus played an important role in the passage of

---

3 Tilton 1974:567. For good historical overviews of these franchise extensions, see Verney 1957; Rustow 1955, 1971:9–26.

4 Rustow 1955:20–24. Although the 1866 qualifications for the Second Chamber were not changed prior to 1909, workers gradually entered the ranks of those qualified to vote as the wages of artisans and industrial workers rose. From 1872 to 1908 the percentage of enfranchised males over twenty-one years of age rose from 22 percent in rural areas and 21 percent in urban areas to 33 and 45 percent respectively. See Simonson 1990:88.

5 The bill was introduced and initially approved in 1907, but final passage required the further approval by the next Parliament.

this legislation. In 1902, for example, the Social Democrats and the trade unions organized a successful general strike explicitly for suffrage reform. For its part, the Liberal Party was making headway in the Second Chamber and repeatedly, though unsuccessfully, introduced measures for political reform. In 1905 the Liberals edged out the Conservatives in the lower chamber as the Social Democrats also started to gain seats, and for the first time a Liberal prime minister formed a government. Yet, although the Liberals favored manhood suffrage, they did not succeed in this effort: Karl Staaff and his Liberal government failed in the attempt to pass a reform of the lower house in 1906.

The reform of 1907/9 was finally passed by a Conservative government, both responding to opposition pressure and pursuing its own strategy. Arvid Lindman and his Conservative Ministry, which took office after the Liberals' 1906 failure, saw an opportunity to pass a political reform on its own terms. The reform represented an accommodation that conceded manhood suffrage in the lower chamber while it also contained several measures that guaranteed ongoing Conservative power, such as proportional representation, and multiple votes and taxpayers' suffrage in the upper house. At the same time, the combination of reforms fashioned in the compromise dealt a major blow to the Liberals, who in this decade remained the other major party, weakening particularly the dominant reformist wing and breaking up their alliance with the Social Democrats, who, unlike their former partners, rejected the reform (Luebbert 1991:70–72, 130).

The Third Reform of Parliament in 1918/20 established universal suffrage without major qualifications in both chambers.[6] Like the 1907/9 reform, the 1918 legislation was the result of the coincidence of interests of various groups, although worker demonstrations were even more central in this final step of democratization. In 1917 Liberals and Social Democrats again formed a coalition in the Second Chamber and the following year put forward a bill to extend the suffrage. The bill, however, was defeated in the First Chamber. It was only after the economic crisis of 1918 and ensuing worker protests for democracy led by the Social Democrats that the Reform Act was passed. Indeed, in November 1918 labor protests reached such a point as to be perceived as a revolutionary threat by Sweden's Conservative Party and the upper classes. In this very month, Conservative leaders renounced their opposition to a fully democratic regime for fear that Sweden might follow the revolutionary examples of

6 In the First Chamber, members were indirectly elected through commune elections. See Verney 1957:213.

Russia, Germany, and Austria-Hungary (Tilton 1974:568). In the end, then, the reforms of 1918/20 passed as a result of a very forceful role of labor organizations, both party and unions, acting in Parliament and in the streets combined with Liberal Party strategy and Conservative Party concessions.

FINLAND

Two episodes in Finnish history potentially mark the transition to democracy. The first is the famous law of 1906 that, virtually in one step, took Finland from a grand duchy in the Russian Empire with an unreformed Diet under tsarist control to a parliament with substantial sovereignty and universal suffrage, the first in Europe to enfranchise women. The second, following a democratic retrogression, is the set of events of 1917–19 that concluded with the 1919 democratic constitution of an independent country. Both of these episodes can be categorized as Joint Projects.

After being united with Sweden for six hundred years, Finland was invaded by Russia in 1808 and, upon Russia's military defeat of Sweden, was incorporated into the Russian empire as a grand duchy, formally retaining its own institutions under the Russian tsar as its constitutional monarch. Yet, despite the autonomy supposedly granted by Alexander I, after an initial meeting the Diet was not convened again until 1863. After this period of rule by a bureaucracy chosen by the tsar, modest reforms toward a more representative system were adopted in 1869, including a commitment to convene a Diet every five years. Although these reforms also expanded the franchise to "underprivileged" estates (burghers and farmers), the electorate represented only about 4 percent of the population (Arter 1987:8). Moreover, until 1886, the Diet lacked independent legislative authority and could only present petitions for legislation to the Russian-dominated Senate (the council that constituted the executive power).

The 1906 electoral reform was the result of the imperial and anti-imperial strategies of the tsar and Finnish liberals, respectively, in combination with working-class demands. From 1890 to 1905, in reaction to the rising power of Germany, Russia carried out a policy of Russification within Finland that affected recruitment in the police, disbanded the Finnish army, increased the use of the Russian language, and finally in 1899 reduced the power of the Diet, centralizing power and placing approval of all legislation with the tsar. This policy had the effect of pitting the liberal Constitutionalists (Young Finns and Swedish liberals), who advocated passive resistance, against the Compliers, who were willing to appease and accommodate Russia.[7] The former collected petitions of opposition, and for this purpose they sought to mobilize the support of the lower classes, particularly the working class, which was beginning to organize and engage in strikes, albeit largely under middle-class leadership.[8] This support mobilization was already an established pattern as labor organization had had its origin in the 1880s when middle-class groups in the Finnish parties had sought to organize a mass base for the nationalist movement (Nousiainen 1971:21; Kirby 1990:524). In order to appeal to worker support in the face of the Russification policy, the Young Finnish Left within the Constitutionalists backed the right to strike and supported universal suffrage, a key goal of the Social Democratic Party (SDP), which had emerged in 1903 out of the Finnish Workers' Party, formed in 1899 as the working class began to act more independently (Alapuro 1988:112). Despite these overtures, the SDP stayed largely aloof from nationalist activity, concentrating instead on building its own membership (Kirby 1990:524–25).

The SDP became more centrally involved in political issues with the 1905 revolution in Russia, which reverberated in many parts of the empire, including Finland. At this point the SDP joined the Constitutionalists in a national, patriotic strike. With Russia weakened both internally from revolutionary unrest and externally from the military defeat by Japan, the strike succeeded in forcing concessions from the tsar. The result was "Europe's most radical parliamentary reform,"[9] with the replacement of the Four-Estate Diet with a unicameral parliament elected by universal and equal suffrage of all adults over twenty-four. Substantial parliamentary sovereignty and hence social reforms were anticipated, although final approval of legislation continued to rest with the tsar (Alapuro 1988:116).

The 1906 reform can be seen as a Joint Project. It resulted from a combination of (1) a Constitutionalist mobilization against the Russification policy and for political autonomy and (2) the mobilization of the SDP and its worker base in favor of their perennial demand for universal suffrage. When the time came, both groups participated and cooperated in the decisive 1905 strike, and both groups championed a full suffrage: the workers, whose own enfranchisement was at stake and the Constitutionalists, among whom "it was widely felt that a legislature with broad popular

7 T. Soikkanen 1984a:65–66; Rokkan 1981:60; Nousiainen 1971:20–21.
8 The largest of these petitions listed over one-fifth of the entire Finnish population (Alapuro 1988:112).
9 Jutikkala and Pirinen 1962:424, cited in Alapuro 1988:115. See also Tornudd 1968.

support could best stand up against Russia" (Tornudd 1968:28). It has also been suggested that the relatively easy grant of universal suffrage corresponded to an explicit strategy on the part of the Russian rulers, who saw it as a way to benefit the still small SDP, which it regarded as "less dangerous than the more restive bourgeois groups" and as a vehicle that could be used against them. The Russians also thought they could thereby win support for the empire as champions of social reforms, against those Finns who would oppose them (Alapuro 1988:113–14). In the end then, the democratic reform was an achievement both of the working class and of different groups of powerholders that supported it for their own strategic reasons.

As radical as the 1906 reforms were, the one remaining constraint made them largely illusory. From 1907 to 1914 the new Parliament passed a legislative program, but this was vetoed by the Russian-dominated Senate, over which imperial control was even tightened. After 1909 a new governor-general purged the Senate, and for the first time its membership became completely Russian (Smith 1958:6). When war broke out in 1914, Russia imposed a military government on Finland. In the 1916 elections, the SDP won an absolute majority, but Parliament was not allowed to convene. Thus the question of parliamentary sovereignty was essentially the question of nationalism and anti-imperialism. The struggle for parliamentary sovereignty and Finnish autonomy and finally outright independence in 1917–18 took place in the rapidly changing context of the unfolding Russian Revolution.

The first move came from above. Within a week of the February Revolution in Russia, the Provisional Government restored Finnish constitutional rights and allowed the Parliament elected in 1916 to convene. The second step came from the rapidly growing workers' movement, from both the party and the unions. The SDP, following a period after 1906 in which it emphasized electoral and parliamentary activity, now rejected collaboration and alliances with bourgeois parties, and at party conferences it stressed "the intensification and broadening of the class struggle" (H. Soikkanen 1984:122). The unions meanwhile forged an increasingly independent and more militant workers' movement, which mounted strikes and mobilized a militia in the face of the void left by the earlier Russification of the army and police. The SDP government introduced a number of reforms, including a Law on Authority, which proclaimed full autonomy (save for foreign policy and military affairs). In the context of high mobilization and revolutionary fervor both in Russia and Finland, the Kerensky government, backed by Finnish bourgeois groups, rejected all the reforms, dissolved Parliament, and called for new elections. At this stage, then, workers were at the center of the struggle for democracy, but it came to naught.

The final step was the achievement of parliamentary sovereignty and national independence, finally accomplished at the initiative of bourgeois groups. Widespread consensus existed over these issues, but in a revolutionary situation with pitched class conflict, each of the sides pursued its own strategy. In the new elections, the SDP failed to take a clear position on whether it should contest the election or support a revolutionary seizure of power. Thus "aided by revulsion in the socialist ranks against the apparent futility of parliamentary politics" and a halfhearted electoral effort, "a united front of a thoroughly frightened bourgeoisie" won a majority (Upton 1973:108–9; Alapuro 1988:158–59). Within days of the elections, the Bolshevik Revolution occurred, making the issue of parliamentary sovereignty more immediate and reinforcing the inclinations of both sides to push hard: on the one hand, the Bolshevik government gave encouragement and limited support to Finnish workers for a revolutionary seizure of power; on the other, the presence of a Bolshevik government made independence from Russia a more urgent priority for the Finnish bourgeoisie, which had a majority in Parliament and no longer had Russian protectors. The SDP was now subjected to strong pressure from below, specifically from the workers who had just decided to form a national armed workers' organization to be completely controlled by the unions. The party issued a set of demands, including the election of a Constituent Assembly and the implementation of the reforms passed by the previous Parliament. Two weeks later the unions called a general strike based on the same set of demands, forcing the SDP to support the strike. However, the party acted to prevent the strike from becoming an attempt at revolution, and on the fifth day, the strike was called off, with only few concessions (Alapuro 1988:167–68). In December the Finnish government declared independence.

One more iteration took place before the issue was put to rest. With the two sides developing a "Red" and "White" militia, respectively, civil war broke out in January 1918, after the SDP declared the government deposed and established a provisional workers' government. Each side appealed to a big-power protector, the Reds to Russia, the Whites to Germany. Following the Treaty of Brest-Litovsk, German troops landed and the Reds were defeated. With no participation of the Reds,[10] a struggle ensued over the form of government to be adopted: one faction invited

10 While the casualties during the brief war were relatively limited on both sides, its aftermath was bloody. It is estimated that about twenty thousand imprisoned Reds lost their lives in the months following their surrender. Of these about eight thousand were

a German prince to be king of Finland, but Germany's defeat in World War I put an end to that possibility. After new elections in 1919, in which the SDP won 80 of 200 seats, a republican constitution was ratified, and the following year Russia recognized Finnish independence.

BELGIUM

The course of democratic reform in Belgium was characterized by a strong working-class role, one that was apparent through many phases as the process unfolded. From the time of the 1830 rebellion and separation from the Netherlands, Belgium was born as an independent country with a liberal constitution, a "broad" suffrage for the epoch, and substantial parliamentary sovereignty. Though the early democratic reforms took place without working-class participation, the working class soon became a strong and consistent force for democracy. Working-class pressure and particularly the use of the political strike were constant features of the process of Belgian democratization from the 1880s on. They played a key role in the reform of 1893 and the subsequent reforms of the 1910s – the 1912 reform that was aborted by the outbreak of World War I but taken up again in 1918. At the same time, an additional and central feature propelling reform politics was the partisan rivalry between Catholics and Liberals. Belgian democracy, then, came about as a result of working-class pressure combined with the electoral strategy and political orientation of Liberals and to a somewhat lesser degree those of the Catholics as well.

Working-class groups favoring equal manhood suffrage emerged as early as the 1860s and began to gather some momentum in the 1870s, especially at the end of the decade when the POSB (Belgian Socialist Labor Party) was formed.[11] A weak federation based on corporate membership, the POSB brought together unions and other workers' associations around the issue of manhood suffrage, for which it organized its first large street demonstration in 1880 (Mabille 1986:167). In 1885, a more unified Belgian Labor Party, the POB, coalesced, also based on indirect membership. The POB began to organize a series of strikes for suffrage reform in the second half of the 1880s and by 1890–92 orchestrated an incessant campaign in the press and on the streets. In 1891, under considerable pressure from the POB, the Catholic prime minister and the king both let it be known that they might accept some type of electoral reform (Terlinden

---

executed while the rest perished in prison camps. The death toll among the Reds during and after the civil war equaled about 14 percent of the maximum union strength in 1917. See Paavolainen 1971:238, 242; Korpi 1981:311.

11 Cudell 1960; Landauer 1959; Mabille 1986; Sztejnberg 1963:198–215.

1928–30). The POB followed up the next year with a general strike, which ended only when the government announced the forthcoming elections of a Constituent Assembly to revise the electoral articles of the constitution. Parliament's rejection of the proposed reform was answered with yet another general strike in 1893, constituting a second show of strength that resulted in the September reforms (Terlinden 1928–30; H. Linden 1920). A government-POB compromise mediated by the Progressive wing of the Liberal Party introduced manhood suffrage along with plural voting, so that 37 percent of the electorate had 58 percent of the votes (Zolberg 1978:122).

In 1893, then, workers were enfranchised, but the issue of electoral reform for equal votes was still very much on the POB agenda. In continuing the struggle, the POB was now able to take advantage of its newly won seats in Parliament, where indeed it overtook the Liberals. Despite this opportunity to pursue reform in a new, parliamentary arena, the streets remained important in the ongoing struggle. The next major success occurred in 1912, following a big Catholic electoral victory, when the POB transformed a wave of demonstrations and rioting into a strike in which nearly half a million workers brought almost all major industry to a halt (Mabille 1986:211). Again, the strike ended when the prime minister agreed to put electoral reform on the agenda. However, the momentum of reform was stopped short by the outbreak of war.

The final step quickly followed the end of the war. By 1918 workers were in a good position to press their demands. Their claim to equal voting weight was bolstered by their role in the fighting. Beyond the moral argument, however, they were politically in a strong position: the POB had participated in the wartime unity government in exile; just days before the armistice, workers had flexed their muscles and struck military production factories; and upon dissolution of the German military government, councils of workers and soldiers in Brussels briefly constituted the only pretender to national authority.[12] It became clear to members of the returning government that social stability and reconstruction depended on cooperation with the POB. Accordingly, with the decisive intervention of the king, a new unity government was formed, followed by the election of a Constituent Assembly based on equal voting. After the electoral reform was written into the constitution, a new democratic government was elected in 1919.

The working class was thus a central part of the story of democratization in Belgium. Yet the process must also be seen in terms of the roles

12 Cudell 1960; Landauer 1959; Mabille 1986.

of other players, particularly the Liberals and, to some extent, also the Catholics. Important in this regard are the competitive strategies of these parties, though attachment to liberal and later Christian social principles played some role, particularly on the part of the Progressive Liberals. In this light, democratization was not only a question of concessions, though the final step in 1918 may largely be characterized in this way.

Virtually from the beginning, the Liberal Party, formed in 1846 as the party of the anti-clerical urban bourgeoisie, was divided over the suffrage, with the Progressives, who favored its expansion, at odds with the Doctrinaires, who did not (Linden 1920:269). In 1848 the first all-Liberal government passed a suffrage reform, reflecting, no doubt, some influence from the February Revolution in France, but also an electoral motivation: the reform had a differential impact on the constituencies of the Liberals and Catholics, doubling the urban electorate while adding only a third to the rural electorate (Mabille 1986:134). As a result, the Liberals stayed in power for most of the next forty years, with the exception of 1852–57 and 1870–78.

Interestingly, the Catholics also supported this reform in the hope of gaining petit bourgeois and peasant votes, though Liberals in the end benefited disproportionately (Linden 1920:276). Nevertheless, the Catholic position presaged subsequent episodes of strategizing with respect to suffrage expansion. In 1864 they introduced a proposal for lowering suffrage restrictions on communal and provincial elections, which was aimed at splitting the Liberals (only the Progressives supported it) and fashioning a Catholic majority, but the king, who opposed the measure, dissolved Parliament, and new elections returned a stronger Liberal majority (Terlinden 1928–30:115). Another iteration a few years later fared better: in 1869, on the same calculation, Catholics founded an Association for Electoral Reform, which favored suffrage reform at the communal and provincial levels, and joined with Progressives to pass a compromise measure in 1870, which had the expected payoff; it further fragmented the Liberals and led to a Catholic victory in the same year, even though the new law had not yet been put into effect (Terlinden 1928–30:129). The Catholic government passed additional minor electoral reforms with the support of the Progressives.

The role of the Progressive Liberals was also important in the 1893 electoral reform. The large Catholic victory of 1884, which put an end to the period of Liberal rule, led to increasing cooperation between the Liberals and the POB by the end of the decade. With the change of government and the apparent setback to the goal of suffrage reform, the

Progressives in 1887 formally, though temporarily, left the party over the
issue and soon came out in favor of full manhood suffrage without literacy
requirements, as advocated by the newly formed POB (Mabille 1986:187).
Two fronts were thus opened in the struggle for reform: the streets, under
the leadership of the POB, and the Parliament, under the initiative of the
Progressives. The first has already been discussed. Of the second, Landauer
states: "It soon became clear that the presence of supporters of universal
suffrage in parliament made a great deal of difference. The government
showed a less unyielding attitude than before" (Landauer 1959:463). The
combination of the political strike and parliamentary action produced the
1893 compromise reform of full manhood but unequal suffrage.[13]

Although the reform measures of the 1910s were more lopsidedly the
result of working-class pressure, even here Liberal strategic calculations
played a role. Proportional representation, introduced in 1899, had the
effect of strengthening the Progressives and the POB; yet Catholics continued to have a large majority of seats with only a minority of votes.
Therefore, both Liberals (reunified in 1892) and labor continued to place
high priority on the issue of electoral reform. With the Doctrinaires
increasingly coming to agree with the Progressive position on reform, a
formal lib-lab alliance was created in 1902, with all Liberals now endorsing
unqualified manhood suffrage in exchange for POB acceptance of enlarged
national electoral districts (to the benefit of the geographically dispersed
Liberals) and the postponement of women's suffrage (which everyone believed would advantage the Catholics) (Carstairs 1980:55). The big Catholic victory and Liberal losses in the 1912 elections diminished remaining
disagreements over tactics. The Liberals became willing to tolerate the
strike weapon which was used the same year to force the government to
take up the reform issue. A further boost to lib-lab cooperation came with
the outbreak of World War I and the formation of a unity government in
exile.

Ultimately, democratization in Belgium can be seen as a Joint Project
of the working class and the Liberal bourgeoisie as both came together on
substantive reforms and undertook coordinated action to achieve them.
The earlier reforms were the result of working-class pressure outside Parliament and Liberal initiatives within it. Once the working class achieved
parliamentary representation through the POB, a parliamentary reform
alliance of Liberals and labor was bolstered by insistent working-class
agitation in the streets. Though the last step can be seen largely in terms of

---

13 While the Progressives encouraged street demonstrations, they did not at this point
   regard the general strike as an acceptable tactic.

post-war concessions to working-class demands, electoral calculations had already led the Liberals to line up on the side of reform some years earlier.

THE NETHERLANDS

Democratization in the Netherlands started quite early, following developments in France. The French invasion of 1795 brought about a brief experiment with democracy in the form of the Batavian Republic, which introduced manhood suffrage for an elected Assembly, but Napoleon soon took a number of steps that established control over the Dutch government, finally establishing a monarchy in 1806 and installing his brother as king. The more durable process of democratization began with the liberal reform constitution of 1848, which introduced a limited franchise for elections to the lower house; by 1868, with the establishment of parliamentary sovereignty, the Netherlands had the basic components of a democratic regime except for a mass suffrage. The subsequent extensions of the suffrage took place in 1887, 1896, and 1917 in the context of two developments: (1) the complex strategies of competitive support mobilization and compromise among parties divided along a religious-secular axis and (2) the growth of a pro-democratic working class with increasing political influence. In this sense, democratization in the Netherlands can be seen as a Joint Project.

Although Dutch politics has often been analyzed as rooted in a segmented or plural society with a dominant cleavage, what seems most striking with respect to the politics of suffrage reform is the way in which that issue cut across what was becoming the principal religious-secular cleavage and produced a complex pattern of partisan cleavages – both among parties and also within them. In this context, each of the major democratic reforms (1887, 1896, 1913–17) took place as a result of broad compromise among the major competing, mobilizing, multiclass parties, the first two reforms leading to limited, unsatisfactory compromise, the last to manhood suffrage.

Mass politics and support mobilization started early in the Netherlands when the dominant liberal-conservative cleavage gave way to a religious-secular cleavage. The change started in the 1860s as the politically dominant liberals became more secular and their opposition to state funding of denominational schools became an important issue for both Protestants and Catholics. The new cleavage led to a pattern of political competition in which mass mobilization became a prominent feature, resulting in the formation of multiclass parties. The key event occurred in 1878 when the Protestants organized the Anti-Revolutionary Party as a

Calvinist mass movement. The Anti-Revolutionary Party "pioneered modern mass-party organization techniques" (Daalder 1987:201) and quickly displaced the conservatives as the main opposition party. This context of competitive mobilization provided an incentive for all parties to seek a suffrage extension in an attempt to find new sources of partisan support. At the same time, however, the pull of class interests meant that the Liberals, the Anti-Revolutionaries, and later the Catholics were all divided on this issue.

The first reform was passed in 1887 by a Liberal-Conservative coalition government with support from most of the Anti-Revolutionaries and some Catholics (Newton 1978:93; Friedman 1943:116). The suffrage, however, remained very restricted, rising from 12 to 27 percent of the adult male population (Lijphart 1975:107). Politicized both by the emergence of a socialist party and the mobilizing efforts of the other parties, the working class became a participant in the politics surrounding this reform. Nevertheless, its independent role remained quite marginal at this time. In 1871 the ANWV was founded as a labor group that was closely tied to the Liberal Party; it rejected class struggle and favored cooperation with employers. In 1877–78 it turned its attention to the extension of the suffrage. Around the same time, the ANWV split, with the right wing joining the Protestant mass movement and the left wing founding what in 1881 became the SDB, the Social Democratic Party, based in the unions and championing a suffrage reform (Buiting 1989:61–63; Windmuller 1969: 8–17). Despite this activity, the 1887 reform reflected the political dynamics of the major, multiclass parties, rather than socialist or specifically working-class demands.

Nor was working-class pressure a part of the 1896 reform. Indeed, in reaction to the feeling of political failure due to the very restricted and unsatisfactory nature of the 1887 reform, the SDB abandoned an electoral strategy and the struggle for the popular vote in favor of trade union organizing and the general strike. As the SDB hardened its rejectionist, anti-parliamentary position, the political or parliamentary faction split off and in 1894 formed the SDAP, which soon eclipsed the SDB. Yet, the SDAP was still young and weak by the time of the 1896 reform. Coming at a time of fragmentation and organizational fluidity within the workers' movement and at a time when the rejectionist strategy was still important and the "parliamentary" wing was still forming, this second reform was passed with little working-class influence or participation.[14]

The expanded suffrage of 1887 provided no clear winners, as might be expected from the fact that the issue internally divided the major parties.

---

14 Windmuller 1969:14–16; Newton 1978:91; Buiting 1990:66–67.

These ambiguities would heighten in the following years. While the Liberal Union remained the largest party, in 1888 it was outvoted by the combined religious parties, which formed the first post-reform government. In 1891 the Liberals regained a majority of seats (Mackie and Rose 1991:330), and the progressive wing of the party, longest associated with a pro-suffrage position, took the initiative in the next reform. Progressive interior minister Tak van Poortvliet attempted to introduce a literate suffrage by reinterpreting the existing law, a proposal that split Liberals, Anti-Revolutionaries, and Catholics into hostile groups of "Takkians" and "anti-Takkians" (Friedman 1943:116). The Liberals split into three (with the right wing breaking away to form the Old Independent Liberals and many progressives joining the Radical League, the result of an older split that had derived from dissatisfaction with the limited 1887 reform). The Anti-Revolutionaries also suffered a permanent split (with the conservative, anti-Takkian wing breaking away to form what later became the Christian Historical Union).

The situation was temporarily resolved by the 1896 reform, a compromise measure that again doubled the electorate, this time to nearly half the adult males (Carstairs 1980:61; Lijphart 1975:107). Although the SDAP supported the campaign for an expanded suffrage, it was still a very small and weak organization at this time, with no parliamentary seats and receiving only 365 votes in 1894. The reform, then, was a compromise among the other parties. All the parties were engaged in competitive electoral mobilization and saw a particular kind of suffrage extension in their interest. In addition, the reform can be seen as an attempt at compromise within parties, which had been seriously divided over the issue and had, as a result, suffered damaging defections. In this context, it seems that suffrage reform may have occurred as a result of compromise within as much as between the parties.[15]

Be that as it may, the compromise failed to settle the issue, as had the previous one in 1887. The final step occurred in the next two decades, and, with the growth of union organizing during this period, the working class entered the scene more decisively. Unsatisfied with the still limited outcome of 1896, progressive Liberals stepped up their campaign for the suffrage, and in 1901 another large group defected to the Radical League. Working-class organizations also joined the battle in a more forceful way. The SDAP quickly began to attract votes and win parliamentary seats, and at the same time it initiated the creation of a new centralized labor

15 I have not been able to verify this last point in standard analyses of Dutch politics. Nevertheless, the structure of the situation is suggestive, and I offer this explanation in the spirit of a hypothesis.

federation, the NVV, which grew rapidly and with which the party had close relations. In 1899 the SDAP had founded the Dutch Committee for Universal Suffrage but left it in 1908 to organize an independent campaign with the NVV. Together, these two working-class organizations mounted a large suffrage movement, with mass petitions and large-scale demonstrations, the most notable being the "Red Tuesdays" of 1911 and 1912, which "undoubtedly helped precipitate the introduction of universal suffrage for men in 1917" (Buiting 1990:74).

By 1913 the left (SDAP, Radicals, and the two Liberal parties) won a majority in Parliament. Yet, it was not this majority that was responsible for the 1917 reform. The suffrage remained a highly contentious and complex issue: Christian Historicals and conservative Liberals opposed any change; the Anti-Revolutionaries favored a suffrage extension weighted toward rural areas; centrist Liberals favored a suffrage extension weighted toward urban areas; and progressive Liberals and the SDAP favored a full extension (Windmuller 1969:32, n. 59). In addition, the question of public funding of religious schools was still a festering and highly conflictual problem. Out of this multifold pattern of issues and cleavages, a compromise solution was again struck. In 1913 the Liberal government appointed two all-party special commissions, one on the franchise, the other on the schools, to recommend a policy. The following year, the electoral commission proposed manhood suffrage combined with an electoral system based on proportional representation. The parliamentary debates took place on both sets of recommendations during the war and the proposals became law in 1917. This final step, then, can be seen as a Joint Project. The campaign orchestrated by working-class organizations – parties and unions, inside and outside of Parliament – played a part. In addition, the regime issue concerning the suffrage and the electoral system was finally resolved in concert with the major substantive issue that had come to dominate Dutch politics for the previous half century. The "grand compromise" was thus the next step in the ongoing pattern of conflict and compromise that had come to characterize party politics in what has widely been interpreted as the segmented, plural society of the Netherlands (Daalder 1987; Lijphart 1975).

GREAT BRITAIN

By 1884 Britain could be said to have become a mass democracy with the working class constituting a majority of voters (Pugh 1978:3), even though it still did not have full manhood suffrage and registration requirements in effect further limited the suffrage. This is the view of most analysts of British history, a point made by Matthew, McKibbin, and Key, who disagree with the general assessment that the 1884 reform instituted an almost universal manhood suffrage and that it was not classes who were disenfranchised, but individuals who were, for the most part temporarily, excluded particularly by the residency requirement for registration.[16] In opposing this view, they suggest that in effect four categories were denied the suffrage (paupers, live-in servants, most of the military, and many sons living with parents) and that the occupational and lodger franchises contained some onerous requirements that affected much of the working class (Matthew, McKibbin, and Key 1976:724–35). In a more recent rebuttal, in turn, Tanner (1990:119–20) calculates that the underrepresentation of the working class probably came to about only 3 percent.

Whatever the extent of the continuing exclusions, the fourth reform law of 1918 substantially reduced (but did not completely eliminate) the existing shortcomings. While most analysts have traditionally viewed this 1918 reform as a minor one, some (including Rueschemeyer et al. 1992 as well as Therborn 1977), date the attainment of democracy only with this act and the substitution of the accumulated body of complicated, anachronistic (Tanner 1990:100), and still somewhat restrictive franchises with the straightforward grant of manhood suffrage. At least as important after 1884 was another remaining issue: the status of the nonelective House of Lords and its veto power. This issue was addressed in 1911, without significant working-class participation. Also controversial was the question of plural voting, provisions for which were reduced but not eliminated in 1918. The 1918 reform came as part of a broad agreement of the parties, that included also the redrawing of constituency boundaries. While the Labour Party favored reform and participated in the parliamentary negotiations, working-class organizations were not a major force in bringing the reform about.

After 1884 the reform issue subsided. It received little popular attention, and was not high on the agenda of any of the political parties, including the new Labour Party. It was not a high priority issue among the working class, with the organized sector largely enfranchised and the

---

16 Pugh 1978:3–4, for instance, states that "among the four and a half million men who were not on the Register at any one time only one and a half million were expressly excluded in law from the franchise; [and] the majority [of these] failed to be registered owing to the complexity of the registration system and particularly to the need for twelve months' continuous residence. A man could thus move back and forth between voting and non-voting, and the dividing line between the enfranchised and the unenfranchised was therefore much less significant than the gross numbers would suggest." Tanner (1990: esp. ch. 4) takes a similar view.

poorer unorganized sector showing little interest (Pugh 1978: 29, 31;
Thomas 1956:78).

The following decades saw active union and socialist organizing, and
in 1900 the TUC (Trades Union Congress, which grew out of annual
meetings begun in 1868) and socialist groups formed the Labour Representation Committee, which became the Labour Party in 1906, specifically to
put forth parliamentary candidates independent of the Liberal party. However, as Thomas has suggested, "after 1884, the extension of the franchise
never again became a central issue in working-class politics. Indeed Labour
and Socialist leaders often spoke as though parliamentary democracy was
already an accomplished fact" (Thomas 1956:77). Indeed, workers were
first elected to Parliament in 1874 (as Liberals). Their numbers grew
gradually in the 1880s, and in 1892 the first independent labor MPs were
elected. In 1906 the Labour Party was formed out of the Labour Representation Committee, and "by 1914 . . . the working class movement faced a
state that was increasingly open to its influence. Parliament contained 42
Labour members" (Price 1990:4, 6, 11). While not yet strong in any sense,
the Labour Party and its constituency was clearly not an excluded actor. In
fact, in 1903 the Liberal and Labour parties made a pact not to present
competing candidates against the Conservatives.

Nevertheless, the reform issue was kept alive by the suffragette movement and by partisan rivalry between Conservatives and Liberals. The
former were eager for a redistribution of seats to eliminate the over-
representation of Ireland (which redounded to the Liberals, who were more
sympathetic to home rule), and the latter were particularly eager to eliminate plural voting (which was said to result in an additional forty to eighty
Conservative seats). In addition, working-class organizations, including the
Labour Party, were on record as favoring a suffrage reform (Seymour and
Frary 1918: 1:166). Reform bills were introduced, but other issues claimed
more immediate attention.

Despite the Liberals' return to power in 1906, no reform was passed
in the pre-war period. Liberal attention focused primarily on the issue of
plural voting, and the House of Commons passed more than one bill to
abolish plural voting, but they did not pass in the House of Lords. This
was a period when the Liberals introduced new social legislation, and a
constitutional crisis erupted over the House of Lords' attempt to reject the
budget. In this context, the Liberals introduced a bill to reduce the power
of the nonelected upper house and enlisted the support of the king, who
threatened to appoint the number of peers necessary to ensure success.
Faced with this threat, the House of Lords abstained on the 1911 measure
that eliminated its veto, leaving it with only the power to delay legislation

(Seymour and Frary 1918: 1:168). Thus, this democratic reform was achieved by the Liberals, with the help of the king. The way then seemed clear for the electoral reform, and in 1912 the party did introduce a serious reform bill, but it foundered on a weak sop to the suffragettes (Thomas 1956:58; Tanner 1990:385).

During this period, the Labour Party took a position in favor of electoral reform and universal suffrage but it was not the central focus of attention.

> Although the party was committed to adult suffrage it did not on the whole bring the Government under pressure to legislate except in so far as its position on the suffrage was an embarrassment to the Liberals. . . . The party's immediate interest lay in the organised, politically aware sections of the working class already on the parliamentary register; nothing was as yet to be expected from domestic servants living with their employers or labourers residing with farmers who bulked large among the unenfranchised, or indeed from many industrial workers in which, in Ramsay MacDonald's words, "poverty and degradation are of the worst type."[17]

In any case, the Labour Party had increased its representation in the 1910 elections, but reached only 6 percent of the seats, hardly a major force in its own right. Labour MPs were the most unequivocal supporters of the failed Liberal bill of 1912 (Matthew et al. 1976:746), and in addition they introduced their own bills, but these did not succeed.

It was the war that brought the issue to a head. Analysts have often suggested that the war precipitated electoral reform, owing to its impact on the working class *qua* producer and soldier. Specifically, two effects of the war are often emphasized: the empowerment of the working class, whose cooperation was crucial for both wartime production and conscription;[18] and the ethical response to the lower classes whose members had fought and risked their lives and thus merited political inclusion.[19] In the British case, the war had an even more direct impact on electoral reform because of its relationship to the specific terms of the existing law. The war ushered in the breakdown of the old electoral system because massive wartime displacement and changes of domicile and occupation disqualified

17 Ramsay MacDonald was the first secretary of the Labour Representation Committee. Cited in Pugh 1978:30.
18 Because of the war effort, working-class organizations achieved an unprecedented degree of political influence. Trade union cooperation was essential to manpower allocation with respect to the rule of entry into employment and conscription.
19 Another effect of the war was partisan cooperation and the entry of the Labour Party into a coalition government. See, for example, Moor 1978:138–40; and Fox 1985:280–82.

many voters in a system where the franchise and registration had occupational and residence qualifications. Matthew et al. (1976:746) argue that
as a result of the war, the old system "was broken beyond repair." Finally,
because of their contribution to the national effort, the war broke some of
the resistance to the enfranchisement of women, who had engaged in the
greatest agitation for reform.

The fourth reform was the result of substantial consensus. It came at a
time of political cooperation and unity behind the war effort: in 1915 the
Liberals had formed a coalition government in which all three parties
participated; and from the outbreak of the war national union leaders had
agreed to forgo strikes and accept compulsory arbitration, though unofficial
labor actions took place as a result of rank-and-file pressure (Powell 1992:
55ff.). In August 1916 an all-party conference was set up to consider the
question of electoral reform. The recommendations of the conference report
of January 1917 were the product of unanimity on all matters other than
women's suffrage (Butler 1953:7); as the Representation of the People Bill
of the same year, they were considered largely uncontroversial, with the
one exception that a proportional representation system was rejected by
Parliament. Remaining restrictions on the franchise produced only weak
protest from Labour MPs. Thus, the wide-ranging reform enacted in 1918,
which enfranchised women for the first time but not on equal terms, was
a compromise, producing an agreement that was "extraordinarily wide"
(Butler 1953:7–12).

The 1918 reform can be seen as a Joint Project. The earlier reform
pattern of Conservative-Liberal competitive bidding for popular support
had changed. The Conservatives had become a party that appealed more
exclusively to landed, industrial, and commercial classes, while the Liberals,
with their base more firmly in the middle class, flirted with an appeal to the
working class but in the end were limited by divisions and fear of defections to the Conservatives. Hence, they were committed to the abolition of
plural voting and in principle to universal manhood suffrage, though they
were somewhat less certain in practice. The Labour Party was less problem-
atically ready to move ahead with an even broader reform and one that
would include women on equal terms. Yet, if we ask the question about the
actual politics concerning the passage of the reform bill, the Labour role
recedes. Indeed, it is a telling comment that histories of the union movement
and of the Labour Party are often silent about the reform: it was hardly a
salient issue around which the working class or its organizations mobilized.
Though the party supported reform in principle, Tanner (1990:120) suggests that "Labour in fact did not anticipate major electoral benefits." War de-
privations had resulted in labor actions that broke the national no-strike

agreements, and an anti-war movement began in 1917. However, the terms of the reform had been laid out before the big increases in strikes and union membership toward the end of the war, before the anti-war movement and the Leeds Conference, and more generally before the activities that followed the Russian Revolution. In the end, the reform issue was kept alive primarily by the pressure of women to gain the suffrage and brought to a climax by the dislocation of war. The result was a broad "enquiry . . . which investigated everyone's pet schemes and proposals" (Tanner 1990: 385) and led to a compromise bill that attracted wide agreement.[20]

GERMANY

Full manhood suffrage was introduced early in Germany, in the middle of the nineteenth century, prior to any effective demand for reform mounted by the working class. Worker organizations, union confederations, and the worker-based Social Democratic Party (SPD) were founded with voting rights already in place, and the SPD was in a position to make impressive electoral gains once the anti-socialist laws were repealed in 1890. The process of democratization therefore was not one of extending the suffrage but one of establishing the equality of the vote and the sovereignty of a parliament in which the SPD already had significant party representation, holding the plurality of seats in the Reichstag elected in 1912. In the end, democracy was achieved with the post-war reforms of 1918–19 as a Joint Project around which multiple interests converged. On the one hand, all the major steps in German democratization reveal elements of a "revolution from above" as those in power saw the reform as a strategy for pursuing their own ends. On the other hand, working-class organizations constituted an active force demanding democratic reform from the time of their founding. If in the earlier steps in the nineteenth century the right called the shots, in the final step Germany was the unusual case in which a labor-based party led the government coalition. In the end, "a majority of the Social Democrats and of their bourgeois allies succeeded in democratizing Germany" (Roth 1963:295).

Bismarck's move to introduce equal manhood suffrage in the North German Confederation in 1867 and again in the unified Reich in 1871

20 Tanner (1990:384, 391, 408ff.) argues that the post-reform rise of the Labour Party owes less to the expanded franchise than to the redrawing of constituency boundaries. Conceived of as a way to protect Tory interests in declining agricultural constituencies, the new boundary guidelines with their attention to "economic interest" had the unanticipated effect of helping Labour by also creating more solidly working-class and mining constituencies. In any case, one should not argue ex post and, on the basis of Labour's subsequent rise, assign it unwarranted weight in the politics of reform.

had precursors in some of the empire's constituent states, where liberal influence resulted in new constitutions providing for assemblies and universal manhood suffrage. However, in the all-important Prussian state, the king, having introduced full manhood suffrage in 1848 under pressure from economic crisis, social unrest, and liberal opposition to the crown, quickly modified it the following year to protect conservative, absolutist interests through a grossly unequal and manipulative three-class system of public, oral voting (Sheehan 1989:623–68; Seymour and Frary 1918: 2:16–21).

The context of the 1867 and 1871 electoral measures was, as Mann put it, the twin processes of incorporation that proceeded simultaneously and interacted in complex ways: the class incorporation of the bourgeoisie into the authoritarian state and the national incorporation of German states into a political confederation (Mann 1993:306–7). By 1861 Liberals had taken advantage of the electoral law to control 235 of 352 seats in the Prussian Landtag (Sheehan 1989:879). This situation led to an impasse, which pitted the monarchy's militarized conception of the state against a liberal conception, as the Liberals in the Landtag rejected military appropriations, a move that was countered in the upper house. In response, Bismarck, named prime minister of Prussia in 1862, turned to a nation-building task with external and internal dimensions. Externally, he consolidated Prussian control over other states by integrating them – into first the North German Confederation and then the Reich – through both military submission and federal representative structures, including a chamber based on universal manhood suffrage. In addition to forging the larger territorial unit, the strategy addressed its internal balance of power in three ways. First, it provided for Prussian hegemony over the larger unit. Second, it overcame the political stalemate within Prussia by weakening the Liberal opposition and building support for Bismarck and the imperial forces: the geopolitical consolidation split the opposition, as the larger bloc of National Liberals in Prussia fell in behind Bismarck on the national question (Craig 1978:2–11). Third, rather than replicating at the confederal/imperial level the Prussian provisions of unequal, class-based voting and indirect elections, Bismarck introduced full and equal manhood suffrage with a secret ballot for direct elections at the confederal/imperial level as a mechanism for enfranchising a population that would vote conservative against the Liberals, thus stemming Liberal power.

The conservative thrust of the reform was further revealed in a central limitation: it did not include a grant of parliamentary sovereignty to the new representative institutions. Indeed, Parliament had very limited power and, without the right to appoint ministers or debate foreign policy, served as a facade for authoritarian rule. Power was effectively concentrated, particularly in the hands of Bismarck, the imperial chancellor, a position that fused the offices of minister of foreign affairs, prime minister of Prussia, chair of the Bundesrat (the Federal Council of delegations from the federated states), and countersignatory to all legislation (Wehler 1985:53–54).

Bismarck's revolution from above was a strategy to preserve the conservative, absolutist order and to unify Germany. As he himself put it, "The masses will stand on the side of kingship. . . . In a country with monarchical traditions and loyal sentiments the general suffrage, by eliminating the influences of the liberal bourgeois classes, will also lead to monarchical elections" (quoted in Craig 1978:45). His great achievement was to deliver the king from an unpalatable choice between parliamentary and military government (Craig 1978:142) and instead, in his own words, to "overthrow parliamentarism by parliamentary means" (quoted in Wehler 1985:53), thereby creating a third alternative that would provide a new basis for continued imperial rule.

Neither the unequal manhood suffrage of 1848 in Prussia nor the equal suffrage of 1867 and 1871 in the Confederation and Reich respectively was the result of – or, indeed, attended by – working-class pressure. Working-class organizing remained incipient. In the 1860s, both unions and political organizations were beginning to develop out of strike movements, organizations for social protection, and education associations. In the second half of the decade organizations began to extend their reach beyond the local level. Out of this organizational effort independent labor parties were founded: the ADAV in 1863 and the SDAP in 1869 (Kocka 1986:338–39). From the beginning both were concerned with the issue of the suffrage. In 1863 Ferdinand Lassalle, the founder of the ADAV, argued in favor of political action through a workers' party and the importance of full, equal suffrage and direct elections. A similar position was articulated in the Eisenach Program of 1869 (Hartung 1950:96, 98). Nevertheless, the precursory working-class organizations did not play an important political role in the 1860s; and when the Social Democratic Party was subsequently consolidated by the unification of the ADAV and SDAP in 1875, Bismarck quickly identified it as an enemy of the Reich. His posture, oriented toward enfranchising conservative rural voters, was far from any compromise or accommodation with or even incorporation of the working class. When the SPD took advantage of the electoral reform, winning 39 percent of the popular vote in Berlin in 1874 and twelve Reichstag seats in 1877 (Nipperdey 1990: 2:355), Bismarck responded with a virulent attack and sought to crush the Social Democrats through the anti-socialist laws of 1878, which repressed Social Democratic leaders, organizations, and activity. Nevertheless, the policy excluded the party's delegates to the Reichstag from the repression, and Social Democrats were allowed to run for electoral office (Nipperdey 1990: 2:355–56).

The 1860s and 1870s had seen the establishment of the principle of full manhood suffrage as part of a conservative strategy from above, and it was not accompanied by other components of a democratic regime, specifically parliamentary sovereignty, civil liberties, or, in Prussia, equality of the vote. The remaining steps were taken at the end of World War I when the Bismarckian state, long in crisis, collapsed and was replaced by a parliamentary democracy.

The longer-run context was the unstable coalitional politics and political recalculations that came with the rise of the SPD. The anti-socialist laws had not realized their intended result of stopping socialism in its tracks. Rather, the toleration for electoral participation had allowed the party to gain electoral strength. In 1890, the year the laws were repealed, the party doubled its percentage of the vote (to nearly 20 percent), gaining the plurality of votes and more than tripling its number of seats in the (malproportioned) Reichstag (to 35, or 9 percent). Thereafter gains continued to escalate, and by 1912 the party won over a third of the vote and 110 seats (or 28 percent) (Rokkan and Meyriat 1969:155–56).

During the same period, union strength mounted in parallel fashion, with membership in the Freie Gewerkschaften swelling from 300,000 members in 1890 to 2.6 million by 1913 and worker actions averaging 104 per year in 1890–93 and then spiraling upward by a factor of 25 between 1909 and 1913 (Nipperdey 1990: 2:554–55). The labor central, however, was principally oriented toward bread-and-butter issues and inserted a "quietist, reformist mentality" into the SPD (Wehler 1985:90): with increasing numbers of Reichstag members recruited from the ranks of the trade unions, the unions prevented the party from continuing its use of the political mass strike, calling it "general craziness" (Craig 1978: 268, Nipperdey 1990: 2:570). Nevertheless, the growing organizational and political strength of the working class particularly in the SPD produced a situation of political impasse and polarization and again challenged conservative, imperial interests.

The outbreak of World War I further weakened the Bismarckian coalition and increased the pressure for realignment. Whereas the pre-war alignment pitted the military, right-wing parties, and employers against the socialists and left-wing liberals, the prosecution of the war pushed toward class collaboration. The kaiser's government, the Supreme Command of the military, and the industrialists all realized they needed work-ing-class cooperation for the war effort. For their part, with the outbreak of war working-class organizations – both party and unions – enthusiasti-cally fell in behind the nationalist cause and supported the war (see Roth 1963:287ff.), though the working-class movement later split over this issue, with the departure of what became the USPD and Spartacists from the Majority SPD (MSPD). With the support of the MSPD and the unions, a pattern of class collaboration did develop during the war, with two important effects. First, it further changed the balance of class power: "From the political standpoint, the war had been a disaster for the employ-ers and a blessing for the unions" (Feldman 1966:473). Second, it made democratic reform a salient issue, as, from the beginning, the MSPD had insisted on reform as a condition of its cooperation.

The immediate context for the reform was the final year of the war, when a number of things came together that affected the strategic calcu-lations of various groups and produced a new alignment representing an accommodation of the right and the moderate Social Democrats, now devoid of, indeed challenged by, their left wing. Three factors were partic-ularly important. The first was working-class protest, led by the groups that had split from the SPD. This radical, militant, and potentially revo-lutionary movement developed in the wake of the Russian Revolution in October 1917 and amid accelerating hardship and deprivation: in the first half of 1918, bread rations were reduced; real wages fell; clothing, shoes, and coal were in short supply; and ongoing political stalemate prevented progress on the promised reform of the Prussian suffrage and a Worker Chambers bill (Feldman 1966:492). Second, with the prospect of military defeat, the Supreme Command saw a continued need for class collaboration and working-class cooperation for the task of demobilization and peacetime conversion (Feldman 1966:435). Third, facing the need to call for an armistice, the government and the army came to view a democratic "revo-lution from above" as a "vital necessity," both to secure the best possible peace terms from the democratic Allies and to sidestep responsibility for the military debacle and for the anticipated post-war difficulties (Feldman 1966:514).

In October 1918 a broad coalition of forces that had supported the government's military venture, including working-class organizations, came together behind a project for democratic reform when suddenly the army and the government "commanded [the pro-reform opposition parties] to take over power" (Craig 1978:397). Various strategies converged to set the reform process in motion. The Supreme Command, searching for a scapegoat, saw a revolution from above as an expedient tactical move: as the Bavarian representative to the Supreme Command said, "It is very good that the left wing parties will have to take the odium for the peace upon themselves. The storm of popular anger will then direct itself against them. . . . Later one hopes to swing into the saddle again and rule on according to the old prescription" (quoted in Feldman 1966:516). The Social Democrats had always pressed for democratic reform, and like the right the MSPD too now saw it in a further light: a means to preempt the forces that had emerged to the party's left and their threatening working-class revolution. The kaiser, who was becoming politically isolated, now thought it necessary to make good on his earlier promise of electoral reform, an attempt at which had recently been defeated. In the beginning of October, the kaiser appointed Prince Maximilian of Baden as chancellor of the empire and prime minister of Prussia. Under increasing pressure from President Wilson, who made clear his unwillingness to deal with the kaiser, and in opposition to the military's consideration of prolonging the war, Prince Max formed a new government, which turned to a more serious reform project. The new government, based on the Black-Red-Gold coalition of the Catholic Center, Democratic, and Majority Social Democratic parties, effected a "constitutional transformation" that included a reform of the Prussian suffrage, ministerial responsibility to the Reichstag, and civilian control of the military – but did not abolish the monarchy (Craig 1978:397; Fulbrook 1990:157).

The democratic reform of October 1918, which represented a realignment of forces, was thus based on a combination of distinct strategies and a common fear of revolution on the part of the army, the government, and the centrist and Majority Social Democratic parties. Working-class organizations were important participants, but they were only one of the strategic actors. Furthermore they were divided over the project, with more radical factions, representing probably 40 percent of the SPD before it split (Roth 1963:292), rejecting the MSPD faction's goal of liberal democratic reforms, and pursuing instead a more radical social transformation based on alternative political structures. Indeed, the Joint Project had to survive a major revolutionary challenge from these groups before it was institutionalized in the new constitution of the Weimar Republic. The revolution from below that broke out later the same month threw the new alliance off balance until it was in effect reconstituted two months later.

The revolutionary challenge began with the 22 October strikes that for the first time overtly opposed the kaiser and struck pro-republican themes (Craig 1978:397–98). By the beginning of November insurrectionary movements took place in several port cities, where councils of workers and soldiers were established, and on 7 November, a Socialist Republic was declared in Bavaria. The response was mounted on two levels.

One level saw the marginalization of the right, effected in two days, on November 9–10. Prince Max preempted imperial options by announcing the intention of the kaiser to abdicate and then passed the government into the hands of the MSPD. Friedrich Ebert, who became chancellor, tried to maintain leadership of the revolutionary movement and carried out an apparent coalitional shift in replacing the Black-Red-Gold coalition government with a socialist government based on MSPD and the USPD. On the formal governmental level, then, a shift to the left occurred as the monarchy was abolished and a republic declared, the center was coalitionally excluded, and, under pressure from the USPD, the move toward a liberal, parliamentary democracy was replaced with the establishment of a Council of People's Representatives elected by workers' and soldiers' councils.

On another level, however, the alliance underlying the Joint Project of October survived, taking its most concrete form in two pacts: the Stinnes-Legien Agreement and the Groener Pact. The Stinnes-Legien Agreement represented a "social partnership" between industrialists and unions. With the fast-moving developments of October, the big industrialists decided to abandon their coalition with the Conservatives in favor of an agreement with the unions. Talks immediately ensued, and the agreement of 12 November, by which the industrialists formally recognized unions, constituted a "truce between labor and management . . . [on which] the Weimar Republic [was] . . . founded" (Feldman 1966:532). The Groener Pact represented an accommodation between the Supreme Command and the Ebert government. Within hours of becoming chancellor and forming a Socialist government, Ebert received a call from Groener, the new supreme commander, offering the army's support to the new government in exchange for which Ebert agreed, inter alia, to limit the revolutionary movement and suppress the workers' and soldiers' councils (Fulbrook 1990:159). Thus, the Social Democrats looked in two directions at once. At the same time that a new leftist coalition was constructed among political parties in the government, a centrist coalition was reconstituted through pacts on the part of major corporate groups.

The tension between these contradictory coalitional responses was effectively resolved the following month. In the middle of December the first Congress of Workers' and Soldiers' Councils was called to chart the future course. The choice pitted the USPD vision of a path to socialism based on workers' and soldiers' councils versus the vision of Ebert and the

MSPD of a liberal parliamentary republic. The sentiment in the Congress of Councils was moderate, with the MSPD constituting 60 percent of the representatives. Opting for the parliamentary system, the Congress of Councils voted to hold elections in January for a Constituent Assembly which would write the new constitution. The Congress also voted to replace the army with a popular militia, but again Ebert reached an agreement with the army, which vigorously opposed such a move. In these ways, the coalition of the October Joint Project was in effect reconstituted. Indeed, the refurbished alliance was able to put down the Spartacist uprising that occurred in January, and with the realignment the USPD ultimately left the government.

In the next half year, the Joint Project was back on track. The January elections to the Constituent Assembly were held on the basis of plans drawn up by the Ebert government and reflected long-standing positions of the SPD, such as proportional representation and universal suffrage for all men and women aged twenty and over. In those elections the MSPD won a plurality of 38 percent of the vote and 163 of 421 seats, while its closest associates of the war period (and the coming period) won a combined 166 (91 for the Center and 75 for the Democrats) (Craig 1978:412–13). Thus, encompassing one faction of a divided workers' movement, a combination of forces similar to that which had formed the Black-Red-Gold coalition came together to write the Weimar constitution (promulgated the following August) and established the basis for Germany's first democratic regime.

CONCLUSION

In the Joint Projects pattern, democratization proceeded primarily through the interactions among "in" groups. Not only the middle and upper classes but also the working class had already been largely enfranchised and even represented in parliament through labor-based, socialist parties. Indeed, what distinguishes these cases is not only the participation of working-class groups as important pro-democratic actors but also the fact that they participated largely from a position of prior inclusion. Two points follow. First, as actors within the parliament, all the parties, including the socialist parties, must be seen both as class actors and also as strategic actors engaged in a political game of partisan competition. Second, the working-class role took on a dual form and operated in a dual arena. It was motivated by a commitment to the substantive reforms that enhance the representation of working-class interests, but also by the mobilization of support by labor-based socialist parties, which were already significant actors in the competitive electoral arena. With respect to arena of action, the working-class role took place both through party negotiations within parliament and through mass mobilizations, in which unions also became active participants.

4

LABOR ACTION IN RECENT DEMOCRATIZATION

The processes of democratization at the end of the twentieth century are particularly complex in that they typically involve "ins" as well as "outs," both the negotiation and protest arenas, and many different class actors among the "outs," including, with the exception of two cases, labor groups. Within this commonality, different patterns can be distinguished according to the role of the working class and the incumbent project.

The country analyses in this chapter suggest that the comparative and theoretical literature has largely missed the importance of the working class and the labor movement in the democratization process in the 1970s and 1980s. The argument, of course, is not that these democratic transitions should be considered a working-class or labor project, that elite strategies were not also important, or that the labor movement and union-led protest were the most consequential sources of pro-democratic pressure. Furthermore, one must also recognize that other groups also engaged in protest, including, variously, human rights groups, nationalist groups, and urban social movements. These last typically organized and mobilized larger working-class groups in poor neighborhoods, rather than in the workplace, and often involved class-related grievances, demands, and identities. However, mobilization of the working class *qua* working class most clearly occurred through unions and union-affiliated parties, and this is the focus in the following analysis. In the overwhelming majority of cases, the roles of unions and labor-affiliated parties were important to a degree that is at most hinted at in the literature. Certainly in most cases their roles were at least as significant as those in some of the earlier cases of Joint Projects, for instance, Great Britain and Denmark.

As discussed in Chapter 1, in explaining the initial sources of democratic transitions, the literature has tended to emphasize an "internalist" account that begins with the divisions and strategies of authoritarian incumbents as they respond to problems of legitimation; in analyzing the process of democratic transitions, the literature has emphasized the centrality of elite bargaining between incumbents and moderate opposition party leaders. This approach can usefully be supplemented by explicating the role of labor in both these phases: (1) its contribution to the delegitimation and destabilization of the authoritarian regime and hence its role in provoking the transition; and (2) the oppositional role of labor during the transition process itself.

With respect to the first phase, the case analyses indicate that in some countries the legitimation and consolidation problems of authoritarian regimes were preceded and at least partially caused by explicit opposition from society, which demanded a response from authoritarian incumbents. Labor protest was often an important factor in generating legitimacy problems; indeed, in some cases labor opposition prevented the consolidation of authoritarian rule from the very onset of the regime. Regarding the second phase, the weight and shape of labor opposition also varied: sometimes it played a leading role, coordinating and galvanizing the anti-authoritarian opposition; in other cases it played a more supplementary role, but nevertheless was important in affecting the pace and rhythm of the transition and providing a more leftist democratic alternative, thereby increasing contestation.

With regard to the role of incumbents in the transition, it is useful to distinguish a spectrum of three alternatives. At one end are cases in which incumbents failed to pursue any explicit and autonomous project from above, thus playing an essentially "negative" role of retreating from former positions and bargaining for the terms of their withdrawal in the democratization process. In these cases, incumbents defensively extricated themselves from power once the regime was destabilized. At the other end, incumbents carried out an explicitly stated transition project that defined a context, a set of procedures, and a timetable for a regime change. Such a project was initiated and implemented by the government. In the middle are cases in which authoritarian incumbents adopted legitimation projects without an explicit or well-defined formula for a transition, though there may have been some notion of future goals and some piecemeal moves in a democratizing direction. In these intermediate cases, defensive, ad hoc steps were taken as the incumbents lost control over the transition process.

On the basis of these dimensions, four patterns can be distinguished, in one of which the labor movement played no effective role. Not surprisingly, a focus on the role of the labor movement produces a different set of typological categories that groups countries in ways quite different from the dominant framework (see Table 4.1). This chapter analyzes these patterns and in addition discusses the multistaged case of Portugal, which eludes any easy categorization within the present framework.

The first pattern, Destabilization/Extrication, is the biggest departure from the conventional understanding in terms of the countries that it groups together and the characterization of the transitions. In these cases, labor protest destabilized and delegitimated the authoritarian regime, and the government was ultimately unable to formulate an adequate response. Rather than labor protest emerging in space opened from above, labor protest itself created space and helped provoke splits among the incumbents. Authoritarian incumbents adopted no transition project prior to this destabilization, and, instead of elite negotiation, the transition is better characterized as forced retreat.

In the second pattern, Transition Game, the incumbents adopted a legitimation project around a controlled electoral arena with approved opposition parties. Within this context, the democratization process proceeded in large part as an elite strategic game carried on between the authoritarian incumbents and party opposition leaders. Yet, popular pressure expressed as electoral opposition and protest was crucial to undermining these incumbent projects. To different degrees and at different stages, labor-led mobilization helped to advance democratization and keep it on track, and it secured the legalization of left and labor-based parties.

A third pattern is Parallel Tracks. If in the first pattern the government had no project, and in the second its project was derailed, in this pattern the government laid out a transition project and carried it through. At the same time, labor was a strong and key opposition actor. Yet it did not affect the timetable laid down from above by the government. While the labor movement was perhaps a more consistent pro-democratic force than other actors in these cases, its activities were the least consequential, compared with the prior patterns. Again, however, it can be said to have contributed to keeping the government project on track and to have expanded contestation.

The fourth pattern is the Interelite Game, in which no labor organizations – neither unions nor labor-based parties – played a consequential role. Rather, these were military governments that in quite different ways alienated the civilian right, which opposed and isolated the government. These transitions took place primarily as a game of interacting elites within the right. In one of these cases, Greece, the government suffered a humiliating military defeat; but, as in Argentina in the first pattern, the regime

Table 4.1. *Patterns of Democratization: 1970s and 1980s*

	Destabilization/Extrication	Transition Game	Parallel Tracks	Interelite Game
From above	No incumbent project Defensive exit	Legitimation project with restricted contestation Derailed	Explicit transitional project and timetable Planned exit	Unimplemented incumbent project amid opposition by civilian right Defensive exit
Labor role	Destabilizes authoritarian regime Opens space Triggers transition Expands contestation	Advances transition Expands contestation	Opens space Leads early democratic opposition Helps enforce project Expands contestation	None
Cases[a]	*Spain 1977* *Peru 1980* *Argentina 1983*	*Bolivia 1982* *Uruguay 1985* *Brazil 1985*	*Chile 1990*	*Greece 1974* *Ecuador 1979*

[a] Portugal 1976 is a hybrid case.

was clearly in trouble beforehand, and in both cases the military venture was more an outcome than a cause of regime breakdown.

DESTABILIZATION AND EXTRICATION

In the first pattern, characterizing Peru, Argentina, and Spain, massive labor protests destabilized authoritarianism and opened the way for the establishment of a democratically elected government. In these cases, the labor movement was one of the earliest and most important anti-authoritarian actors, leading an offensive in the form of strikes and protests against the regime. Regime incumbents were unable to ignore such opposition or formulate a successful response to these challenges from below, a task that generated or greatly intensified deep divisions among authoritarian incumbents. The government had no particular project for liberalization or democratization before labor protest mounted and, sooner or later, came to represent a significant challenge to the stability and viability of these regimes. The prominent role of the union movement stemmed both from its specific grievances and from the special organizational resources it had to create space within the authoritarian regime and to take a leading role in coordinating broader anti-regime protest.

The labor movement, of course, was not the only source of protest. In Spain nationalist groups tried to destabilize the regime through terrorist incidents, and in Argentina human rights groups were most effective in conducting nonviolent vigils that undermined any moral claim of the regime and attracted widespread international attention and sympathy. In all three countries, however, the labor movement mounted ongoing and escalating protest that destabilized the regime in two ways – by challenging its ability to provide a basis for social peace or order and by undermining its cohesion as it confronted this challenge. Incumbents then made the decision to relinquish power and pursued a defensive extrication in which the goal was ultimately to step down, salvaging whatever terms they could.

These terms varied, with the Peruvian and particularly the Argentine incumbents coming away with much less than the Spanish incumbents, who as civilians were capable of transforming themselves into democratic actors. In Peru, labor protest propelled the regime into crisis, and the government then moved quickly to announce elections for a Constituent Assembly, which, although the military hoped to wield influence in it, was nevertheless given responsibility for directing the transition. In Argentina, unions organized protests, which, along with an economic crisis and

ongoing human rights vigils, exacerbated splits within the military government and destabilized the regime. The government tried to forestall
the regime crisis by invading the Malvinas. When that failed, the government quickly called for the elections that marked the regime transition. In
Spain, labor protest produced a severe challenge to the regime even before
the death of Franco and undermined the initial responses of Juan Carlos
and Arias after Franco's death. Suárez then came to power and within four
months built a consensus around a mechanism and timetable for replacing
the authoritarian regime. It is notable that in all these cases, contacts and
negotiations between the authoritarian government and the pro-democratic
opposition parties continued after the extrication decision, and these discussions included left and labor-affiliated parties.

PERU

Labor organizations were centrally involved in the failure of Peruvian
authoritarianism and the course of its transitional process. Heightened
labor mobilization, the unintended consequence of the government's initial
reformism, opened splits within the armed forces that were institutionally
threatening, as different military factions were attracted by the possibility
of conflicting civilian alliances. Against this background of escalating
protest and institutional vulnerability, a successful general strike in 1977
convinced military leaders that they could not maintain either stability or
their own cohesion. It thereby convinced them to convert vague references
to an eventual return to civilian rule and an incipient dialogue with
established political parties into an explicit timetable for a democratic
transition.

Unlike most cases in this chapter, the authoritarian regime in Peru
did not initially engage in the systematic repression of labor. Rather,
during the first phase of military rule under the leadership of General
Velasco (1968–75), Peruvian authoritarianism had a distinctly "populist"
character, and the government encouraged labor organizing.[1]

Rather than being anti-labor as such, the military targeted attention
on its decades-old enemy APRA, the continent's classical, pioneering populist party. APRA had historic ties to the labor movement, and the
military's anti-Aprista strategy meant an assault on labor organizations
affiliated with the party. In its attempt to carry out a major reform agenda,
the military regime sponsored rival organizations for rallying popular

1 For a good overview of the Velasco administration's relationship with labor, see Haworth
   1983. More generally on Velasco's reforms, see Lowenthal 1975; McClintock and Lowenthal 1981; and Stepan 1978.

support – SINAMOS and the Workers Central of the Peruvian Revolution (CTRP) – and even favored the Communist-led General Confederation of Peruvian Workers (CGTP), as a means to build an important constituency mobilized against the dominant landed and agroexport elites, as well as against the APRA-backed Confederation of Peruvian Workers (CTP), heretofore the country's major labor confederation. At the same time, however, the Velasco government moved to establish corporatist structures that placed state agencies in charge of workers' organizations and the management of labor-capital disputes. In this regard, the military government aimed to moderate radical elements and undermine the strength of independent parties within the labor movement (Haworth 1989:202).

The political strategy boomeranged, leading to a process of societal polarization, which was reproduced within the armed forces. The military's economic reforms and political strategy encouraged an accelerating spiral of political mobilization. From 1968 to 1975, the total number of recognized unions almost doubled, and the number in the industrial sector more than doubled (Stephens 1980:177). However, the government was unable to channel this mobilizational effort and failed either to consolidate an organizational basis for popular support or to control popular mobilization and protest. The reforms "accentuated class conflicts and provoked extensive mobilizations of peasants and workers, which were opposed by rural and urban entrepreneurial associations, the traditional parties, and . . . the national press. These class and sectoral conflicts had profound repercussions in the officer corps, provoking a process of ideological differentiation" (North 1983:251–52). At the center of the ideological divisions within the military was the issue of autonomous social mobilization.

Although the labor movement was not the only participant in the growing social protest, it was an important one. The initial reaction of the Peruvian Communist Party (PCP) and the CGTP to Velasco had been one of guarded support for his reform efforts. While offering support, the PCP and CGTP nonetheless "called for 'an authentic, popular nationalist and democratic government,' which the military regime was not yet thought to constitute" (Haworth 1983:107). By 1973, a conjuncture of factors – including the onset of a severe economic downturn, increasing attempts to replace the CGTP with the state-controlled CTRP, and Velasco's illness – combined to move the union movement into a position of increased opposition (Cotler 1986:154; Haworth 1989:202). In that year strikes increased substantially (roughly double the average for the previous five years),[2] creating a general climate of instability. A leading military general in the cabinet identified the government's primary problem as "strikes without a

2 See the strike statistics in Palmer 1980:114.

reason" (cited in North 1983:267). In the next two years, strikes became larger and more political in nature (Stephens 1980:211).

Polarization and protest escalated, amplified by a growing economic crisis and the adverse effects of the stabilization measures adopted by the government. The year 1975 opened with a police strike, supported by and coordinated with Aprista student leaders. The strike and the deaths that occurred when army troops were called in to put it down were followed by riots in central Lima. The events, including an attack on the offices of SINAMOS, symbolized the government's loss of control (Graham 1992:57–59). In this context, the Velasco government fell in August 1975.

General Morales Bermúdez succeeded to power, ushering in the "second phase" of Peruvian authoritarianism, which represented a sharp reversal of the earlier reformism. Within the first year, economic policy turned toward a more orthodox form of stabilization, and the government was reconfigured to eliminate the reformists. The new government was weak, divided, and isolated, and by March 1976 it moved decisively to seek civilian allies among the business sector (Pease García 1979:136–44). At the same time, the government opened a dialogue with the traditional parties, which began to pressure for a transition.

Under the Morales Bermúdez government, state-labor relations had quickly become antagonistic, and in short order organized labor became a central anti-authoritarian actor. From the beginning, the new government adopted anti-labor policies, carrying out repression against the labor movement more characteristic of the other authoritarian regimes discussed in this chapter.[3] Relations further deteriorated with the June 1976 economic package and the government's declaration, two days later, of a state of emergency. The labor movement responded with a series of mobilizations in the second half of 1976, including strikes by fishermen, municipal workers, and telepostal workers (Pease García 1979:225–27).

Though these were not successful, strike activity symbolized the labor movement's new posture of direct and confrontational opposition against the authoritarian regime. Given the repression, combined with declining real wages and the state's role as the largest employer, ongoing labor conflicts took on "a highly political character. For the unions, the restoration of democratic freedoms became as important a demand as traditional issues involving wages and dismissals" (Reid 1985:69).

The mounting strikes and ensuing societal polarization posed a particular problem for the new regime, opening further the splits within the

---

3 On the anti-labor policies of Morales Bermúdez, see Pease García 1979; and Haworth 1983:110.

military. On one side were progressive officers who saw in the strikes the possibility of a rapprochement with sectors of the civilian left; on the other side were those opposed to strikes and autonomous mobilization. "No officer was willing to push internal disputes to the point of provoking a rupture within the armed forces" (North 1983:269). In February 1977, in the Plan Tupac Amaru, the government announced its intention to hold elections for a Constituent Assembly, a demand earlier made by APRA and put forth five months earlier by the unions affiliated to the party. However, the Plan, which explicitly criticized Velasco's earlier economic direction, did not include any electoral calendar (Pease García 1979:200, 209).

The single most important event in triggering the Peruvian democratic transition of 1980 was the dramatic and highly successful general strike of 19 July 1977 (the first in Peru since 1919 and the largest strike in the country's history).[4] This strike united nearly all trade union bodies along with many other groups loosely composing what had become known as the popular movement. It paralyzed industrial activity in Lima and affected other cities in the country as well. In addition to workplace concerns, the strike demands included a call for basic democratic freedoms (Pease García 1979:235). According to Henry Dietz, "The 1977 strike carried the unmistakable message that attempts by the military to slow or avoid a transfer of power to civilians would result in only greater turmoil that would further undermine the military's already weak credibility" (Dietz 1992:241).

In the aftermath of the strike, members from the traditional political parties and economic elite used the presence of working-class mobilization to argue that a return to democracy was necessary to restore political order and economic growth (Cotler 1986:163). Indeed, as an immediate result of the July general strike, "Morales Bermúdez was obliged to announce a timetable for a return to civilian rule" (Reid 1985:70; see also Pease García 1979:247). Nine days later, he announced that Constituent Assembly elections would be held in June 1978, and in August the government lifted the state of emergency. With this act, the military government had clearly made a decision to extricate itself and proceed with a transition.

The labor movement remained at the forefront of the anti-authoritarian opposition. Until the Constituent Assembly elections of June 1978, strikes and popular mobilization continued, including further general strikes in February, April, and May 1978 (Haworth 1989:208). "The low-income

4 McClintock 1989:351. Also see Pease García 1979:232–37; and Reid 1985:71–72.

sectors who were hardest hit by the regime's austerity policies, latched onto the activities of the unions. The political parties, while opposing the regime, were thrown into a position of collaborating with it in order to be allowed eventually to attain power through elections. The unions, meanwhile, provided an effective opposition to act as a catalyst for the transition to civilian government" (Graham 1992:62; see also Reid 1985:68).

During the final phase of transition, mobilization declined "because the assembly marked an important step in the military's road back to the barracks – the one aim which united the fragile coalition of groups which made up the 'popular movement' " (Reid 1985:76). Nevertheless, unions and labor-affiliated parties continued to play a role. APRA, the party with historic ties to the labor movement, won 35 percent of the vote to the Constituent Assembly. By 1977 the APRA-affiliated CTP still claimed more than a quarter of the labor movement, but had clearly been surpassed by the Communist-led CGTP (Sulmont 1980:147; see also 210–11). More important, given this shift in partisan affiliation of the labor movement that had occurred during the military regime, the left won 33 percent. Further, the Constituent Assembly solicited advice from many social groups, including union leaders, and during this period the military government kept up contacts with party leaders, especially those of APRA, which the military had singled out as its major interlocutor, but including those of the left (Dietz 1992:241–46). In July 1979 all citizens over eighteen years of age were enfranchised, and the elections that followed in May 1980 led to the inauguration of a civilian government elected under the new constitution.

ARGENTINA

It is generally argued that the 1983 return to democracy in Argentina stemmed directly from the defeat of the Argentine military in the Falkland Islands/Malvinas War. According to this view, the disastrous failure of the ruling generals "precipitated the sudden collapse of the regime and thus led to a new democratic transition in 1983" (Cavarozzi 1992:222). While it is certainly the case that the democratic transition followed regime collapse in the aftermath of military defeat, such a characterization ignores the factors that brought on the military venture in the first place. Analysts have suggested two points at which labor may be interpreted as having played an important role. First, labor protest contributed to a division within the military between hard-liners and soft-liners, a division that, according to many analysts, the decision to invade the Malvinas was in turn intended to overcome (Fontana 1984:35; Colombo and Palermo 1985:

81). In an additional argument, some analysts have suggested that labor protest directly led the generals to implement plans for the Malvinas invasion. With or without this second argument, union-led protest was an important factor in destabilizing the military regime.

Since the 1940s, when Perón came to power on the shoulders of working-class support, the labor question had been at the very core of Argentine politics, and it certainly remained central in 1976, when the military intervened to overthrow the first Peronist government it had allowed to come to power in the intervening decades. Massive worker demonstrations and strikes had occurred throughout the Peronist government from 1973 to 1976, and, as Epstein (1989:26) points out, the inauguration of military rule was a response to this worker activism: "the image of a weak government at the mercy of the trade unions . . . convinced the military of the need to act politically to end what to them was an unacceptable situation."

The immediate response of the new military government was repression. Many unions were intervened and thousands of labor leaders killed, disappeared, or jailed. The repression decapitated the most prominent and combative labor leadership, leaving behind the previously more moderate and "participationist" leaders in less central economic sectors in addition to the collaborationist leaders in the intervened unions (Fernández 1985: 73–74). The importance of the labor question could be seen not only in the speed and scope of the repression but also in the fact that a new labor law to deactivate the labor movement was under active consideration by the military government within a month of the March coup. Despite the clear centrality of this issue, most transition analysts have, as Munck points out, largely missed these dynamics, though, as he adds, some have stressed that "the military regime in Argentina always feared the possibility of a social explosion led by the workers" (G. Munck 1990:384–85, n. 16).

The first interpretation of labor's role in the Argentine transition centers on its contribution to heightening military factionalism and thereby reducing the junta's ability to consolidate an authoritarian regime. Early military factionalism was closely linked to divisions over how to handle the labor question, and the labor issue was directly connected to the economic model adopted by the new government headed by General Videla:[5] based on economic liberalization and free markets, the model constituted an assault on unions that was ultimately embodied in the new labor law. An alternative approach, taken by a military faction centered

5 Several analysts have seen the economic model not only as a technocratic response to the economic situation but also as an explicit political strategy to weaken the power of the working class. See, for instance, Villarreal 1987; and Smith 1989.

around the allies of General Viola, invoked an older pattern of state-labor relations worked out under the previous military regimes, in which labor moderation could be bought with some concessions regarding a still limited but more positive role for unions, rather than an all-out attack. Thus, though factions within the military formed along various lines, the major cleavage that was to emerge cannot be understood apart from the historic and ongoing position of labor in Argentine politics.

Despite incipient factionalism, military unity was maintained through the initial years of the "dirty war," a period of hard-line dominance. The weakness and ineffectiveness of the soft-line faction was seen in the two documents published at the end of 1979: a political document and a labor law, neither of which, quite pointedly, produced any project for political liberalization or opening. Indeed, the labor law has been described as completing the unprecedented onslaught against labor (G. Munck 1998: 98–102). Nevertheless, both the repression and the pending law failed to "solve" the problem of union power. Instead, in different ways, both led to labor responses that brought to the surface the embryonic factions within the military.

The repression was extensive and effective, but it did not completely put an end to labor opposition. Even after the coup labor activity had continued. "Belying the image of a society immobilized by repression, individual strikes began almost immediately after the 1976 coup."[6] At the outset workers in some of the stronger unions had staged a series of "defensive strikes" designed to prevent government assaults on strategic labor sectors. More important, however, the repression of the national labor leadership had two interesting effects. First, the newly emergent national leadership, which either had survived or had replaced those who had been removed, paradoxically reinforced military factionalism. This group of labor leaders was not free of divisions: one wing, primarily based in the unions the state had intervened, was more cooperative and willing to submit to military initiatives, whereas leaders from the other wing took a more critical position. Nevertheless, the common willingness of both wings to negotiate or enter into dialogue with the government in the post-coup period facilitated the traditional corporatist strategy of the regime's labor minister, General Liendo, a representative of the softer-line faction. As labor opposition surged in 1977, however, divisions within the military widened over labor policy, with harder-line leaders more actively opposed to the labor-military dialogue, calling for Liendo's ouster in order to block

6 McGuire 1995: fn. 15. See also Epstein 1989:26–27; R. Munck 1987:212; Pozzi 1988: 86; Fernández 1985:91–93.

labor's political access and influence (Pozzi 1988:150–52; Abós 1984:37). The second effect of the repression of national labor leaders, combined with the emergent labor leadership's willingness to pursue a rather supine negotiating strategy, was that it created space for a new generation of leaders whose increasingly critical stance toward the national labor bureaucracy reflected shop-floor pressures for greater combativeness. These leaders arose both at the level of factory commissions, particularly in sectors dominated by conservative labor leaders, and at the level of provincial labor organizations in smaller cities.[7]

Based on these new sources of labor activism, in late 1977 a wave of strikes spread throughout the country in a variety of economic sectors. From October to December, some one million workers participated in "marginal, semiclandestinely organized" strikes, sometimes aimed at the union bureaucracy (Fernández 1985:91). The result was "a change in the correlation of forces between the workers' movement and the military regime" (Pozzi:1988:81). The strike wave pushed the more critical national leaders toward a more confrontationist and mobilizing stance. By March 1978 the Commission of "25" was formed, organizationally uniting a more oppositionist group of national labor leaders. In a public speech in December 1978, Saúl Ubaldini, leader of the "25," declared that the country's problems could be solved "only through a government elected by the people" and demanded the "establishment of a full democracy" (cited in Senen González 1984:97, 111–12).

The 1979 labor law also had the unintended consequence of providing the impetus for increased labor opposition. On 27 April, 1979, when the new labor law was being considered, the "25" organized the first general strike under the military dictatorship. The labor law also spurred a flurry of renewed activity at the national level. In September, in anticipation of the law, the "25" and the heretofore apolitical or "professional" CNT united to form the CUTA; and, in reaction to the published law, the CUTA immediately undertook overtly oppositional activities on a number of fronts: it announced a "plan of action" to fight the new law through "national plebiscites" in the workplace; it initiated contact with political parties, labor lawyers, and the ILO; and it undertook organizational work, developing regional labor groupings. Divisions remained within the CUTA, and the moderate CNT wing did little to implement the "plan of action"; furthermore, some of the organizing efforts at the regional level reflected a competitive strategy taken on the part of the "25" against the CNT (Pozzi 1988:128–29). Nevertheless, the brief unification of the labor

7 Epstein 1989:26–27; Fernández 1985:91–93; Pozzi 1988:130, 135.

movement, the new posture it formally adopted, and the activities of at least one of the wings represented a significant change. At the same time, labor activity increased at the more decentralized level of individual unions.

In this way, unions moved to take an initiative in mobilizing opposition and attempting to coordinate other social sectors, at the same time that the political parties rejected the initiative and business groups were divided (G. Munck 1998:112–24; Pozzi 1988:94,128). It should be remembered that the increase in oppositional activity that occurred in response to the labor law was a result not of a policy of political liberalization (the very labor law was indication that the hard-line faction remained dominant) but rather of what Munck has referred to as the declining despotic power of the state, as the dirty war unleashed against the left and labor wound down (G. Munck 1990:269). This mobilization kept the labor question alive, a question that continued to divide the military.

Open divisions within the ruling authoritarian regime emerged in this context of labor protest as well as economic deterioration. The incipient cleavage within the government became more concrete under the impact of financial crisis, economic recession, a substantial increase in rank-and-file labor protest, and an impending presidential succession. The fragile labor unity having collapsed in May 1980, one labor faction, coordinating its activity through the Intersectorial CNT-20, was willing to enter a dialogue with the Viola military faction;[8] the other, oppositionist labor faction, now organized as the General Labor Confederation (CGT), "displayed growing boldness, worked to develop thicker organizational networks through contact with various actors within society, and made direct calls for a change in labor policy and of the regime itself" (G. Munck 1990:305–6).

In this context, the presidential succession of the soft-liner General Viola in March 1981 became the focus for ideologically based antagonisms among top officers. The discontent of the navy was particularly pronounced since, in addition to having been cut out of "its turn" in the succession, it was identified with a hard-line approach and opposed Viola, who favored a more pragmatic economic policy and more normalized relations with political party and conciliatory union leaders (McGuire 1995:186).

The ongoing opposition of the labor movement contributed to Viola's inability to consolidate power. Initially split over the possibility of cooperating with the Viola government and still organizationally divided, both wings of the union movement came to agree on an overtly oppositionist

8 Abós 1984:78; Fernández 1985:81; Pozzi 1988:129,133.

and pro-democratic stance when it became clear that the conciliation and dialogue promised by Viola would not be forthcoming. In July 1981, the CGT mounted another general strike, and under its leadership, the opposition fostered an intractable climate of instability and a sense that "civil society was getting out of control" so that opposition to Viola grew even within his own branch of the military (G. Munck 1990:318–19). On 7 November the CGT called another mass mobilization. The depth of opposition that it expressed surprised its organizers as well as the regime (Pozzi 1988:98). Two days later Viola was forced to resign.

General Viola's removal exposed deep divisions within the regime that were compromising the military's institutional control of government. With the defeat of the soft-liners, the new president, General Galtieri, returned to a hard-line authoritarian stance and in the face of ongoing divisions launched the Malvinas invasion in order to placate the navy, which had favored it, and thus restore cohesion in the military.[9] The first interpretation, then, is that "diverse views on how to deal with society produced internal divisions within the Armed Forces" (G. Munck 1990: 326; see also Pozzi 1988:101). Labor's pro-democratic opposition and protest prevented the military regime from consolidating power and finally led to its destabilization by reinforcing and intensifying these splits, which the disastrous military escapade was intended to repair.

A second interpretation suggests that labor protest *directly* prompted the decision of the generals to initiate the Malvinas invasion. Aside from its adverse effect on military cohesion, this argument points to the role of accelerating union-led protest in destabilizing the military regime by demonstrating not only the regime's lack of social support but its inability even to maintain order. As Ronaldo Munck put it, "the military adventure of the generals cannot be explained in purely 'military' terms. . . . It was the constant level of working-class resistance since 1976, which was moving from a defensive to an offensive phase by 1982, which alone explains [the] bizarre political gamble by the armed forces" (R. Munck 1989:78).

Opposition and protest increased after the ouster of Viola and the self-conscious return of the military regime to its hard-line "sources." The union movement – the CGT as well as the Intersectorial – took steps to coordinate joint action with the parties, which since July 1981 had been organized in the Multipartidaria. On 30 March 1982, along with human rights groups and political parties, the CGT initiated the largest demonstration since the 1976 coup. The leading role of the workers' movement

---

9 McGuire 1995:187–88. McGuire further suggests that the invasion was also intended to generate support for a positive project of a military party.

has been suggested by Pozzi (1988:101), for whom the protest "demonstrated how the workers' movement constituted the motor of antidictatorial resistance," triggering the participation of other social sectors. Throughout this whole period, the political parties in particular took a more reactive rather than initiating role (Abós 1984:78–80, 92).

By the time of the 30 March protest, it had become clear that "the CGT's massive demonstrations were threatening the stability of the government" (G. Munck 1990:327). On 2 April, the Argentine armed forces activated plans for the Malvinas invasion. Although the protest itself did not precipitate the decision to invade, it was symbolic, and in some sense the culmination, of a longer process of societal destabilization of the regime, in the face of which Galtieri resorted to igniting a long-standing nationalist cause behind which he hoped to rally the country: the issue of British control of off-shore islands. Leading accounts by journalists and participant observers also trace the invasion directly to societal mobilization and increasing regime destabilization (R. Munck 1989:79; G. Munck 1998:139–40).

In either interpretation, the invasion was a desperation move to preserve a regime already in trouble, and the pressure from at least one faction of the labor movement was, directly or at a step removed, a major source of the problem. The invasion was launched either with an eye toward addressing splits within the military that were exacerbated by labor protest, and/or in an effort to deal with the challenge of accelerating popular mobilization in opposition to the authoritarian regime, mobilization in which the CGT played a central initiating and coordinating role. Thus, union-led protest was critical in destabilizing the authoritarian regime, a point that is missed with a focus on regime collapse by military defeat. As O'Donnell and Schmitter (1986:18) have also recognized, "It is more accurate to interpret [the Malvinas invasion] as the result of an already tottering regime launching a *fuite en avant* than as a cause for the regime's having reached such an impasse."

The military gamble, of course, failed. Not only did Argentina lose the ensuing war against Britain, but the invasion failed to defuse labor protest. Though the labor movement supported the military campaign itself, it remained active in opposition to the regime. By mid-June 1982, with the clear-cut loss in the war and ongoing massive mobilization, the discredited military quickly moved to extricate itself by installing a "caretaker" government and announcing that general elections would be held in October 1983 on the basis of the 1853 constitution.

The Argentine union movement was an active player in the remaining phases of the transition. First of all, through mobilizations and strikes it kept up constant pressure on the military regime. Union locals maintained a general climate of militance as almost every organized labor sector struck at least once, with civil servants in the Justice Ministry striking seventeen times. This local militancy contributed to ongoing mobilizations at the national level, particularly as the two labor centrals competed for position. These national protests included, in addition to the Multipartidaria's March for Democracy, two successful general strikes and a large demonstration to commemorate the pre-Malvinas mobilization. Although mobilizations called by the centrals tapered off in the last months as the national leadership got involved in negotiating the transition, at the local level union militance continued at an extremely high level of activity (Senen González 1984:187–95).

The negotiating role of the national labor leadership is the second point. The interim government of General Bignone more extensively attempted to negotiate the military's extrication than is generally recognized (McGuire 1995), and union leaders were key players in these events. On the one side, three plans to shape the subsequent government were rejected by the Multipartidaria, of which the union movement was one of the main members. On the other side, though they continued to be denied by the reputed principals, rumors and charges were widespread regarding a military-union pact in which the military would receive an amnesty against human rights abuses in exchange for Peronist control of unions as they were normalized after the long period of government control. Regardless of the actual existence of the pact, labor leaders were a major interlocutor in the post-Malvinas period as "the junta made a special effort to negotiate the transition with Peronist union leaders" (see McGuire 1995:189). As McGuire has suggested, had the Peronists won the elections as widely expected, these negotiations would have received greater prominence in analytic interpretations along with, in Drake's words, the role and prime interest of the unionists "in reaching minimal understandings with the armed forces to assure an orderly election and transfer of power" (McGuire 1995:190; Drake 1996:173). As it was, Radical party leader Raúl Alfonsín denounced the pact and, being a more appealing candidate with a background in the human rights movement, won the elections of October 1983. His inauguration marked the completion of the democratization process.

SPAIN

According to most authors, Spain is a prototypical case of democratization by elite negotiation.[10] Indeed, the Spanish transition to democracy in 1977

10 See, for example, Huntington 1991:125–27; Share 1986; Share and Mainwaring 1986; Linz 1981; Medhurst 1984; Stepan 1986:74; Smith 1987:183; Di Palma 1990:6–8; Gunther 1992; and Karl and Schmitter 1991. The interpretation of the Spanish case

is in many ways the case that inspired the elite-centered approach to the analysis of contemporary democratization. The dominant interpretation of Spain sees the process of democratization as beginning roughly with the death of Franco in November 1975 and the accession of Juan Carlos as king. According to this prevailing interpretation, in the uncertain environment that followed Franco's death, skilled elite leadership explains the crafting of a successful democratization. Particularly important was the ability of regime moderates – most notably Adolfo Suárez – to pursue democratic negotiations simultaneously with both the moderates from the "democratic opposition" and the *continuistas* of the Franco establishment.[11] Further, the fact that Suárez pursued these negotiations and reforms in an incremental fashion had the effect of garnering support for this carefully crafted democratization.

This interpretation misses the crucial role played by labor through the various stages of regime change. First, by the early 1970s, even before the death of Franco, labor pressures for an end to authoritarian rule had put the regime in a deepening state of crisis. Second, the dramatic labor protests served to undermine regime attempts to establish a system of "Francoism without Franco." Finally, labor protest expanded contestation by ensuring the inclusion of the Communist Party in the new democracy, and in addition, once the regime was destabilized, elements of the labor movement helped define a more moderate opposition strategy that enabled Suárez to negotiate the final agreements leading up to the democratic elections of June 1977. As Maravall (1982:14) states:

> Popular pressure "from below" played a crucial part in the transition, especially that coming from the workers' movement. It was a causal factor in the Francoist crisis, in the non-viability of any mere "liberalization" policy, in the willingness on the part of the "democratic right" to negotiate the transition and carry through reform up to the point of breaking with Francoism, and in the initiative displayed by the Left up to the 1977 elections.

The Spanish labor movement was well positioned to open space within the authoritarian regime and to lead pro-democratic protest for two reasons. The first was the advantage brought by the leadership of the Communists, who could draw on a tradition and experience of unusual

---

that comes closest to the analysis presented here is Maravall 1982. See also Foweraker 1987, 1989, and Tarrow 1995; both have criticized the elite-centric interpretation and offered a more interactive approach that incorporates social movements, including labor mobilization.

11 These negotiations were largely informal discussions. In fact, a formal pact was not negotiated during this period. The Moncloa Pacts were economic pacts – essentially between Suárez and the left – that came after the political transition to democracy was completed.

organizational capacity and underground strategizing. The second was the existence of an official union structure, which, though corporatist, verticalist, and designed as an alternative "representative" structure that would contain workers' organizations within appropriate, conciliatory, and even legitimating channels, could be infiltrated, reoriented in unintended directions, and used to push the boundaries of oppositional activity.

As early as 1948 the Communist Party decided to take advantage of the elections to workers' committees at the factory level and work within the official union structure. Under this impetus, the official unions became unintended sites of more genuine demand making and representation of workers' interests and grievances, even within the officially created spaces. In this way, corporatist structures began to erode, and at the same time the labor movement began to recover its capacity for collective action.[12] The first dramatic labor eruption was the Barcelona transport boycott and strike in March 1951. By the mid-1950s, rising working-class militance and wildcat strikes had led to a pattern of informal, unofficial interchange and coordination between workers and employers, which was essentially recognized by the 1958 law that officially began to open up the process of collective bargaining.[13] The following decade of the 1960s witnessed a huge increase in labor mobilization, eventually to the point that Spain had one of the highest per capita strike rates in Europe. During this time, "strikes became a regular feature of Spanish life," even though illegal and punishable under the Penal Code (Carr and Fusi 1979:139).

The strikes facilitated the creation of a parallel structure, the Comisiones Obreras (CCOO), which established a formal organization in the mid-1960s but was promptly outlawed in 1967. Illegal, it continued to act as the leading representative of the labor opposition. Although the CCOO continued to use and be protected by the legal spaces made available by the state inside official unionism, it was more overtly oppositionist with an "essentially antiregime character" and put greater emphasis on mobilization, a "participatory movementlike quality," and illegal protests and strikes (Fishman 1990a:96–97,113). Thus, in different but symbiotic ways, both the legal unions and the illegal CCOO became important sites of opposition and channels for undermining authoritarianism.

At least by the mid-1960s, the agenda of the labor movement broadened from wage and shop-floor issues to democratic liberties. In October

---

12 Fishman 1990a:90–94; Balfour 1989; Witney 1965:39ff.; Amsden 1972; Foweraker 1987.

13 The appointment of technocrats to the cabinet at the expense of the traditional dominance of the Falange in February 1957 – which is sometimes viewed as the initial steps in liberalizing the regime – has been linked to labor protest. See Preston 1986:7.

1967 the CCOO led a demonstration in Madrid in which "more than 100,000 workers marched through the streets of the capital shouting 'free trade unions,' and 'Franco no, democracy yes' " (Gilmour 1985:93). The end of this decade also saw a shift in the strategy of the labor movement from limited protests to tactics aimed at toppling the regime. The Communist Party and affiliated labor leaders began to discuss openly the possibility of a *ruptura democrática*. This important transformation reflected a belief among many in the opposition that it was possible to overthrow the regime through a working-class insurrection.

In part as a consequence of ongoing labor protest and the labor strategy of *ruptura*, serious divisions emerged within the regime between soft-liners, who believed that the regime must be opened to survive, and hard-liners, who resisted any change. Hard-liners were initially dominant, and the 1967–73 period saw a return to increased levels of repression (Foweraker 1987:105). Franco decided to pursue the long-term continuation of authoritarianism through the establishment of a future Francoist monarchy with Juan Carlos as king. Yet repression was ineffective in reducing social protest. During 1970 worker strikes occurred in dramatic proportions, totaling over 1,500 in number.[14] At the same time, terrorist activities were on the rise. According to Carr and Fusi (1979:192), Prime Minister "Carrero responded to these conflicts and challenges with tougher police measures. . . . The government had no political answer to this increasing level of conflict." In reaction, soft-liners became increasingly vocal in pressing for a change of policy. In late 1972 and early 1973, Franco and Carrero Blanco responded in speeches that suggested some type of political opening would be forthcoming.

Sustained labor protest in 1973 helped keep the government on the defensive, searching for a new formula for stability. With the assassination of Carrero Blanco in December 1973, Franco appointed a moderate, Carlos Arias Navarro, whose strategy was to establish some type of *dictablanda*, or softer dictatorship, but labor activism was crucial to preventing the stabilization of such a political system. Strikes increased dramatically under Arias, as 1974 witnessed the largest number in Spanish history. In 1975 the strike record was once again broken. In reaction to this labor protest, the hard-liners retrenched, favoring a severe crackdown on the protests and driving a deeper wedge in the regime. It was in this context that Franco fell ill. According to Carr and Fusi (1979:205–6), "When the news of Franco's illness broke . . . everything seemed to show that the regime was in crisis. The government was floundering in a vain attempt to contain

14 For strike data, see Maravall 1978:33.

within the political system severe conflicts, knowing that if it failed to do so it was doomed."

In the opening months of 1976, labor strikes and demonstrations once again reached new, unprecedented levels. Carr and Fusi (1979:210) assert that "the ministry remained impotent" when confronted with this labor offensive, in which an estimated fifty million hours were lost to strikes from January to March alone (Maravall 1978:33). In this context of regime destabilization, "the strategies of mere liberalization could have little chance of success" (Maravall 1982:10). In this way, labor protest in fact undermined the strategy of limited liberalization pursued by Arias. When he resigned in July, it had become clear that "if a catastrophic clash between the irresistible force of the left and the immovable object of the right was to be avoided, it was essential that rapid progress be made to the introduction of democracy" (Preston 1986:91).

By the time Suárez became prime minister, the labor movement had done much both to destabilize the authoritarian regime and to reject any government attempt to respond in a way short of a democratic transition. It seemed clear that the government had to find some means of effecting a speedy transition to democracy. In about two months, Suárez did just that and got his cabinet to approve a transition project that committed the government to holding elections in less than a year. In another brief two-month period, the project was approved by the Cortes (legislature).

These events are worth pondering. The task – and triumph – of Suárez was, as many have emphasized, nothing less than convincing the Cortes to agree to its own replacement in a very short time. How was this possible? The real question is not, Was Suárez a skilled negotiator, full of *virtú* and enjoying some added dose of *fortuna*? Surely he was. The question, rather, is whether what he did can be seen as an extrication – did Suárez, in other words, negotiate an extrication, even though he did it very well and ultimately with positive implications for democratic consolidation? It is difficult to imagine an entrenched Cortes participating so quickly in its own demise without reference to the high level of oppositional mobilization and regime crisis that had been reached by that point. The two speeches referred to in some analyses, however brilliant they may have been, hardly seem up to this portentous task. The context in which they were given must be invoked to make sense of these developments. The importance of the "Communist Party and the trade union movements controlled by it," along with the nationalist challenge, has been explicitly, however parenthetically, recognized by analysts like Linz and Stepan, who, even as they emphasize the agency of Suárez, nonetheless refer to the "fear of a vacuum of authority, of a sudden transfer of power to the then quite radical opposition forces" in prompting Suárez and the reformers to act (Linz and Stepan 1996:92).

Not only did labor opposition play an important role in provoking the transition, but it also shaped the way it unfolded. Even before Suárez came to power, the democratic opposition – led by the Communist Party, affiliated trade unions, and the Socialist Party – recognized that it could not directly overthrow the government and abandoned the strategy of *ruptura democrática* in favor of a *ruptura pactada* (negotiated rupture), which envisioned a provisional government and a constituent Cortes to determine the successor regime.[15] The reform project that Suárez proposed in October 1976 and that the Cortes passed in November in part paralleled this project, providing for the election of the Constituent Assembly but rejecting a provisional government. Once Suárez had engineered a consensus behind the transition project, the rest followed quickly according to the timetable adopted. In June 1977 free elections to a democratic Cortes were held, and the new constitution that was subsequently written provided the institutional structure of the new democracy.

In addition, labor mobilization was central in opening the new democracy to the participation of the left. While many favored a proscription of the Communist Party, Suárez argued for its legalization in terms of the balance of political forces made clearly apparent in the streets: "The reality [is] that the Communist Party exists and is organized. The struggle against it could only be carried out by repression." He further pointed out that the result of proscription would be "to see our jails full of people" and presented a choice between "ballot boxes" and "unrest in the streets" (quoted in Linz and Stepan 1996:97).

Although in the final months of the transition, labor and the left opposition lost power to the more moderate opposition, their role in bringing about and shaping the transition should not be underestimated. They had precipitated the transition, and in many ways their *ruptura pactada* strategy gave the transition its particular form. Indeed, discussions and negotiations took place between the government and left parties, including the labor-based Communist Party.

As for the other cases, the argument here is certainly not that labor single-handedly brought about the demise of the authoritarian regime, no less constructed the new democracy. Nor is it that labor was the most

15 See Preston 1986:95; and Carr and Fusi 1979:214. Carr and Fusi state that the expression *ruptura pactada* was coined by Communist leader Santiago Carrillo in an interview in March 1976.

important of an admitted array of reformist players (including industrialists, students, Basque and Catalon nationalists, the king) if such a ranking could be determined. Nevertheless, labor had exerted constant pressure on the regime for about ten years, and this pressure continued during the years of the transition itself. Despite the widely noted "moderation" of labor in these years, Pérez-Díaz notes the "explosion" in the level of industrial conflict and collective action in 1976–79 and a rise in real wages at a rate almost double that of the OECD average in 1973–79 (Pérez-Díaz 1993:238–39, 242). Labor "moderation" can thus be seen as more indicative of a pro-democratic approach than of labor passivity.

Within a year of becoming prime minister, then, Suárez oversaw the transition to a democratically elected regime, and labor opposition was an important part of that story. It is certainly the case that Suárez used the legal instruments of the Francoist system to bring about its liquidation and demonstrated impressive leadership skill in his ability to negotiate a broad consensus around the transition. Yet, to begin the story of Spanish democratization from this point and to emphasize continuity and skilled leadership is to focus on the final step of a much longer process and to miss the important role of labor and the degree to which it succeeded in destabilizing the authoritarian regime, making impossible a reform that stopped short of democratization and forcing incumbents to undertake a rather speedy extrication *qua* regime change.

TRANSITION GAME

The Transition Game, labeled to acknowledge a certain degree of conformity with the dominant framework in the "transitions" literature, includes the unusual cases in which the transition process began with an incumbent project for legitimation. There followed a protracted series of moves and countermoves and formal and informal negotiations between authoritarian incumbents and moderate opposition party actors, the former pursuing projects to institutionalize their rule, the latter seeking to undermine those projects and advance a democratic transition.

Nevertheless, in this pattern the labor movement was more central to the transition than has been acknowledged in general or theoretical statements, though its weight varied considerably among the cases. It was less important, though not insignificant, in Brazil and quite substantial in Uruguay. In Bolivia the labor movement was an even more central protagonist and was so from the beginning. There, and later in the transition process in Uruguay, the labor movement constituted the best organized group in the opposition, led the anti-regime protest, and was an important player in the wider negotiations. It affected the timing of the democratization process and pushed it forward, sometimes when it had stalled. In all three countries, the labor movement helped to undermine the limited incumbent projects and expanded contestation.

In Brazil and Uruguay, the strategic game arose in a particular context in which from the very onset the military rulers sought legitimation through a facade of civilian rule operating through a chosen set of politicians and a restricted electoral arena. In this way, the government project defined a game it would play with selected political parties, whether long-established (Uruguay)[16] or newly formed under government guidance (Brazil). Counter to their expectations, however, it was a game these governments could not control. In both cases popular opposition found space in the limited and controlled electoral arena that remained open: the 1980 plebiscite marked the first failure of the government project of Uruguay, and the opposition gains in the 1974 elections portended the failure of the government project in Brazil. Henceforth, both regimes were thrown on the defensive, with incumbents continually scrambling to alter their project and change the rules of the political game in the face of an opposition increasingly on the offensive.

Given their sanctioned space in the regime legitimation projects, party leaders were poised early on to play a role as opposition actors in Brazil and Uruguay; and given the pattern of repression, the labor movement appeared on the scene later. Nevertheless, once it surfaced, union activity helped advance the course of the transition. Furthermore, in both cases the activities of the labor opposition worked to undermine government attempts to control and limit the party system and created room for the entry of a political left. This was particularly important in a context in which formal (Uruguay) or informal (Brazil) negotiations between government and the leaders of major parties could well have led to an agreement to exclude left parties. Nevertheless, in Brazil labor protest gave rise to a new socialist party based in the new union movement, and in Uruguay the reconstitution of the labor movement and its protest activities provided a front for the banned Frente Amplio, its participation in various opposition fora, and finally its legalization and participation in the final negotiations, allowing the stalled transition to proceed.

---

16 In Uruguay, the parties were dissolved in 1977, but selected members of the traditional parties were appointed to form a new body that replaced the closed legislature.

In the Bolivian variant, labor opposition to the regime erupted before the party arena opened and was central in derailing the government's project for electoral legitimation. Bolivia constitutes the unusual case among those in the 1970s and 1980s where coups followed the transfer of power to civilians, and hard-line military rule was reestablished. The rapid sequence of moves that followed in this historically unstable country was a game among military, labor, and party actors, with the first two often the primary players. In the final iteration the Bolivian regime imploded, collapsing for a series of reasons but ultimately being forced into a speedy extrication primarily through ongoing labor mobilizations.

BRAZIL

The labor role in Brazil was less important in terms of its impact on the course of the transition itself. It formed a part of the larger opposition and helped to derail the government project, but its most important contribution was in expanding contestation. In a political setting in which the major parties were historically nonprogrammatic and the Marxist parties were banned, an important segment of the labor movement gave rise to and secured the legalization of an avowedly socialist party that articulated a leftist program and laborist aspirations.

In Brazil, the first steps toward political opening were initiated autonomously by the authoritarian incumbents, who came to power in a 1964 military coup.[17] At the outset, the military sought to legitimate its rule, first holding indirect presidential elections, then in 1965 moving to institutionalize a restricted party system based on two officially recognized and approved parties, followed two years later by a new constitution. By 1968, with hard-line generals gaining political power, a more harshly repressive period was inaugurated, in response to opposition stemming both from politicians in what was supposed to be a safe, controlled party arena and from popular mobilization, including the first labor strike and a guerrilla threat.[18] In 1974, the military soft-liners once again gained the upper

17 Good overviews of the 1964–85 military period are found in Skidmore 1988; and Stepan 1989.
18 Interestingly, the major sources of opposition came not only from the MDB, the factionalized official opposition party, which sometimes cooperated with and sometimes criticized the government, and sometimes participated in and sometimes boycotted elections held under continually changing and manipulated rules, but also from Carlos Lacerda, who, from the right, had been probably the most outspoken and strident opponent of the more "populist" pre-1964 democratic governments. In 1967 he organized the Broad Front and announced his candidacy for president.

hand, and, during the presidency of General Geisel, instituted a process of political liberalization, known as "decompression." Thus, for ten years, political dynamics and rhythm followed the relative political fortunes of hard-liners and soft-liners within the military and the activities of leaders within the officially recognized parties in the limited legislative and electoral space that was allowed.

The decompression policy ushered in a period of political opening in which repression was eased and greater political criticism and opposition activity became possible. The immediate result was the unexpected success of the official opposition party in the 1974 elections as the government party retained the majority but lost the two-thirds necessary for amending the constitution. Further opposition gains followed in the 1976 municipal elections. Many groups in civil society began raising oppositionist voices in favor of a democratic transition. In the face of this failure to engineer a carefully controlled political opening that would favor the government party, the government briefly closed Congress and decreed the so-called April package of 1977. These constitutional changes further manipulated the electoral law to make the reform project safe for the continued dominance of the government party and thereby to keep the project on track and prevent its derailment by either regime hard-liners or opposition forces.

At this point the labor movement burst onto the political scene with renewed militance and strike activity. Although not very visible, given the repression following the 1968 strike, the labor movement had developed a new form of resistance in the early 1970s. Especially within the multinational automobile plants, workers carried out slowdowns and in-factory strikes to protest wage and employment policies (Moreira Alves 1989:53). In 1977 the unions mounted a wage recuperation campaign, which exposed and protested the manipulated cost-of-living figures the government had been using to index wages. Given the government role in setting wage policy and its duplicity in the use of the inflation index, this action around bread-and-butter issues had direct and broader political implications. The following year, the "new unionism" erupted when the metalworkers' in-factory strike triggered a series of other strikes that eventually encompassed nearly one-quarter of a million workers over a nine-week period, and over one-half million workers by the end of that year (Moreira Alves 1985: 194–97). One of the largest strike waves in Brazilian history followed in 1979, as more than three million workers participated in over one hundred strikes (Moreira Alves 1985:199; see also R. Munck 1981:226–27). The new unionism "signaled the existence of massive, organized discontent

with the regime, and it constituted powerful evidence that democratization was necessary to resolve the potential for social conflict" (Keck 1989:
42).

By the late 1970s, a substantial and diverse opposition movement had
already emerged. Thus, although the workers' movement did not by itself
provide the opening wedge of protest, it did contribute to the overall
process of democratic transition. As Noronha has suggested, the strikes of
the late 1970s were a direct challenge to the regime and can be seen as
expanding the scope of the transition both by extending the pro-democracy
struggle beyond the electoral arena and by challenging the government's
mechanisms of corporatist control. In both the short and long run (though
not without setbacks), the strike constituted a successful blow against the
government's industrial relations system regarding unions' right to elect
leaders, strike, and bargain collectively. The military project, in Noronha's
words, "neither included nor foresaw, at least in the short term, an increase
in union freedom. In this sense [the 1978 strikes] . . . raised the level of
the *abertura's* policy debates by forcing the question of labor union freedom
to be included on the agenda" (Noronha 1992:2:85–86).

In addition, the Brazilian labor movement made another contribution
to the transition: it intensified and helped to change the nature of the
opposition. Before its resurgence in 1978, many other groups had taken
advantage of the Geisel decompression policies to oppose the military
regime. These included the Church, the bar, the media, and, somewhat
later, elements of the business community. This opposition mostly took a
verbal form through manifestos, articles, and so forth. While political
leaders and intellectuals in the opposition had been debating ways to
establish links to the popular sectors, "the massive strike waves of 1978
and 1979 changed the context of the debate. The problem . . . ceased to be
only a question to be debated among intellectuals; it became instead a
matter for negotiation among increasingly organized constituencies. Many
working-class leaders were no longer willing to leave the act of interpretation to others – they wanted to create an organizational opportunity for
workers to speak for themselves" (Keck 1989:58–59).

The new union movement was not the only mass movement to emerge.
A genuine grass-roots urban social movement in the form of CEBs (eccle-
sial base communities) promoted by the Church had been proliferating
throughout the country. Indeed, the new unionism in large measure
emerged from these same organizing efforts, and the two social movements
developed in a pattern of mutual support. From 1973 the CEBs had been
active in the Cost of Living Movement culminating in 1977–78. "Among

its accomplishments was helping to regain the streets for public protest" (Skidmore 1988:183). Hence, the labor movement did not initiate either the opposition movement or mass protest. Its dramatic reemergence, however, placed it at the forefront of the broad segment of social movements then emerging in opposition to the authoritarian regime. According to Keck (1989:51), "the rebirth of the labor movement . . . happened dramatically enough to gain ascendancy quickly in the social process and claim a leadership role in the broad tissue of movements then appearing."

Initially factory based, the protest movement led by labor spread in two complementary directions. First, it extended beyond the union sector proper, stimulating greater activism within the larger working-class neighborhoods and communities (Seidman 1994:208). From the 1978–79 strikes the new unionism galvanized a broader opposition, winning not only passive support but the active involvement of church groups and the larger community in providing material support. "In the process of supporting the strikers . . . a functioning network of alliances was established among grass-roots organizations, social-movement organizations linked to the church, and the labor unions" (Moreira Alves 1985:203).

Second, and relatedly, demands became broader and more overtly political as the labor movement moved beyond an emphasis on shop-floor, wage, and industrial relations issues and championed the demands and concerns of the lower classes more generally. In the wake of the strikes labor leaders became important "national political figures articulating broad political demands."[19] When the government abandoned its two-party project, union activists took advantage of the new political space by organizing an explicitly socialist Workers' Party (PT).

As a new actor on the scene, the PT had an impact on the projects of both the government and the opposition. With respect to the former, it frustrated the government's attempt to exorcise the left. At the same time it undermined the strategy of the opposition, and especially of the leading opposition party, the PMDB, the successor of the "official opposition" party in the government's original two-party system. Prior to the formation of the PT, the opposition tended to see the PMDB as the only viable opposition party and to call for opposition unity under its leadership, conceiving of the struggle for democracy in unidimensional, polar terms – a struggle taking place between pro- and anti-regime forces (Keck 1989: 124,127). The PT refused to join or merge with the PMDB and insisted

---

19 Seidman 1994:37. See also Moisés 1990:114 for an argument that the 1978–80 strikes placed the new unionism at the forefront of the larger democratic movement.

on providing an alternative opposition voice that would assert a discourse of citizenship and class and a program of popular participation, emphasizing the importance of popular organizations (Keck 1989:139–40). In this way, the new unionism gave rise to a new party actor and increased contestation in the party/electoral arena.

The strike movement culminated in 1980, when the metalworkers called a strike that, with a much higher level of organization and closer coordination with the urban popular movement, was sustained for forty-one days. Hard-liners within the government engaged in provocative moves, but Kucinski (1982:155) argues that popular sympathy for the strikers prevented a coup and changed the balance of power within the regime, isolating the hard-liners. After that, the transition was more firmly on course.

Labor organizations, then, came together with broader social movements organized around lower-class neighborhoods to form large mass opposition movements that engaged in protests for democracy. The new unionism itself exerted substantial popular pressure on the government. Although the level of strikes fell off in the early 1980s when the government stepped up the repression and the economy went into recession, by 1983 resurgent labor protest was evident in a strike of over three million workers. The following year, labor and social movements mounted a massive campaign for direct presidential elections. The campaign was not successful in its immediate goals, but it did contribute to deepening the succession crisis faced by the regime and to forcing the government to allow an opposition victory when the Electoral College chose the next president in 1985 (Keck 1989:37). Thus, organized labor was a participant in a mass movement for democracy that was broadly based in a variety of social groups. Beyond that, the new unionism played a more independent role in affecting the transition by expanding political space for a new force on the left, creating and securing the legality and participation of the union-based Brazilian Workers' Party, giving voice to a popular constituency, articulating a different perspective, and thereby expanding contestation.

URUGUAY

Uruguay's authoritarian regime did not have its origin in a definitive military coup, but rather in a two-sided process of the erosion of democracy and the gradual takeover by a military gaining increasing autonomy as it conducted an "internal war" against urban guerrillas. This onset gave rise to a military-dominated regime that continued to seek electoral legitimation and the collaboration of political parties. As in Brazil, the Uruguayan military committed itself to regularly scheduled elections and developed projects to outline and mold a new regime. In this way, the military chose political parties as protagonists in its regime project while repressing other social actors. Nevertheless, the labor movement became an important pro-democratic actor in the transition process, constituting an anti-authoritarian force at the very outset and subsequently figuring prominently in the events leading up to the installation of a democratic regime in 1985.

In the gradual coup that unfolded in the years prior to 1973, the military increasingly held de facto power behind a civilian facade. It has been suggested that even the 1971 elections were held at the pleasure of the military, which sought electoral legitimation (Rial 1984: 1:57). In 1973 the "coup" was completed when the military closed Congress and dissolved political parties. Even then, however, the military's continued orientation toward legitimation through the traditional parties (excluding the left) was evident:[20] the elected president was retained in office, a commitment to holding the elections scheduled for 1976 was reiterated, and a Council of State made up of members of the traditional political parties was nominated to replace the legislature. In 1976 the tattered remains of the electoral facade were swept away with the postponement of the elections and the appointment of a new president. However, this move was taken as a first step in the elaboration of a new political project, one that continued to rely on electoral legitimation and the cooperation of the traditional parties.[21] In accordance with this plan for "limited redemocratization" under military control (Rial 1984: 1:73–74), the junta charged a new body, consisting of the Council of State along with the junta, with drafting a new constitution. It also set a timetable that foresaw a plebiscite on the constitution in 1980 and elections the following year based on the participation of the traditional parties, which between them would nominate and present a single candidate.

The legitimacy project failed. When the plebiscite was held, voters defeated the constitution, throwing the government project off track. With this unexpected defeat, the project from above entered a new phase, and the government came up with another plan. Once again relying on party collaboration, the military initiated conversations with the traditional

20 These were the Blancos and the Colorados, which had dominated Uruguayan politics since the nineteenth century.
21 It is interesting that the dismissal of the president in 1976 was due to the military's preference for this party-based legitimation and its opposition to the president's proposal for a nonparty, corporative regime.

parties[22] and proposed a transition in 1985 according to a new constitution it would negotiate with the parties. To rehabilitate the parties, which were a key component of this plan, a new law, written in collaboration with party leaders, called for primary elections in 1982. The primaries dealt the military its second defeat: instead of resulting in the intended purge of the parties that would favor the collaborating factions, the outcome was a victory for the factions less friendly to the government.

The following years have been analyzed in terms of the "coup poker" strategies of the parties, the alternating harder and softer lines of the government, and the moves and countermoves of an elite strategic game. With stops and starts, formal negotiations took place between the military and party leaders, culminating in the 1984 Naval Club Pact, signed by the participants – which in the end came to include the left parties, except for the Communists.[23] In accord with the agreements laid down in that pact, elections were held later that year and a new democratic government took power in 1985.

Uruguay is one of the few countries where a formal agreement of transition was negotiated between the regime and party leaders of the democratic opposition. The model of elite negotiation and strategic action therefore seems particularly appropriate. Yet this account misses the story from below, in which the labor movement plays an important part. That organized labor was an avid pro-democratic actor can be seen in its initial resistance. In 1973, on the day the military made its final move to assure political control by closing the legislature, workers began a general strike against the dictatorship, thereby emerging as the only group to register its opposition publicly. For two weeks thousands of workers occupied factories, perpetrated acts of sabotage, and closed down the economy until the strike was broken (Gillespie 1991:52). If the labor movement was silenced in the following years, it was due to the ensuing repression in which unions were dismantled and many leaders were arrested or in exile.[24]

With the repression, the role of mass actors disappeared for the next seven years. Their reemergence can be discussed in connection with three

---

22 In addition to the traditional Blancos and Colorados, one other small "acceptable" party was included.

23 One of the few points on which the military was finally able to prevail in the negotiations was the exclusion of a popular Blanco as presidential candidate in upcoming transition elections. The negotiations around this issue led to the inclusion of the left parties, which were willing to accept this condition, and the boycott of further negotiations by the Blancos. Although the Blancos dropped out of the negotiations, they came to accept the terms of the pact, in practice if not in principle.

24 Of the Latin American countries with repressive military regimes in the 1960s and 1970s, Uruguay had the highest level of arrests per capita in the years following the military takeover. See Gillespie 1991:50–51.

events. The first was the stunning defeat the military suffered in the 1980 plebiscite. This project from above failed not because of opposition parties, which hardly had an opportunity to mobilize, but because the electorate used the vote to reject that project (Rial 1984: 2:57). The terms of the plebiscite were hardly fair. The government mounted a massive media campaign at the same time that the levels of repression and fear remained high, and those engaging in any political activity ran a substantial risk of arrest. Only at the last minute were the traditional parties allowed to campaign. And yet the constitution was rejected by the people. It has been suggested that although unions were severely repressed at the time, workers played an important clandestine role in mobilizing for the "no" victory (De Sierra 1992:218).

The second event was the party primaries of 1982, when again the people used the vote to deliver a defeat to those factions of the two participating traditional parties that were open to collaboration with the military government. A union role in this outcome is suggested by a new law of the previous year that authorized unions at the enterprise level. Though the law was very restrictive, in a contested decision workers decided not to reject it, hoping to use the law both to organize and to gain some legal protection. Furthermore, from the outset, these unions had a political program of democracy. The primaries, then, took place in a period of increasing labor reactivation and mobilization (De Sierra 1992: ch. 8).

Third, and more definitively, was the reactivation of social movements and the appearance of organized mass protest. The limited liberalization following the plebiscite created space for opposition groups in civil society to begin to mobilize. Starting in April 1982 the cooperativists became one of the first mass movements to organize and make its presence felt, first mobilizing for particularistic issues and, by the end of the year, engaging in more explicitly anti-dictatorship protests. At the same time, the union movement was beginning to be revived, first at the enterprise level and then at the national level when the Inter-Union Plenary of Workers (PIT) was formed. Given its organization and links with the grass roots, the PIT had a special capacity for mass mobilization and became one of the most important axes in the struggle against the authoritarian regime (Chagas and Tonarelli 1989:231–32). On May Day 1983, the PIT carried out the first major demonstration since 1973, attracting an estimated 100,000 to 200,000 people (Chagas and Tonarelli 1989:220; Gillespie 1991:131) and explicitly calling for the immediate return of democratic liberties (Gargiulo 1989:226). The May Day demonstration catapulted the PIT to the leadership of the social movement and, according to Caetano and Rilla (1991:91), represented a qualitative change in the politics of transition.

For the next year, mass actors, especially the PIT, set the pace and led the pro-democracy opposition. In the face of constant pressure from mass protest, the military was ultimately forced to retreat. In the 1980 plebiscite and the 1982 primaries, popular action had dealt the military severe blows, each time forcing it to scuttle its political project. Each time, however, the military came back with a new political plan. In the beginning of 1983, the military still thought it could mold a new regime and set out to write a new constitution during the course of the year (Caetano and Rilla 1991:91). That goal too was thwarted, and by the end of the year important sectors of the military had dropped the idea of a political project and began to focus instead on the problem of "the best exit" (Caetano and Rilla 1991:95).

These tendencies seem to have been given a decisive impetus by the general strike called by the PIT in January 1984. The result of the strike was a substantial change in the balance of forces. Up to that point, the military persisted in taking a hard line and was unwilling to compromise in the Parque Hotel negotiations it initiated in May 1983. When those negotiations broke down, the military increased repression in the context of the growing mobilization. After the general strike of January 1984, however, the balance changed substantially. Shortly thereafter the government lifted censorship and allowed the Communist leader of the left-wing Frente Amplio to return to the country.

The strike also changed the relationship between the traditional parties and the social movement. Sanguinetti, the leader of the opposition faction of the Colorado Party, in effect apologized to the PIT for his party's opposition to the successful January strike and proposed a reorganization of the democratic opposition to coordinate the activities of the parties – including the left – and the PIT in a new Multipartidaria (Chagas and Tonarelli 1989:240; Gillespie 1991:135).

During the next months the Multipartidaria entered pre-negotiations with the government while it maintained the pressure through a series of symbolic one-day strikes, the most important occurring at the end of June. The government made a series of concessions, and, at the end of July 1984, legalized the Frente Amplio and its constituent parties, except for the Communist Party and the Tupamaros. Negotiations came to a rapid conclusion in the Naval Club Pact, which was signed in August and in which the military gained few concessions, except that the most popular Blanco candidate as well as some Frentistas were excluded from running in the transition elections that quickly followed in November.[25] PIT protest was thus important not only in pushing the transition forward but also in the

---

25 While the military also salvaged a few transitory arrangements, it was explicitly recognized that these would remain in effect only until the another constitution was written by the new government and ratified in a plebiscite in 1985. See De Sierra 1992:26–27.

formation of the Multipartidaria as a more inclusive democratic opposition that could negotiate the end of authoritarianism.

BOLIVIA

Bolivian political history is remarkable for two traits: its extreme instability and a labor movement of perhaps unparalleled strength relative to other social forces, in one of Latin America's least developed economies. With its strength in the mining sector, the militant, syndicalist labor movement has historically been capable of effective, disciplined, mass mobilization. In Bolivia, the main political actors have been the military and the workers.[26]

Against this background, it is perhaps not surprising that democratization in the 1970s and 1980s was anything but a smooth process and that the labor movement was a central actor in the unfolding events (although it is surprising what scant attention it has received in most accounts).[27]

The complex pattern of democratization in Bolivia challenges the analyst. It has been seen as a combination of a failed transition, undermined by labor protest, followed by democratization as a *faute de mieux* (Whitehead 1986), or as an exhaustion of the military option (Conaghan and Malloy 1994:96). It is an interpretive decision to treat the Bolivian events as a single transition or as several. The sequence of events between 1977 and 1982 includes the following: a legitimation project by the authoritarian incumbents, fraudulent elections, a coup, another coup, elections for a new democratic government, a coup against the new civilian government, restoration of the civilian government, new elections, another coup, and the reinstatement of the elected government.

The Bolivian transition began with an incumbent project that was derailed by labor protest and other opposition, and ended with a transition in which labor protest quickened the pace, helped to keep it on track, and expanded or ensured a wide scope of contestation. The kaleidoscopic events are seen here in terms of three episodes, in each of which the labor movement played an important democratic role. The first episode is the military government's legitimation project, an episode in which the labor

26 In the Latin American context, Bolivia is similar only to Argentina in the way social forces have confronted each other directly with relatively little recourse to the electoral system. They are the prototypical examples of Huntington's praetorianism, in which "each group employs means which reflect its peculiar nature and capabilities. . . . Workers strike . . . and the military coup" (Huntington 1968:196).

27 See, for instance, Conaghan and Malloy 1994; and Whitehead 1986; as opposed to Dunkerley 1984.

movement helped to open up public space and political dialogue, to undermine a controlled and limited transition, and to realize free elections in 1979. The second is the turbulent year of civilian rule from July 1979 to July 1980, during which the labor movement prevented the success of the Natusch coup and defended the previously scheduled 1980 elections against military plotting, although another coup succeeded immediately after the elections. The third episode is the 1982 transition from the harsh military government that came to power in 1980, a transition in which the labor movement was a leading pro-democratic actor.

Some interpretations see the labor movement in quite a different light. To the extent analysts treat the role of the labor movement at all, they tend to see a militant and mobilized labor movement as destabilizing a fragile transition (Whitehead 1986). Thus, some see labor activity as derailing the 1978 transition attempt by the Banzer government, as undermining the Guevara government elected in 1979 and thereby paving the way for the Natusch coup, and as enfeebling the subsequent Gueiler government and similarly helping to create the conditions that led to the 1980 García Meza coup. The current interpretation differs. Analytically, it insists on the distinction between democratic transition and democratic "consolidation" or persistence. Substantively, it emphasizes the willingness of the labor movement, in the course of these events, to depart from its orientation as a syndical actor, which had eschewed the electoral arena and party politics, and to take on an active pro-democratic role, to be willing to compromise its commitment to syndical democracy in order to press for electoral democracy.

The project of General Banzer aimed to legitimate the military government, which he had headed since the coup of 1971. Under some pressure to seek legitimacy in the face of internal military discontent and economic problems and, like other generals in this pattern, with some minimal nod to a constitutional cloak, in 1976–77 Banzer embraced a formula for completing a six-year presidential term mandated in the constitution. Conveniently opting to reckon from the *autogolpe* of 1974, he planned a controlled transition culminating in a 1980 election, which he was confident of winning and which has been seen as a calculation for "prolonging his personal ascendancy by 'constitutionalizing' his rule" (Whitehead 1986:58).

Two factors undermined the calculation with respect to the timetable and the outcome, respectively: pressure from the Carter administration pushed the elections up to 1978; and labor protest mobilized the opposition and deprived Banzer of his electoral victory. Starting in 1975, the FSTMB, the federation of mine workers, had begun to open political space under the dictatorship, reestablishing its organization and successfully demanding a return of the local radio stations the military had closed. The following year it called a strike for wage demands, which was supported by strikes of factory workers. With one mine holding on for twenty-five days, the military occupied the mines and brutally repressed the strike, although it was forced to yield in recognizing the base committees established by the FSTMB (Malloy and Gamarra 1987:93–94). It was in the wake of this seemingly reestablished control that Banzer put forth his transition project. In December 1977, three months after the elections were brought forward, the wives of four miners carried out a hunger strike to demand an amnesty and military withdrawal from the mines. The hunger strike rapidly became a broader movement for trade union rights and succeeded in undermining the repressive system of union control. "The hunger strike was the single most important factor in bringing the *banzerato* to an end and laying the basis for mass mobilisation over the coming period" (Dunkerley 1984:241). Confronted with a remobilized and repoliticized society, Banzer relied on blatant fraud to declare victory for his officialist candidate. In response, the FSTMB workers threatened to strike at the same time that the opposition parties, more tamely, refused to recognize the electoral results. The Banzer project had failed.

In the chaotic events that ensued, a number of groups converged to advance the immediate holding of new elections. Among these the FSTMB was prominent, holding a forty-eight-hour strike in response to a coup and the attempt to renew the dictatorship (Dunkerley 1984:251–52) or at least to delay elections until 1980. Many pro-democratic forces then converged in protest, and, following a coup by a supportive military faction, elections were held in July 1979, marking the first democratic transition.

In the event, the resulting government was weak and did not endure, falling victim to a coup the following November. Its fragility should be seen as a consolidation issue, not a transition issue, which is the present subject. Still, one may ask about the culpability of the COB, the Bolivian labor central that was reconstituted in May 1979, when it held its first Congress since 1970. Some analysts hold the COB primarily accountable, emphasizing the polarization and policy impasse that resulted when the labor organization rejected the government's approach to the International Monetary Fund (IMF) and presented an alternative economic package. Yet the explanation for democratic failure should be seen in terms of the specific situation: the 1979 elections had resulted in a tie, and after seven votes the hopelessly deadlocked Congress failed to elect either of the two contenders, both of whom embarked on hunger strikes to defend what they considered their victory. When the president of the Senate was made

interim president until new elections could be held the following year, the
new democracy was born without legitimacy, devoid of any governance
capability, and structurally unable to pursue contentious economic policies
that were per force on the agenda. Furthermore, particularly in this context
it was the government as much as the COB that decided not to pursue a
compromise policy, and indeed the COB charged the government with
democratic failure in seeking extraordinary powers to pass its economic
policies and in intending to close the legislature and govern only with
military support.[28]

The second episode in which the Bolivian labor movement was an
important, indeed a decisive, pro-democratic player involved the defeat of
the Natusch coup that overthrew the new democracy and the defense of
the subsequent elections scheduled for 1980. Natusch intervened with the
support of some social groups and politicians, and initially made overtures
to both the Congress and the COB, promising to collaborate with both.
The COB, however, acted immediately and forcefully to oppose the coup
and defend the democratic order. Within hours it called a general strike,
which shut down La Paz and the mines, and it sustained the strike for
seven days *despite* Natusch's offer of co-government to the COB and acceptance of its economic package in exchange for the end of democratic rule
(Dunkerley 1984:266–67).

Faced with this intransigent opposition, the Natusch strategy turned
brutal and bloody. Government troops blew up the COB building and
killed or wounded hundreds of people in the "Massacre of All Saints." Yet
the COB continued the strike until the Congress, the military, and the
COB all agreed to negotiate a political solution. When the military proposed a tripartite government, the COB again rejected the offer, under
substantial pressure from the miners and the rank and file generally.
Although the Congress was more open to the scheme, it was unworkable
without the COB. The failure of the proposal (combined with U.S. pressure
and the impending political trap of responding to the renewed IMF calls
for unpopular policies) convinced Natusch to resign. Within sixteen days,
then, the coup was defeated and the democratic regime was restored. While

---

28 Lazarte 1989:151. Analysts are often too quick to blame the labor movement for
    destabilizing elected governments. After all, it takes two sides to have a policy impasse
    – and in a different day and within certain circles the "other side" (e.g., the IMF) was
    the object of culpability. Furthermore, one might do well to remember that the real
    radical mobilization by the Bolivian labor movement was mounted against the policies
    of the "new," "fragile" democracy after 1982 in the context of political crisis and
    inflation calculated in the thousands of percent. Yet this radical and militant strategy
    of the COB to "deepen" democracy (see Mayorga 1990:169) did not cause democratic
    breakdown.

both the parties and the United States were an important part of the opposition to Natusch, it would seem that the COB had a special pro-democratic role in directing the mass mobilization[29] and in twice rejecting participation in a potentially viable nondemocratic government. When Natusch resigned, the COB issued a statement referring to "the workers who with their blood successfully defended the democratic process . . . the restoration [of which], despite its limitations, is of enormous importance for the working class" (cited in Lazarte, 1989:152; my translation).

In something of a repetition, another weak government came to power when the legislature chose the head of the Chamber of Deputies as interim president, again until the scheduled 1980 elections, now seven months hence (June 1980). Also in a seeming replay, polarization over economic policy continued, as one of the government's first decisions was to implement the IMF agreement, a move that provoked an oppositionist reaction that included not only labor strikes, but also a shift to the left by the middle class and, more dramatically and unexpectedly, a militant rural mobilization on the part of a reconstituted and independent peasant movement. At the same time, conservative forces within the military asserted themselves, and the period was rife with rumors of military coups.

In this context, the COB emerged as a crucially important pro-democratic actor, ensuring the path to the 1980 elections. First, in order to defend the fragile government and the democratic process, it moderated its mobilizational activities against the government's economic policy and did not form a larger worker-peasant agitation campaign. Second, with rising rumors of a coup by the extreme-right military faction, the COB and the main parties moved to defend the democratic regime by issuing a "Call for the Defense of Democracy" and founding CONADE, whose strategy was mass mobilizations like those that took place against Natusch: general strikes and road blocks, forms of collective action that the COB was uniquely capable of calling and directing. Finally, when García Meza, the most prominent member of the hard-line faction within the military, became the new army commander and made public statements that seemed to prepare the ground for another coup, the COB (without the larger CONADE) and the military high command, along with the president, signed a pact pledging respect for the constitution, dialogue and respect among the signatories, and a joint commitment to the democratic process and new elections. The elections were held as scheduled and the leftist UDP won.

29 As the COB put it, "the parties at no time had the capacity to defend the democratic process with popular mobilizations" (Lazarte 1989:151, my translation).

The pro-democratic forces did not prevail for long, however: in little more than two weeks García Meza staged a coup, which the CONADE general strike call and continued strikes in the mines were unable to defeat when faced with a ferocious armed assault, massacres, and an attack on COB headquarters. The third episode, then, is the 1982 transition from the harsh García Meza dictatorship.

Most interpretations have emphasized that the García Meza government fell of its own weight: dependent on drug trafficking, highly repressive, kleptocratic, and internationally isolated, the government was unable to maintain any semblance of public authority in the context of widespread opposition that included the business community as well as factions within the military. Given the weakness of the regime, two more heads of state rotated in power before the military was forced to concede to the civilians. Still, it is instructive to inquire about the nature of the pressure exerted against the government.

The first presidential change, and the defeat of García Meza a year after the coup, were largely the result of a military rebellion, though supported by an indefinite general strike in the mines and factories. In the following year, the role of the labor movement became more central as, according to Dunkerley (1984:340), the axis of conflict shifted back to the working class. From November 1981 to February 1982, the labor movement, led by the miners, carried out a series of strikes that forced the government to abandon its labor repression, recognize independent unions, and legalize the COB, thus opening political space and allowing union and political leaders to return to the country. The government could not withstand the mounting pressure and was forced to concede to elections, first scheduled for 1984, then brought forward to 1983. The next rotation produced a military government that would oversee the military withdrawal and the 1983 elections. Again, however, popular mobilization for an immediate democratic transition derailed that plan. In September 1982, amid widespread strikes and street confrontations in La Paz, the COB called a mass march to be followed by an indefinite general strike. The massive response convinced the military to yield immediately, and by the end of the day it agreed to reinstate the 1980 Congress (Dunkerley 1984: 336–43).

Looking at the whole 1976–82 period, many analysts, such as Whitehead, seek to explain the relative failure of democratic transition in Bolivia, emphasizing the reversals and setbacks along the way, and placing much of the blame on popular movements for which "formal democracy may not be an entirely convincing end" (Whitehead 1986:67). But one might be impressed with precisely the opposite. The COB strongly committed itself to upholding the electoral process against both military threats and more revolutionary tendencies within the left and the labor movement. An unusually strong, traditionally syndicalist labor movement shifted from its workerist orientation and entered the political arena in order to press not only for union or worker demands but for electoral democracy; and it used its enormous mobilizational capacity to that end. In the process, it may indeed have "delayed the transition," but the unsuccessful "democratic transition" of Banzer was a scripted, controlled project from above. The union movement was an important force in condemning the Banzer project, bringing about open elections in 1979, rejecting cooperation and thereby defeating the Natusch coup, reinstating and defending the elected government, clearing the way for the scheduled elections of 1980, and finally defeating the García Meza dictatorship. One should not lose sight of the fact that taken as a whole (1977–82), the transition was successful – messy, but successful – both in the sense of producing a more open and indeed "democratic" transition than originally contemplated and in the sense of persisting, a trait that speaks more for Bolivia than for many other countries.

PARALLEL TRACKS

Another pattern is characterized by the implementation of an explicit government transition project according to its own specified timetable and with minimal negotiations between incumbents and the opposition. In this pattern more than the others, then, the transition takes place according to the rules laid down by authoritarian incumbents, to use J. S. Valenzuela's (1992) terms. An interesting feature of this pattern is that while the transition follows an explicit government project and occurs within parameters defined "from above," union-led protest emerges as an important pro-democratic force, opening political space and, at some points, playing a key role in leading, mobilizing, and coordinating the opposition, even if it is not successful in altering the course of the transition from the rules defined by the regime. In other words, the labor movement is an important, and perhaps the most consistent, force for democracy, but it is unable to alter the incumbent project. It does, however, contribute to increasing the risks to the incumbents inherent in their own project (the risk of standing in elections that were earlier scheduled with confidence), and enforcing that very project in the face of those risks or setbacks. Furthermore, it could be argued that the labor role helped ensure the participation of left and labor-affiliated parties in the new democracy, again expanding the scope of contestation. The label – Parallel Tracks – highlights the largely nonintersecting trajectories of the authoritarian incumbents and the labor organizations. Although the pattern corresponds to only the Chilean case, it does constitute a logical typological category in terms of the two dimensions of labor role and incumbent project.

CHILE

The Chilean transition to democracy in 1990 followed the broad outline laid down in the military government's 1980 constitution. Although Pinochet did not anticipate the outcome of the 1988 plebiscite rejecting a continuation of his presidency and although some of the specifics remained to be negotiated, the democratic transition unfolded within the framework of the government's 1980 project. At the same time, the labor movement, given the special organizational resources at its disposal, played a leading role in opening political space for the formation of a broader democratic opposition, and in leading and coordinating protest and opposition at important junctures. Although it did not remain at the helm in the same way, it continued to be a part of a broader democratic opposition movement, which, unable to alter the government's timetable, nevertheless ultimately defeated Pinochet at his own game. Then, as part of an implicit threat of collective action, it enforced a democratic outcome.

The government's transition project emerged out of Pinochet's efforts to institutionalize military power and his own personal leadership following the coup of 11 September 1973. During the first years of the military regime Pinochet gradually consolidated his power as president, establishing an institutional framework whereby he personally oversaw all key governmental decisions (see A. Valenzuela 1991). By 1976 Pinochet's personal authority was so great relative to the power of the military institution as a whole that some observers have likened his rule to patrimonial domination (see Remmer 1989:149–70). The important point for present purposes is that divisions within the government were muted and the incumbent role in the process of Chilean democratization would largely revolve around the individual decisions of Pinochet (Garretón 1989a:126–28).

Once having secured his position within the regime, Pinochet next sought to institutionalize the regime in power. The first major suggestion of his plan for achieving this end came with the July 1977 Chacarillas speech, in which he suggested that the regime would go through several liberalizing phases, ultimately culminating in civilian rule by 1985. This proposed plan, however, did not yet constitute a transition project. It remained vague, lacking specific formulations for how the transition would proceed. As important, at this point Pinochet had no intention of allowing for anything more than a "protected" democracy, which would exclude the left and within which the military would maintain substantial leverage (Garretón 1989a:137–38; Arriagada Herrera 1986:118–24). The plan sketched in 1977 was never implemented, and 1978–79 witnessed an internal debate within the government over the future course of the regime and the nature and timing of its institutionalization. By 1980, there was an "imminent need" for Pinochet to take some action (Garretón 1989a: 138). In the middle of the year Pinochet decided in favor of a new constitutional proposal and announced it would be submitted to a plebiscite for approval in one month.

The 1980 constitution put an end to internal debate within the military and was the cornerstone of the project from above. It extended Pinochet's rule until at least 1989 and ensured that he would maintain dictatorial powers. After 1989, the continuation of the current regime would be contingent on the results of a plebiscite to be held in 1988. A vote of approval would enable Pinochet to remain in power until 1997. In the event of a negative vote, the constitution called for competitive elections for president and Congress within a short period of time.

Pinochet adopted the new constitutional and transitional framework amid international pressure as well as internal debate. The Carter administration exerted pressure with its greater attention to human rights violations, as did party internationals, particularly the Christian Democrat and Socialist internationals. In addition, international labor organizations such as the ILO and the AFL-CIO mounted vigorous and highly publicized criticism of the government's abridgment of labor rights. Their activities included the threat of a boycott of Chilean imports and exports (see Campero and Valenzuela 1984:266–67, 282–83; Barrera and Valenzuela 1986:249–53).

During this period the labor movement began to reorganize and become more oppositionist. Some observers argue that until 1982 the Chilean dictatorship ruled without significant opposition,[30] but political opposition had begun in the early years of the military government. After the coup, the government carried out a purge of the left and instigated a period of harsh repression against the labor movement, which Drake (1996:132) has called a "pogrom against Marxists." The vacuum was filled by the nonleftist labor leadership from the Christian Democratic Party, who found an "initial affinity" with the military government (Barrera and Valenzuela 1986:230). By the end of 1975, however, these conservative labor leaders,

30 For example, Drake and Jaksic 1991:4; and Garretón 1989b:265–66.

began to come out in opposition to the dictatorship under pressure from local union leaders and the rank and file. Ten of the most prominent of these leaders formed the Group of Ten in an attempt to find a more independent voice. In mid-1976, they issued an open letter to the junta, defending workers' interests against the government's economic policy and its political exclusion of the labor movement. The letter, and the government's quick rejection of its contents, clearly left the Group of Ten with "no other alternative . . . than the pursuit of a confrontational and oppositionist course in order to retain a place among the leading sectors of Chilean unionism."[31]

Thus, by 1977 growing opposition within the labor movement was already apparent. Furthermore, this "definitive break of the nonleftist union leaders with the government" provided a basis for their cooperation with the leftist labor sectors, and the different factions "began to draw closer together rapidly on the basis of a commonly shared opposition to the military regime's economic and labor policies" (Barrera and Valenzuela 1986:245). The growth of labor opposition was sustained by the activities of the Catholic Church, which had given significant physical, legal, and social protection to labor leaders and had "kept alive" the trade union movement after 1973 (Angell 1996:187). Through its Vicaría de la Pastoral Obrera, the Church provided moral, material, and political support to union leaders, leftist as well as Christian Democratic, creating space for reconciliation and unity among the bitterly divided partisan groups within the labor movement (Lowden 1996:77–78).

In the aftermath of the 1977 Chacarillas speech, labor opposition stepped up on a number of fronts. First, that speech provoked a response from the Group of Ten that went beyond more narrowly construed workers' issues and directly addressed larger regime issues, explicitly rejecting Pinochet's call for a "protected and authoritarian democracy" and the transition process he set out (Barrera and Valenzuela 1986:245). Second, a number of new, oppositional labor organizations became active, including most importantly the CNS, which provided space for more oppositionist labor leaders. The slogan of their joint May Day celebration in 1978 was "freedom, participation, pluralism: the pillars of democracy" (Falabella 1990:233). Third, during late 1977 and 1978, a variety of rank-and-file labor protests were mounted by workers in the large copper mines as well as among textile, port, and construction workers. These collective acts of resistance were more limited stoppages, slowdowns, and other public demonstrations of grievances rather than outright strikes, but they nevertheless

31 Barrera and Valenzuela 1986:244. See also Campero and Valenzuela 1984:254–60.

became an opening wedge in creating political space in the context of repressive authoritarian control (Campero and Valenzuela 1984:262–65, 276–77; Barrera and Valenzuela 1986:248–49). Finally, labor reactivation within Chile was paralleled and supported by the activity of a number of international labor organizations. International ties were particularly important in the case of Chile, where the trade union movement, including salaries, training programs, and travel abroad, was largely funded by these organizations (Angell 1996:190).

After repression failed to break domestic labor activism and only heightened the pressure from abroad, the government was led to restructure institutions for managing industrial relations by holding union elections and introducing new labor legislation in 1978 and 1979. In October 1978, in the hope of catching the opposition off guard and depriving it of an opportunity to organize, the government called for union elections to be held just four days hence. Furthermore, the government barred the election of anyone who had previously held office or had been affiliated with a political party. The government thus tried to respond to democratic pressures and deflect international condemnation by reintroducing union elections but in a form calculated to produce a cooperative, nonleftist union leadership.

The attempt, however, backfired. The new labor legislation did introduce a legal framework that provided for highly constrained and weak unions (Campero and Valenzuela 1984:125–50; Vergara 1985:215–29). On the other hand, it also permitted the reactivation of local leaders and rank-and-file workers. Interview evidence suggests that "the new generation of leaders [were] opponents of the military government, that they retain[ed] partisan affiliations or at least identities and sympathies, and that the relative weight of the ideological and political leanings among them remain[ed] mostly unchanged from the previous period" (Barrera and Valenzuela 1986:250–51) when the left had been predominant. Further "the frequent union assemblies turned into channels for the expression of workers' opinions over a broad range of local and national questions" (Barrera and Valenzuela 1986:259). In addition labor policy had the effect of encouraging concerted action and cooperation. In August 1979, the various labor currents united to form the Defense of Labor Rights Command, which was unable to secure more favorable policies but did succeed in creating a "climate of resistance" or a "symbolic power" that later social mobilizations would build upon (Campero and Valenzuela 1984:318; Falabella and Campero 1991:135).

The labor movement continued its leadership of the Chilean opposition after the government's 1980 project was in place. In 1981 the CNS presented a National Petition with a list of reforms to democratize the union movement and alter economic policy, an act the government answered by jailing the top CNS leader. In 1981 and 1982 the government passed further labor legislation that liberalized the labor market (e.g., allowing employers to fire workers at will and eliminating previously guaranteed wage and salary increases) (Barrera and Valenzuela 1986:258). The result of these measures, in conjunction with a severe economic downturn, was that "workers . . . perceived themselves as a class repressed by economic and legal structures imposed by the authoritarian state. . . . Even the rank-and-file saw the need to obtain the workers' reinclusion in the economic and social system, a reinclusion that required a democratic reorganization of the political system" (Ruíz-Tagle 1989:88). In 1983 labor opposition increased. In May, the CNT was formed to unite the center and left unions behind a democratic agenda. In the same month the Confederation of Copper Workers (CTC) initiated a massive protest "with the goal of showing the workers' rejection of the economic and political system on a massive scale" (Ruíz-Tagle 1989:90). Labor leaders called for the participation of all popular organizations and even the public at large. The objectives of the movement were generalized to appeal to all sectors, the principal one being the return to democracy. The overwhelming success of the protest led labor leaders to call quickly for a second protest, which also attracted broad citizen participation. These protests became monthly events.

Labor action thus was central in opening political space for the opposition. Actively joining the protests were urban social movements that had formed as survival strategies of the poor in the face of economic crisis. In calling for these protests, "the union movement . . . became the cement binding different social forces that had been passive, or that had earlier acted in a disorganized way" (Ruíz-Tagle 1989:90). Furthermore, the mobilization allowed the parties to reestablish themselves. As one prominent Christian Democratic politician later said, "Because of labor, the political parties managed to get organized again. The party leadership was able to return from exile. . . . That was permitted because of those protests; it wouldn't have happened otherwise . . . [and subsequently] the labor movement worked very closely with the parties."[32]

This was the high point of union leadership of the protest movement. In August 1983 a new site of political activity opened when the government, on the defensive, appointed a right-wing politician to the cabinet to attract the support of and open a dialogue with civilian groups. The

---

32 Interview conducted by Carol Medlin, 3 July 1995.

following week, the Democratic Alliance was formed as a coalition of groups that included the renovated Socialists but explicitly excluded the Communists. It entered negotiations with the government. At the same time, the monthly protests increasingly came under the influence of more militant "ultras," whose base was in the poor neighborhoods rather than the unions. Neither of these avenues proved able to budge the government or alter Pinochet's project: Pinochet refused to negotiate any concessions with the Democratic Alliance, nor were any forced by the protests, which were increasingly met with repression until they petered out in 1986. Though it ceded leadership of the democratic movement, labor-led protest had opened space for a broader democratic opposition: the protest had reactivated the party leaders and provided an impetus to diverse and more narrow popular organizations to come together as a coordinated network and political actor, which forged a broader social movement and in 1986 formed the Civic Assembly.

The transition proceeded according to the government project, and the focus of activity turned to the scheduled plebiscite, which the parties decided to fight, after some initial uncertainty owing to suspicion about the conditions, conduct, and fairness of the vote. In February 1988 a group of sixteen parties came together as the Coalition of Parties for the No Vote, a broad front that led the opposition to Pinochet's ratification. Following the victory of the "no" vote on 5 October 1988, Pinochet ultimately respected the consequences and proceeded with the steps he himself had laid out in the 1980 constitution. Accordingly, general elections were scheduled for December 1989. In the intervening year, many new rules and institutional arrangements were established, including the electoral law, rules for judicial appointments, and the scope of military autonomy. Though these were negotiated with the opposition and some compromise was therefore necessary, it is striking that these decisions were not taken by a new Constituent Assembly, relatively few concessions were made, and the process remained more controlled by the government than in other cases. The transition to democracy took place with the assumption of power by Patricio Aylwin of the Christian Democratic Party on 11 March 1990.

INTERELITE GAME

In Ecuador and Greece, labor groups played no consequential role in the course of democratization. It is in these two cases (in perhaps the country in Latin America and the country in southern Europe that have received the least attention in the democratization literature) that we find the clearest examples of transitions driven by elite interaction, in which elite groups are the only major protagonists. In both countries, far from reaping the support of the right, the military government provoked its opposition. From the beginning, it was not popular pressure but groups within the right that pressured the military governments, leaving them isolated and divided. Although neither government could consolidate its power and both were forced to withdraw from power, they managed to retain substantial control in shaping the transition and influencing the choice of incumbents in the successor government.

Both countries had traditions of "oligarchic electoralism" through the first half of the twentieth century, though these broke down into more unstable patterns by midcentury with the rise of new social and political forces, and in 1967 in Greece and 1972 in Ecuador the military intervened in the context of that challenge. The directions taken by the military were quite different but had the common effect of alienating the civilian right. In Ecuador the military's reformist orientation was opposed from the right (including the private sector, right parties, and military factions); in Greece a militant anti-communism combined with dogmatic anti-parliamentarism deepened divisions within the rightist triarchy (military, parliamentary right, and monarchy) that had held power through exclusionary regimes, which denied political space to new centrist parties and, even more harshly, to the working class. While in many of the other cases party and sectoral groups on the political right eventually joined the democratic opposition, in these two countries they constituted a key source of opposition to the military regime virtually from the outset. In both countries, the opposition of the civilian right prevented the consolidation of the military regimes, which were among the shortest-lived of the authoritarian regimes considered in this chapter. These democratic transitions took place as a process of interelite negotiations, although in Greece student demonstrations and a humiliating military defeat in Cyprus altered the final steps.

The absence of significant participation by the labor movement in these events can in part be explained in terms of the political situation it faced. In Ecuador, a smaller and weaker labor movement initially benefited from the new reformism and was not inclined to oppose the government. In Greece, a previously more politicized and activated labor movement had been repressed along with the Communist Party following the Greek civil war of 1946–49, the onset of the cold war, and the implementation of the Truman Doctrine. Through corporatist union structures the state had succeeded in penetrating the union movement, controlling the major labor confederation, intervening in union financing, and resolving most issues between employers and workers, although the immediate pre-coup period did see a dramatic resurgence in labor activism. Virtually all the transitions from authoritarian rule in the 1970s and 1980s took place in the context of labor-repressive regimes, and some regimes also had extensive corporatist controls. Depending on the depth of repression and degree of labor strength, it often took the labor movement a long time to carve out space for action through gradual organizational work. In Greece with relatively little time, given the comparatively short colonels' regime, the labor movement had not recaptured its voice by the time of the transition.

GREECE

For all the harsh repression, the Greek military government that came to power in 1967 was politically weak and unable to consolidate its rule. Facing divisions within the military (both within the army and from the other branches) and a withholding of support or even opposition from the king and the parties of the right, the government of junior army officers quickly developed a liberalization project in a bid for some sort of legitimation. The transition developed as a strategic game among elite factions, though one abruptly punctuated in the final year by an outbreak of student protest and a foreign policy debacle that altered the relative power of the key actors and changed the final course of the transition, precipitating in the end a hasty extrication by the disintegrating regime.

The colonels' coup came against a long background in which the right had held power in exclusionary governments, denying political space not only to the working class but even to new centrist parties. The extended period of rightist rule survived a perceived threat of communism and working-class activism, dating from the 1920s, and the civil war of 1946–49, after which anti-communism became a central orienting feature of the government. In 1963, however, the right suffered an electoral defeat to the center-left Center Union, and the new government turned in a reformist direction, embarking on Keynesian policies and easing up on the prior pattern of heavy labor repression and control. Labor strikes, which had started rising in 1962, more than doubled by 1966, with the rate of lost days quintupling over the same period (Katsanevas 1984:99). The demands presented in these strikes were related both to inflation and to political goals.[33] The military government established in 1967 "was an attempt by the Greek Right to safeguard its political ascendancy by forestalling a democratization of the political system" (Diamandouros 1986:145). Nevertheless, with the ascendancy of the military and the consequent internal

---

33 Campbell and Sherrard 1968:278; Diamandouros, personal communication.

reordering of power among the three rightist forces (monarchy, parliamentary right, and military), the conservative coalition lost its coherence. The appeal to anti-communism was now unable to counterbalance the government's hostility to parliamentarism in the eyes of a political right that had long maintained hegemony through parliamentary institutions. With the right itself divided, the military regime was unable to establish either a solid base of support or political legitimacy.

Starting the year after the coup and reflecting splits within the right (rather than popular pressure), the colonels undertook a liberalization project in an attempt to bolster and legitimate the regime. In a move similar to those subsequently taken in Chile and Uruguay, a new constitution was prepared: with provisions for continued military control, it tried to restore the coherence of the right, through provisions for parliamentary trappings and a monarchy, and to mobilize or demonstrate popular support, through approval in a tightly controlled plebiscite. Though it won the plebiscite, the government delayed the enforcement of its own constitution, and in 1973, following a coup attempt, the government of Papadopoulos developed a second project. This project was at once more "authoritarian" and more transitional, envisioning a "presidential parliamentary republic," headed by a " 'superpresident' who retained control of defense, internal security, and foreign policy" (Diamandouros 1986:152; Danopoulos 1989: 359). Elected to the new presidency in an unopposed plebiscite, Papadopoulos did embark on a course of political liberalization, lifting the state of siege, enacting an amnesty, restoring civil liberties, and providing for a new, civilian government to be formed by rightist Markezinis until the new elections promised by the end of 1974.

This project, however, failed to win supporters and only deepened divisions within the military. In the end, it was derailed by the November 1973 student uprising that "further isolated and divided the military" (Linz, Stepan, and Gunther 1995:110), provoking a harsh reaction and, following a coup, the ascendancy of the army hard-liners. The coup de grace and the disintegration of the regime came with the July 1974 Cyprus debacle, in which the Greek military was unable to respond to the Turkish invasion provoked by the Greek-led coup on the island.[34] In the event, the Cyprus developments meant that an overtly military mission was now ascendant and led to the reassertion of control by the military command,

---

34 While tensions had been escalating for some time and were given a new boost by Turkey's claims of rights to newly discovered oil in the Aegean and by Makarios's demand for withdrawal of Greek officers of the Cypriot National Guard, most analysts interpret the Greek government's "mindless response" (Clogg 1992:167) as a desperate effort to rally nationalist sentiment (see also Danopoulos 1989).

who had been marginalized from the government since the junior officers' 1967 coup. The Joint Chiefs of Staff pursued an immediate transition, within days handing power to Karamanlis, the rightist leader who had dominated Greek politics from 1955 to 1963.

The Greek case differs from the others in the final bargaining power of the military and its ability to exclude the center-left. On the one hand, "the military urgency of immediate extrication" may indeed have meant that the military "was not able to impose any confining conditions on the civilians" regarding the *"military-as-institution"* (Linz et al. 1995:111; my emphasis). Further the military failed to transfer power to its supporters or to impose any conditions on Karamanlis, who succeeded to the presidency as part of the extrication. On the other hand, through the decisions of a handpicked council charged with determining a transfer format, the military government was uniquely able to sideline in the transitional process the country's political parties, which together had captured nearly 90 percent of the last vote before the coup (Diamandouros 1986:158). The military rejected the proposal of the leaders of the Center Union, which had ruled before the coup, and of the National Radical Union to form the transitional government, instead recruiting Karamanlis to form a "non-party" government. Though he engineered a successful transition which culminated in free and fair elections within four months, it is probable that, as the opposition argued, the prominence and popular gratitude that Karamanlis reaped from his role in overseeing the final steps and the speed with which they were held gave him an unfair advantage and delayed the return of the center-left to power (Clogg 1986:205).

While in some sense it is obviously the case, as most analysts argue, that the Greek transition occurred as a result of regime collapse occasioned by military failure, the debacle represents the final agony of a regime already doomed and indeed already in the throes of withdrawal, providing for elections and a transfer of power to a civilian government. The same could be said about the student demonstrations. Neither in the end changed the timetable of transition or the capacity of the departing military to put in place a rightist transitional government.

ECUADOR

With a very small and weak working class and little tradition of institutionalized political parties, Ecuador's transition was an elite affair. It was sparked primarily by pressure from the private sector, which had felt deprived of political access and policy influence under the military regime and which opposed the government's reformist orientation. Yet the business community and the political right, which had played the major role in bringing about the transition, did not fare well during it: the military government retained sufficient control of the process to marginalize their influence and prevent a return to the old structures and oligarchic politics (Conaghan and Malloy 1994:94).

The Rodríguez Lara government, which came to power in a military coup in 1972, took a reformist direction somewhat along the lines of Velasco two years earlier in neighboring Peru. Even the mild reforms, however, were opposed and blocked by the business community, which became more class conscious and cohesively organized during the military government (Conaghan and Malloy 1994:71). By 1975 an economic crisis provoked intensified opposition, as business interests and the center and right parties formed the oppositionist Civic Front and called for an end to the government. The labor movement, whose three major confederations achieved some unity the previous year with the formation of the United Workers' Front (FUT), was unable to counterbalance this pressure. In terms of the dynamics of democratization, the labor movement tended to support the government as much as oppose it, its primary demand, backed by a general strike in November 1975, being the fulfillment of the government's own reformist agenda (Isaacs 1993:88).

The transition came in the context of pressure from the right, intensified by business mobilization in reaction to the November labor strike. The decision to undertake a transition came in two steps. Politically isolated and facing a complete lack of popular support as well as divisions within the military (as reflected in the unsuccessful conservative coup attempt in August 1975), Rodríguez Lara made a "last ditch effort to appease his critics by promising a return to civilian rule" (Corkill and Cubitt 1988:38). The tactic was unsuccessful, and in January 1976 the military removed Rodríguez Lara, established a governing junta, and announced its own plan for democratization.

Despite its withdrawal and extrication as a regime that had never been able to consolidate power, the Ecuadoran military government, like the Greek officers, retained some capacity to shape the transition. The government adopted a transition project, labeled a Process of Juridical Restructuring of the Nation, that was designed to prevent a return to old structures and to leave behind a more open political system than the pre-existing regime. For three months a series of public meetings, or "dialogues," was held to elicit comments and suggestions by parties and social groups: the business chambers advanced a scheme for a constituent assembly and a slow transition that would advantage the parties of the right, while the center and left parties favored a quicker move to new elections. The government rejected the plan of the right and instead established three civilian commissions charged with proposing a political framework for a constitution and electoral laws, commissions on which it gave the leadership role to reformists and allocated business interests a single seat (Conaghan and Malloy 1994:92–94). In 1979 new elections were held, and the reformists won. The labor movement played little role in the unfolding of these events, joining the pro-democracy movement only after the military junta had already announced its intentions and in reaction to a crackdown on labor mobilization.

PORTUGAL

The democratic transition in Portugal is not easy to classify. It occurred in the brief, very fluid period following the 1974 coup by the Armed Forces Movement (MFA) that brought an end to the longest authoritarian regime considered here. The authoritarian regime had lost all support and had clearly become bankrupt. Portugal is not the only case characterized by coups or other methods by which actors within the state ousted reluctant heads of government to advance a transition when the authoritarian regime was in trouble. Like those other cases, the post-coup government immediately announced a transition timetable. Yet Portugal does not readily fall into either of our other patterns where collapsing regimes led to extrications: Destabilization/Extrication (where the labor movement played a leading role in destabilizing the regime) or Interelite Games (where it played no effective role at all). The working class was centrally involved in the Portuguese transition. Labor protest was important in the form of both union-led strikes and a grass-roots working-class mobilization, which was increasingly taking matters into its own hands at important points in the process. Drawing on the working-class movement, the radical military faction and the Communist Party vacillated between a more liberal democratic outcome and more social revolutionary goals. In a way somewhat reminiscent of Finland in 1918, the ultimate achievement of the democratic regime conformed mostly to the project of the liberals to the "right," although it reflected a compromise hammered out by all parties, Yet, in Portugal, as in Spain, the Socialist and Communist parties were participants in the transition and their participation had the effect of "driv[ing] democratization in a more inclusionary and reformist direction once it was uncorked from above. . . . [Workers'] belligerence made it more likely that democratization would come about and that it might include their organizations, parties, and demands" (Drake 1996:61).

The Portuguese transition can be considered in two steps. The first is the April 1974 coup by military officers who committed themselves to hold elections for a Constituent Assembly within a year. The second consists of the complex and fluid politics after the coup, through the Constituent Assembly elections of April 1975, to the establishment of moderate civilian government the following autumn, and finally to the elections under the new constitution in the spring of 1976. With regard to the coup one may ask what part, if any, the working class played in generating the conditions that led the officers to overthrow the authoritarian regime. Analysts differ on the factors that destabilized the regime. Two things are clear. First, there were many sources of discontent around nonlabor issues, from corporate grievances within the military to deep divisions within the regime that immobilized the government of Caetano.[35] These concerned the basic direction of Portugal's future trajectory, pitting the "colonialists" against the "Europeanist" opposition, which had a large following in the military so directly involved in the increasingly unpopular and apparently unwinnable colonial wars. By 1973 the regime was in crisis, evidence for which included a series of bombings; a right-wing coup attempt; opposition by liberals in the National Assembly; an opposition boycott of elections in protest over inadequate government concessions to the pro-democratic opposition;[36] publication of a book by General Spinola criticizing government policy and resulting in his ouster as deputy chief of the General Staff; and a wave of illegal strikes, which began in October and was sustained over months.

This last, then, raises the second point: there is no question that working-class mobilization shook the regime. Labor strikes became a pervasive feature of Portuguese society beginning in the mid-1960s and especially after the transition from Salazar to Caetano in 1968 and an initial liberalization, when Caetano permitted free union elections and the formation of a horizontal labor organization, the Intersindical (Stoleroff 1988; see also Raby 1988:241–44). In late 1973 working-class activism expanded even further, precisely the time when some observers place the beginning of the deterioration of the Caetano regime. According to Baloyra (1987:32), "between December 1973 and April 1974 the country was paralyzed by frequent strikes," and Maxwell (1995:43) suggests that "the

---

35 See, for example, Maxwell 1986; Schmitter 1975; Bandeira 1976; Graham 1993; Nataf and Sammis 1990; and Lomax 1983:113.

36 Under the authoritarian regime, electoral rituals were regularly carried out with just enough openness to register an occasional degree of opposition and even thereby to embarrass the government, but not to prevent the victory of the entire government list. See Pimlott and Seaton 1983:46.

security services were preoccupied with widespread labor unrest . . . [which] was spreading not only among industrial workers but also for the first time among office workers and civil servants." There is some suggestion that these strikes led MFA officers to act when they did, before the "population" seized power on its own and put the country in a state of civil war (Lomax 1983:113).

At the very least, the reactivated labor movement contributed to a general climate of instability and crisis in which the coup occurred. The question remains, however, whether these strikes had a pro-democratic content. Stoleroff (1988:12–13) maintains that they did have a "democratic . . . political character" and that most trade unionists before 1974 embraced " 'anti-fascist,' democratic perspectives." Yet it is difficult to gauge the pressure these strikes exerted explicitly for democracy. Though perhaps less successful than their Spanish counterparts, the underground Communist Party had established itself in the official union movement, and it became the dominant force in the unions and the Intersindical once Caetano allowed free elections. The Communist union leadership sought to build a larger, class-conscious workers' movement that would act politically (Logan 1983:140). The political, anti-regime orientation of the Communist Party was clear; its democratic, as opposed to socialist, vocation was not. The more consistent pro-democratic opposition was taken by the more moderate Socialists (whose support was not based in the working class) under the leadership of Mario Soares.

After the coup, new political alignments rapidly evolved, pitting the moderates in the PPD, the CDS, and the military faction around General Spinola against the radicals in the MFA and the Communist Party. The working-class movement must be seen at two levels. The first was a grassroots outpouring of grievances that involved strikes, factory occupations, and seizures of property – spontaneous actions that attempted to change the structure of class relations (Logan 1983:142). At another level, labor organizations, both unions and the Communist Party, called for moderation, warning that it was important to protect the "democratic gains." Indeed, the Communist Party joined the new Spinola government and, from its control of the labor ministry, tried to enforce a more moderate position. Nevertheless, the party was more oriented toward preventing a countercoup than in moving toward liberal democracy.

This priority quickly became clear as events pushed the radicals toward more vanguardist positions. The radicals in the government soon got the upper hand and forced out the moderates, including General Spinola. Even as they were consolidating their position within the government, a January 1975 poll showing popular support for moderate parties drove a deeper

wedge between democratic and more radical socialist trajectories. As polarization increased, the MFA announced that it did not intend to withdraw
after a new government was elected but would retain an institutionalized
political role. After a failed coup attempt by the Spinola faction, the MFA
concretized those plans by signing a pact with the political parties (though
only the Communists showed any enthusiasm) on a three- to five-year
transitional period of a guided democracy in which the MFA would hold
substantial power in putting the country "irreversibly on the road to
Portuguese socialism."[37] The victory of the moderates in the April Constituent Assembly elections further challenged the attraction of democracy for
the left. The MFA's Revolutionary Council began to consider other
schemes of alliances between government and workers' committees as a
basis for the revolutionary process. In July they approved a plan for "direct
democracy" based on workers' control of firms and government committees.[38]

In the end, the democratic transition came about when moderates
reestablished a dominant position and limited this advance toward a mili-
tary-guided democracy. As polarization proceeded, the balance of power
shifted to the moderates. By September a new compromise government
was named in which the power of the Communist Party was eclipsed and
civilian participation reflected the moderate electoral victory of the previous April.[39] Moderates also gained influence within the MFA.

The new constitution represented a compromise among the dominant
social forces. It was the result of the deliberations of the Constituent
Assembly (in which the labor-based Communist Party had won a place,
though its relative position was hardly impressive compared with its earlier
preeminence), and it was also the result of earlier pacts the MFA had forced
upon the parties at the moment of the radicals' zenith. In due course,
legislative and presidential elections were held as scheduled in April and
June 1976, and a new government was promptly inaugurated – albeit one
in which the ongoing power of the military continued to be institutionalized until the review scheduled for 1980.

Through it all, the working class had been a major protagonist. It had
been active in the anti-fascist opposition before the coup, and once the
dictatorship fell, the working class headed a massive wave of mobilization
and protest that undermined the corporatist structures of the Salazarist
regime. As Stoleroff (1988:19–20) writes, "the union movement came to
life in such a way as to establish itself as one of the principal actors of the

37 Quoted in *Portuguese Revolution, 1974–1976*, 1976:97.
38 Ibid., 102–5.
39 Ibid., 114.

transition to democracy and to determine in a large part the class character of this process." In Drake's (1996:64) words, "workers pushed the army's 'revolution' to the left," and they were able to ensure that, "more than in the other cases . . . , the governments that succeeded capitalist authoritarianism in Portugal implemented much of the workers' agenda." Furthermore, as Schmitter (1986:7) acknowledges, the burst of mass mobilization that followed the coup made it "virtually impossible" for the transition to stop short of full democratization. Thus the role of labor protest and the activities of party and union organizations were somewhat eclipsed at the end but had been central during much of the process, had served to advance it, and had affected the final compromises.

CONCLUSION

The foregoing analyses suggest that our conventional understandings of recent democratization should be supplemented by a consideration of the role played by labor organizations, largely ignored in theoretical and comparative analyses, though not in monographic accounts of individual cases. This labor role was not limited to an "indirect" one, in which the government responded to labor protest focused on workplace demands. Rather, the union movement, or important parts of it, was typically one of the major actors in the political opposition, explicitly demanding a democratic regime. More than merely one component or "layer" of a resurrected civil society that moved into the interstices of political space opened by incumbents and followed the lead of many other groups, the union movement was sometimes able to create political space for anti-authoritarian, prodemocratic protest. In some cases, union-led protest for democracy contributed to a climate of delegitimation that provoked the initiation of the transition; in others it helped derail the legitimation projects of authoritarian regimes. Protest continuing to the end of the transition, rather than creating an authoritarian backlash, often kept the transition moving forward. Finally, while the protest of other groups also put the regime on the defensive, labor-based organizations went further in affecting democratic transitions in two ways: in many cases labor-based parties and sometimes unions won a place in the negotiations, and they derailed the transformative projects of the authoritarian rulers to exclude any future participation of left and labor-based parties, thereby expanding the scope of contestation in the successor regimes.

5

COMPARING THE PATTERNS: THE WORKING CLASS AND DEMOCRATIZATION

The struggle for a democratic regime has been one of the most important processes of political change across two centuries of Western history. It has constituted a major political drama of the opening and closing years of the twentieth century, with substantial institutional continuity across the two periods: after evolving more slowly during the nineteenth century, the democratic institutions being adopted at the end of the twentieth century are remarkably similar to those that were the center of political struggle nearly a century earlier. European countries and their eighteenth- and nineteenth-century colonial offshoots have witnessed an extended experience with the struggle to adopt democratic institutions. Yet the processes through which such regime change takes place remain poorly understood, and they continue to be debated.

The goal of the present analysis has been to examine the role of the working class in the process of democratization and to do so in a way that integrates a literature that has been rooted alternatively in either class or strategic frameworks and has asserted (or implied) that the working class was alternatively the major, even decisive force in democratization or at most a rather marginal player in a process dominated by elite strategies. Democratization is a complex, multifaceted process involving a large variety of groups, actors, and interests, and following different trajectories. Several patterns can be distinguished, involving different combinations of class actors engaging in different arenas of action.

The role of the working class in democratization has been analyzed in the two historical periods that have been the main empirical sources of theorizing: Western Europe and South America in the nineteenth and early twentieth centuries and in the 1970s and 1980s. This study has attempted to clear some conceptual ground, to outline some dimensions for analysis, and to suggest the way in which quite different patterns of democratization occur within both historical periods. The comparative analysis does not support the general proposition that working-class pressure is a decisive or even necessary, no less sufficient, factor in democratization, or that mass democracy is dependent on mass pressure. On the other hand, working-class participation in democratization has often been a component of the process, so that a generalized image of democratization as an elite project or a process of elite strategic interaction is also misleading, even for the recent cases. Accordingly, the comparative analysis does not support the suggestions that the working class was consistently decisive in the historical cases in the nineteenth and early twentieth centuries and relatively marginal to what was fundamentally an elite process in the 1970s and 1980s. Within periods, then, democratization has followed quite different patterns, and these patterns should be located in a theoretical space that combines both elite and mass action.

This study has attempted to move toward an integration of distinct analytic perspectives on the basis of three dimensions of analysis: class, political status, and arena of action. The focus particularly on the working class and its role in relation to elite strategies allows us to delineate a new set of patterns on the basis of these dimensions. Figure 5.1 summarizes the major dynamics that have been discussed in connection with these patterns. It depicts the commonalities shared within each pattern and may not capture the additional "corners" that may have come into play in particular cases. For instance, labor-based organizations were central actors in the final negotiations in the Uruguayan Transition Game. Further, since a detailed, overall characterization that would lay out the role of all actors was not undertaken, the diagrams do not represent a complete characterization. Rather, as a summary of the particular analytical focus of the foregoing, they reflect the fact that the role of non-working-class groups was not systematically examined (e.g., nationalist groups in Spain, students in Greece, as well as some popular groups that did not come together around worker or class identities). As with working-class organizations, the weight and role of these other groups varied substantially across cases, and further research will have to integrate these groups comparatively and systematically.

In three patterns the process of democratization proceeded without working-class participation. Middle-Sector Democratization and Electoral Support Mobilization are quite straightforward patterns in which the initiative comes from middle- and upper-class groups, though these are quite

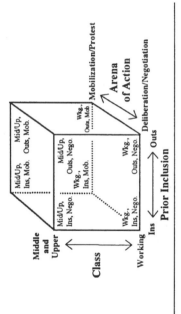

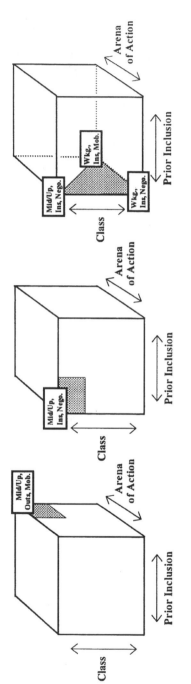

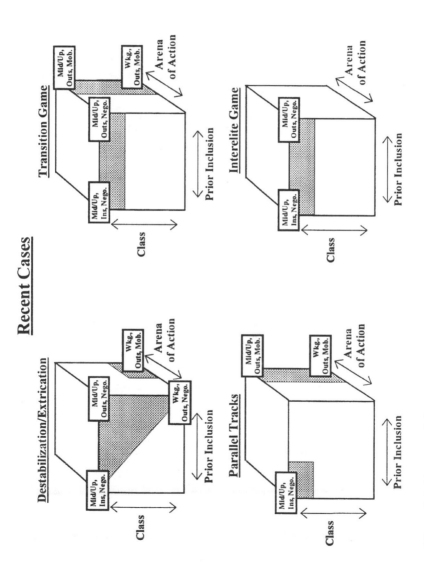

Figure 5.1. Patterns of democratization

differently located in terms of their political inclusion or exclusion and, correspondingly, they have distinct goals and operate in quite different arenas of action. The pattern of Interelite Games includes the recent cases without significant working-class participation, in which middle- and upper-class "outs" played the leading role but, unlike most cases of Middle-Sector Democratization, they act primarily in the negotiation arena and the incumbents retain greater influence over the outcome, at least initially.

The other patterns involve the working class and are thus more complex. The pattern of Joint Projects is characterized by the interacting political strategies of the "ins" representing many class groups, including the working class, whose organizations act on two fronts: labor-based parties engage in strategic interaction with other parties in the negotiation arena, and in addition parties and unions present demands in the protest arena. The Destabilization/Extrication process occurs in two stages: the first is labor mobilization that destabilizes the authoritarian regime; the second, following the extrication decision, is negotiations between representatives of all classes and the authoritarian incumbents, whose strength varies. The importance of these negotiations also varies, from Argentina, where an older constitution was reinstated, to Peru, where a new constitution was written. In Transition Games a rigged, incumbent-defined negotiating arena, to which only parties with middle- and upper-class constituencies are admitted, is undermined by its own contradictions and further derailed by the mobilization and protest of labor and other groups. In Parallel Tracks little interaction takes place: incumbents take the initiative in defining a long-term transition, and the "outs" protest following the initial example and leading role of labor groups. The protests do not manage to alter the transitional project, but in Chile they succeeded at the end of the process in electing the opposition and rejecting the incumbents.

The following discussion further summarizes and compares these patterns. It turns first to a discussion of the labor role in democratization and explanations concerning the conditions under which labor groups became a force for democratization. An institutional and path-dependent explanation is suggested: labor participation in democratization can be seen as an outcome of antecedent regime and the nature of past democratic experience. Subsequent sections address the point in the process when labor activity occurred, the form it took, and the institutional outcome. Although the working-class role in the Joint Projects was often central and even dramatic, it was also likely to be more incremental, while in the recent cases labor organizations participated in more sweeping regime changes and were often uniquely able to open political space, sustain continual pressure to keep the transition moving forward, and expand contestation in the successor regimes. Finally, we return to the importance of analyzing democratization in terms of a framework that integrates class and strategic perspectives.

PARTICIPATION OF LABOR ORGANIZATIONS

First, we may review whether the working class or labor organizations played a role in the process of regime change or democratic reform.[1] In both historical periods the participation of labor groups in democratization was in part related to institutional factors. It was related first to prior experiences (or the lack of such experience) when democratic institutions were adopted and to lessons learned from the way democratic institutions had earlier functioned in practice. Second, the antecedent (pre-reform or pre-transition) regime had an impact in the way it raised class issues and gave labor groups special resources, for instance, allowing labor-based parties to gain parliamentary seats or social movements to acquire particular capacities.

HISTORICAL CASES

Among the historical cases, three patterns were distinguished, two of which can be characterized as democratization from above, in the sense that these were not popular victories of lower-class groups but came about through the initiatives of elite social strata. These two patterns represent democratic reform without working-class participation. Middle-Sector Democratization occurred through the action of an ascendant but still excluded group seeking political inclusion and access to power, often in the mobilization/protest arena. Regime change was a result of pressure on the part of the political "outs," but in social terms these were an elite stratum of rising middle-class groups, not the working class. Though the goal can be seen as their own inclusion, these were liberal movements whose

---

1 It may be appropriate briefly to remind the reader what is meant by a labor or working-class role in democratization, as elaborated in Chapter 1. A central aspect is some notion of worker identity. Thus, I do not mean participation by individual workers as citizens, but some sense of class interest or workers' collective action. Typically (but not necessarily – the noted exception is France in 1848) such action was taken on the part of labor organizations – unions or labor-based parties. A further criterion is that labor participation must be consequential to regime change.

principles often included the notion of full manhood suffrage so that the reforms were not restrictive with respect to class enfranchisement but rather were consistent with mass democracy.

In Electoral Support Mobilization democratic reform occurred at the initiative of the "ins" operating in the deliberation/negotiation arena and seeking to build a support base and win the backing of the lower classes, often as a strategy of partisan competition. These were political strategies of political entrepreneurship, in which the suffrage was not demanded from below but extended from above. In general the working class was not an initiator of these events, or even much of an actor in them, except as a target of elite strategy. Among the cases in these two patterns, the working class assumed a pro-democratic position in only three: most notably in France in 1848, and also in Britain and Norway. Thus, the portrayal of a working class confronting an unwilling elite has been overdrawn.

In the third pattern, Joint Projects, the working class participated more centrally in the process of democratization. Across these cases, the importance or weight of the working class and its organizations varied. This point leads to another: these cases were analyzed as Joint Projects to reflect the fact that, though the balance of force varied from case to case, the reforms were the result not only of the working class. They were also driven by the positive strategies of other groups and political parties as they sought either to protect their own electoral position or to pursue some goal such as national autonomy – as in Finland, and, in a different way, Germany. As with the other two patterns, the image of democratization as a struggle against an unwilling elite is overstated: certainly there may be opposition to democratic reform, but in some cases it came about, in the end, as a broadly consensual "grand compromise," and in others it was the product of lib-lab coalitions of working-class as well as middle-class parties. An important point about this pattern is that it took place as a reform process among political "ins" of various classes, and this included labor-based parties with seats in parliament.

Working-class participation was thus not a generalized feature of early democratization, but one of three distinct patterns. It was a more common component of recent democratization: in all but two cases these were also kinds of "joint projects" in the sense that many class groups including labor groups were involved, as were both "ins" and "outs." Yet these recent cases differ in that the working class and other classes were "outs": if the Joint Projects of the historical cases were strategic games primarily played among the "ins," in the recent cases the "outs" had the more prominent role.

How are we to understand where working-class groups played a role in the politics of democratic change? Timing and antecedent regimes were important factors, but not in the ways initially suggested on the basis of assertions in the literature. Let us examine these two factors.

Timing is the most obvious factor in considering a labor role: it was unlikely in the earliest episodes of democratization and likely in the later historical and the recent cases. Timing serves as a stand-in variable for economic development, and it suggests the proletarianization hypothesis: the working class tended to participate in the struggle for democracy only after the formation of a sizable proletariat.[2] Thus the historical episodes with working-class participation tend to cluster around a particular juncture in world historical time when the second industrial revolution was, so to speak, gathering steam: factory production was spreading and with it a change in labor process and a growth of the proletariat. An obvious caveat has to be added: this explanation can be explored only for the "late" historical cases; that is, this explanation cannot stand on its own but must be combined with other factors that explain why democratic reform in these cases did not occur earlier through one of the other patterns – or why space for democratic reform still existed in this relatively late time period.

The proletarianization hypothesis has substantial support. However, it is only a partial explanation of labor participation. The French reform of 1848 reminds us that working-class participation is not dependent on a high level of proletarianization. Furthermore, these socio-economic factors do not perfectly separate those cases of early twentieth-century democratization in which the working class participated. If we take the percentage of the economically active population (EAP) in agriculture, forestry, and fishing in 1910–11 as an (inverse) measure of the economic and class changes that were occurring in the years up to the time of these reforms (see Table 5.1), then we see that the relationship is far from perfect, with Argentina and Uruguay being among the most advanced in this socio-economic measure but without a labor role and Finland, with a labor role, being the least advanced. A measure like gross domestic product (GDP) per capita helps correct for the omission of agricultural workers, but data were not available for Uruguay. It shows a roughly similar

2 This hypothesis is somewhat different from that put forward by Rueschemeyer et al. 1992. They in effect invoke proletarianization to explain democracy as an outcome. Specifically, they see it as an intervening variable that explains the modernization finding: the correlation between economic development and democracy. By contrast, I am asking to what extent does proletarianization explain the labor role in democratization – to what extent does it help us distinguish those cases of democratization in which the working class participated in the process from those in which it did not.

Table 5.1. *Economic indicators by labor role in early twentieth-century democratization*

	No role			Some role		
EAP in agriculture, forestry, fishing in 1910–11						
Higher				Finland	69.3	
↑	Portugal	57.4				
	Spain	56.1	(1920)			
	Italy	55.4				
				Sweden	46.2	
				Denmark	41.7	
	Norway	39.6				
				Germany	36.8	(1907)
				Netherlands	28.3	(1909)
	Uruguay	26.5	(1908)			
				Belgium	23.2	
	Argentina	17.6	(1914)			
Lower				Great Britain	8.8	
GDP per capita in 1913						
Lower	Portugal	1,354				
↑				Finland	2,050	
	Spain	2,255				
	Norway	2,275				
	Italy	2,507				
				Sweden	3,096	
				Denmark	3,764	
	Argentina	3,797				
				Germany	3,833	
				Netherlands	3,950	
				Belgium	4,130	
Higher				Great Britain	5,032	

Sources: For EAP, Mitchell 1980, 1983; Rial 1980. For GDP, Maddison 1995.

pattern with perhaps a somewhat stronger relationship. More specific labor force data that afford measures that are conceptually more satisfactory but more partial with respect to coverage tend to separate out the four most advanced European countries where labor organizations played a role in democratization, but show little relationship among the remaining cases.[3]

3 Early labor force data are not readily available for all cases. For partial data on percent EAP in manufacturing, labor force in industry, and labor force in manufacturing, construction, extraction, and transportation and communication, see, respectively, Pounds 1990:444; Flora et al. 1983: 2: ch. 7; and Mitchell 1980, 1983.

Other factors must supplement this explanation. It is not only a question of social structure or the proletariat as a numerical force, but also the way the working class comes to constitute itself as a political force. Important here are the different terms in which identities were conceived and interests constructed, the analysis of the situation, and the proposed solutions (see Katznelson 1986). Timing is also a stand-in for sources of ideology and discourse and the invention of social or political technologies, such as organizing in unions and labor-based parties and repertoires of action, and in this regard, of course, the effect of the Socialist International is important. Markoff (1996) has more generally suggested the transnational nature of many social movements, particularly those for democratic reforms. However, we are still confronted with the problem of explaining the historical cases of late democratic reform where the working-class did not adopt a pro-democratic position or choose actively to pursue democratic reform. What, in other words, are the paths of diffusion?

At this point, the factor of region becomes apparent: workers participated in these late episodes in northern Europe but not in Latin countries. Ideology and organization help us to distinguish the social democratic path of the northern working classes from the anarchosyndicalist path of the Latin working classes. Accordingly, in the northern countries the working classes embraced a political role and fought for democratic reform, a position that the Latin working classes were more likely to reject. The regional basis of this difference may suggest, simply, that diffusion is easier among neighboring countries or possibly among countries in a closer language family or among countries with denser existing lines of communication and interaction. These factors related to transmission, however, do not seem satisfactory.

Given the importance of the Socialist International for both regions and the transnational lines of communication it established, some additional explanation of paths of diffusion seems necessary regarding the receiving end rather than the transmission mechanisms. The preceding analysis has suggested an additional, institutional factor in explaining the social democratic path in the north and the anarchosyndicalist path in the south, or what, in Przeworski and Sprague's (1986:13) terms, are the contrasting answers to the question that was at the center of socialist debates and that confronted national labor organizations in the face of democratizing processes: whether to participate. It points to the importance of the antecedent, pre-reform regime and prior national experience with democratic reform.

In some of the Latin countries, democratic constitutions had been introduced relatively early, before the emergence (or "making") of a working class, as part of an elite strategy from above; and labor groups subsequently were skeptical of these institutions as appropriate vehicles for working-class demands. Further skepticism was engendered by the way elite groups, once it looked as if control might indeed slip away from them, resorted to informal mechanisms (patterns of deference, clientelism, and patronage, as well as fraud) to limit competition, divide electoral benefits, and effectively limit the political rights of lower classes, in cases where these were formally granted. Analysts have often viewed the presence of these democratic deficiencies as grounds for excluding these as cases of democratization. The present point is that under some conditions such informal mechanisms are quite a common *outcome* of democratization, understood, as here, not in terms of democratic consolidation but in terms of the introduction of a particular set of regime institutions.

The foregoing case studies have provided ample evidence of these developments. In Spain, El Turno was the informal oligarchic response to a legal, formally adopted democratic order; pre-1912 Argentine politics also secured oligarchic control despite a democratic constitution. In Uruguay, competition among the oligarchic parties was interwoven with a long history of pact making by which those parties effectively monopolized the party-electoral terrain until the last quarter of the twentieth century. In Portugal and Chile, informal practices secured elite political dominance despite a broad, if not full manhood, suffrage. In Italy, the Trasformismo system, which reinforced formal restrictions in the pre-1912 period, was also a clear indication of the disempowering effect of informal practices. Where such practices developed, labor groups subsequently opted for syndicalist strategies, rejecting the potential benefits northern labor groups could anticipate in political democracy.

The countries in the north had quite different experiences with working-class participation prior to those reform episodes. With the exception of Denmark, they had not tended to experiment with early democratic constitutions. Consequently, informal practices to limit mass political influence did not develop in the same way, and the major limitations were embodied in law. Like legal segregation in the southern United States, this situation may have generated a more optimistic assessment in which the problem appeared the same as the solution: legal provisions. In these countries, labor organizations participated in the fight for reform.

Another important institutional factor distinguishes those historical cases where labor played a prominent role in democratization: the countries in the Joint Project pattern generally had quite distinct antecedent regimes prior to these episodes of democratic reform. Uniquely in these cases, by the time labor groups joined the democratization process, the working class was an included actor. (The exceptions were Belgium in 1893 and Finland in 1906.) The labor-based parties that participated in democratic reform had "in" political status, and the weight of the working class in the democratization process in no small measure depended on the degree to which a union-affiliated party had already won parliamentary seats. This relationship does not simply reflect the difference between episodes of democratization that occurred before the second industrial revolution, the formation of unions, and the founding of socialist or labor parties (countries in which there were hardly any cases of a labor role) and those that occurred afterward. Rather, this correlation can be observed among the latter as well (see Table 5.2).[4]

Like liberal and conservative parties, labor-based parties already operating in a competitive electoral arena pursued strategic as well as substantive goals. So it is not only that once these working-class parties were formed they fought for manhood suffrage, as many have noted. A further point is that the prior enfranchisement of much of the working class often demonstrated to these parties that the suffrage could be beneficial, and it gave them a position within the formal, legally constituted political system from which they had gained important political resources and political power to wage that further struggle, as well as strategic interests in doing so. This point provides a further insight into the "northern" decision to participate and the Latin indifference.

RECENT CASES

As a group, the recent cases of democratization were like the Joint Projects in two respects: in most of them labor organizations were actors in the democratization process, and in most the patterns were complex, involving many class groups, "ins" and "outs," and both arenas of action in many of their combinations. Four patterns of democratization were distinguished, and labor groups emerged as pro-democratic actors in all but one of them. In Destabilization/Extrication union groups took the initiative to open space in the authoritarian regimes and destabilized them or prevented their consolidation. Once authoritarian incumbents took the decision to extricate themselves from an unsustainable situation, labor groups – unions and/or parties – continued to be active, sustaining strikes and participating in final negotiations. The Transition Game began with a series of moves between authoritarian incumbents seeking legitimation and a set of (non-labor-based) party leaders who received special recognition as part of the

---

4 In Spain the PSOE had only 10 percent of the parliamentary seats in the pre-authoritarian regime, and neither the PSOE nor unions played a big role in the anti-authoritarian fight, though the former won a plurality in the Constituent Assembly elected in 1931 after the fall of the dictatorship.

Table 5.2. *Seats held by labor-based parties in early twentieth century democratizing reform*

Country	Percentage of seats in lower house	Prior election	Year of reform	Comments
Joint Projects				
Belgium	0	1892	1893	
	21	1912	1918	Wartime unity government in exile
Denmark	28	1913	1915	Plurality of vote but second in seats, in GC
Finland	0		1906	
	40	1919	1919	Plurality but in opposition
Germany	28	1912	1918	Plurality of vote, in GC
Great Britain	6	1910	1918	
Netherlands	15	1913	1917	In GC
Sweden	6	1905	1907/9	In opposition
	15	1908		In opposition
	37	1917	1918/20	Plurality, in GC
	33	1920		Plurality, in GC
Other patterns				
Argentina	0	1910	1912	
Italy	8	1909	1912	
Norway	0	1897	1898	.6% of vote
Portugal	n/a		1918	Reform following coup
Spain	10	1923	1931	Last election pre-dictatorship
	24	1931		Plurality; CA
Uruguay	0	1917	1918	.005% of vote (PS)

Notes: GC = governing coalition; CA = Constituent Assembly.
Sources: Mackie and Rose 1991; Flora et al. 1983; Carstairs 1980; Payne 1993; Martin 1991:1235.

incumbents' blueprint. With differing weights across time and case, the protest of unions and social movements in addition to electoral opposition derailed these schemes. The Chilean experience was described in terms of Parallel Tracks: union-led protest opened oppositionist space for larger protests that came to include other lower- and middle-class groups. This pro-democratic opposition was unable to deflect the transitional path laid out by the authoritarian incumbents. In only two cases (Greece and Ecuador) were labor organizations not an active pro-democratic force.

In almost all the recent cases, then, labor organizations participated in the pro-democratic opposition, though their impact or weight varied, as it did among the earlier Joint Projects. It is difficult to say that labor participation was consistently more consequential in one historical period than another. Probably nowhere among the recent cases did it have the force that it did in Germany – and perhaps in Belgium and Sweden; but it is not entirely a simple matter to compare the impact of those mobilizations and general strikes with those in, for example, the recent cases of Uruguay and Bolivia. On the other end of the spectrum, it is difficult to compare the role of Chilean unions in leading pro-democratic demonstrations at some points with that of British labor organizations. In approaching such a question, it is obviously necessary to establish comparable criteria for the two sets of cases. However, analyses of each historical period have tended to be undertaken within different conceptual frameworks in a way that has stacked the deck in terms of these judgments and comparisons, overplaying the role in the earlier period and underplaying it in the later, and conversely underemphasizing the role of elite strategies in the one and focusing on it too exclusively in the other. We return to these issues later.

The near universal participation of labor organizations in the recent cases can be explained with reference to the same factors we have invoked already: timing and antecedent regime. The exception of Greece raises an additional factor: the "strength" of the labor movement. Especially as a relational concept, this is a difficult factor to assess in a nontautological way that avoids ex post inferences from the outcome. Still, its importance cannot easily be dismissed. The underlying strength and organization of the Argentina labor movement was clearly the resource that allowed it to recover protest space relatively quickly, despite the "dirty war" of which it was a major victim. By the same token, a combination of repression and controlling corporatist structures, which were effective for a long time in Brazil, Portugal, and Spain, continued to eliminate the capacity for political opposition of the Greek labor movement during its briefer authoritarian period.

As we saw for the historical cases, timing can be invoked as an explanatory factor with respect to both economic and ideological issues regarding world historical time. The ideological issue seems straightforward: although these transitions preceded those in the Communist bloc, much had already occurred to change thinking within the left and to make more radical, nondemocratic alternatives less attractive, not to mention less likely. Eurocommunism had become an important pro-democratic current in these regions of the world and the Communist model was seen as less successful and appealing. Many exiles from the countries in these recent cases went abroad, where the positive and negative experiences in the West and in the East respectively both pushed in a pro-democratic direction (Silva 1993). This was a time when the United States began to view its interests as consistent with promoting democracy abroad, when Carter's human rights policy won respect in South America, and when liberal democracy came to have greater international prestige and valuation.

Again we may view timing as related to industrialization and proletarianization. Recent democratization occurred at the end of what we might view as the century of proletarianization. To the extent labor participation is premised on a sufficiently large proletariat, the recent cases fall within the range observed among the Joint Projects. As a group these countries did not tend to replicate the labor force structure of the early industrializers, but maintained instead a larger service sector and an industrial sector that absorbed relatively less labor in the course of late development. Nevertheless, although at the time of recent transitions the industrial labor force as a percent of the EAP was not as high as it was in Belgium and Britain in 1910, it ranged from a low of 18–20 percent in Peru and Bolivia (about the same as Sweden in 1910) to a high of 34 and 40 percent in Argentina, Portugal, and Spain (about the same as the Netherlands and Germany in the 1910s).[5]

In recent democratization, as in the historical period, antecedent regime and past democratic experience are important factors in understanding labor participation. These antecedent regimes as a group were arguably the most closed or restricted, as they excluded most social groups. A few of these (Portugal, Spain, Brazil) kept open a formal party arena, but these arenas were highly restricted with respect to the parties allowed to enter and were ineffective and powerless, amounting to mere fig leaves for naked authoritarian rule. More important was the class coloration of these regimes. In both their fascist and bureaucratic-authoritarian guises, the raison d'être of these post-democratic, authoritarian regimes was to exclude labor influence and power, to remove labor interests from the political arena.

Two points follow. First, that these anti-labor regimes were not simply restrictive but actively exclusionary is indicative of a prior experience in many countries in which labor organizations had had at least some access to power or political influence. Labor-based parties had participated in pre-authoritarian regimes, often with substantial success; indeed, it was often that success – or the threat of success – that had precipitated democratic breakdown. Paralleling the point made for the historical cases, the earlier

5 Flora et al. 1983: vol. 2; World Bank 1983; UN/ECLAC 1997; ILO 1990.

experience under democratic regimes did not leave them completely skeptical about democracy. Second, and perhaps more important, under these regimes, labor unions and labor-affiliated parties typically bore the brunt of the repression and were the targets of attempts to restructure the union movement, the system of industrial relations, and sometimes the party system. It is hardly surprising, therefore, that labor organizations would see redemocratization at least in part in class terms and become active participants. The exception of Ecuador is instructive in this regard: the absence of the labor movement from any anti-authoritarian, pro-democratic struggle can be seen in light of the unusual reformist character of that authoritarian regime, which brought a more sympathetic, pro-labor orientation than previous elected governments. The ambivalence of the Mexican labor movement concerning democratization of that inclusionary regime can also be understood in these terms: antecedent regimes characterized by dominant labor-based parties present quite different calculations and dilemmas.[6]

POINT OF INTERVENTION

We may also ask at what point in the democratization process labor groups played an important role in regime change. Among the historical cases in the Joint Projects pattern, the working-class groups typically entered the process quite late, in the last step or two. Indeed, as has been seen, a notable feature is that this participation usually occurred when the working class was already at least partly enfranchised, and a labor-based party already had representation in parliament (the exceptions are Finland in 1906 as well France in 1848 in a different pattern), sometimes very substantial representation.

Among the recent cases, the labor role came into play at different points in the transition process. In the pattern Destabilization/Extrication, it started early, at the very beginning in the sense that, depending on the case, it prevented the consolidation of the authoritarian regime or was instrumental in delegitimizing it. Thus, it constituted a major factor in creating the legitimacy concerns and the strategic split among the incumbents with which the transitions literature typically begins its analysis. In these cases – as well as in Portugal, Bolivia, and Chile, where it also participated early in the process – the labor movement did not merely

6 A similar dilemma faces, for example, the Chinese working class incorporated into the iron rice bowl. For a discussion of the Mexican labor movement and democratization in the context of a labor-based one-party regime, see Collier 1999.

move into space that was opened by liberalizing regimes but was able to create that space. Elsewhere, as in Uruguay, where unions were effectively repressed or controlled, they arrived on the scene later – only after some space was opened from above. Relative levels of repression and the pre-existing strength of unions explain a great deal about the initial quiescence of the labor movement and the degree to which this quiescence may have been overcome. In either case, whether they had created and expanded space or moved into already opened space, union-led protest continued to exert pressure to keep the transition process going. In many cases labor protest was protracted and lasted virtually to the end of the transition, advancing the process much more consistently than provoking backlashes.

The idea that "maximalist" pressure that rejected compromise would threaten the transition or that protest, while useful in early stages, would risk derailing it toward the end might be revisited. It is true that Portuguese labor organizations were "revolutionary," but the effect, as in the historical cases, was not to retreat into authoritarianism but, in a manner reminiscent of some of the historical cases, to reinforce the notion of democracy as an alternative. In Bolivia, the demands of a strong syndicalist labor movement may indeed have been part of the dynamics of a transition in which coups and authoritarian reimpositions were a notable feature. Yet one must not be teleological about a democratic end point in analyzing the process of regime change. As always it is impossible to run the counterfactual, but one cannot unproblematically assume that the coups were interruptions of a democratic path, or that if the labor movement had been more moderate, an "equally democratic" transition would have occurred earlier. Bolivia was one of the cases where a game of coup poker in fact resulted in coups; yet it could just as easily be argued that the overall effect of the labor role was to undermine the undemocratic or limited democratic projects of the incumbents and, as a result of labor's overtly pro-democratic pressure, ultimately to pave the way for a more democratic transition, to which the military finally conceded when confronting the COB's call for an indefinite general strike.

Elsewhere, labor organizations did not adopt a "maximalist" position, but they did tend to keep up pressure to the end. Unprecedented levels of labor mobilization were sustained in Spain up through the 1977 elections; labor protest continued in Peru until the Constituent Assembly elections and in Argentina until the new elections; demonstrations that included labor participation accelerated in the final stages in Brazil and kept up the pressure in Chile; and in Uruguay the labor movement continued to flex its muscles through a series of one-day strikes, and the 1984 general strike substantially changed the balance of power and forced the military to a more concessionary posture. The widely analyzed role of moderate party leaders willing to come to an agreement with the authoritarian incumbents and thereby provide the conditions that facilitate authoritarian withdrawal is only part of the story. Another part is the continual pressure exerted by labor groups pursuing their interests – at once particularistic and broader – in labor, human, and political rights. In challenging the "myth of moderation" that pervades the literature on democratization, Bermeo (1997) has suggested that popular challenges may be less likely to derail democratic transitions than has often been assumed. One might go even further and suggest that collective protest may have often pushed forward the transition and helped to prevent a retreat.[7]

In later stages in many cases, labor organizations in the form of labor-based parties also participated in the final negotiations concerning the transition. In Peru and Portugal, labor-affiliated left parties won a place in the constituent assemblies that deliberated the terms of the new democracies. In Argentina and Uruguay, union leaders participated in the *multipartidarias* that were established in each country to negotiate with the authoritarian incumbents. In constructing a consensus for a transition in Spain, Suárez entered into talks with all the major political actors, and these certainly included the labor-affiliated Communist Party.

FORM OF PARTICIPATION

In the recent cases as well as the northern European historical cases, working-class participation in democratization was characterized by a kind of dual militance in terms of organizations and in terms of arenas of action: it took place through both labor-based parties and unions; and it took place in both protest and negotiating arenas. France in 1848 is the unusual case that alerts us to the possibility of working-class action that is not coordinated by or does not occur through the vehicle of parties and unions. In most cases, however, working-class participation did occur through those organizations. The different patterns of democratization varied in terms of the relative weight of parties and unions and the relative importance of the two arenas. These differences were related to the antecedent regime.

Where the antecedent regime had already afforded the opportunity for labor-based parties to gain a presence in parliament, as in most of the

---

7 Tarrow (1995), suggests that in contrast to the sustained protest in Spain, the failure of the Italian workers' movement to maintain a high level of protest and mobilization after 1921 contributed to the breakdown of democracy and the rise of the fascist right.

historical cases in northern Europe, the party acting in that negotiating arena quite naturally became an important avenue of working-class participation. Often, however, this parliamentary role was coordinated with and supplemented by very important activity in the streets, and in some cases the political strike was an important weapon. Although unions were activated in the mobilization of this protest, in some cases these tactics were championed by the parties, while unions were more reluctant and cautious, focusing primarily on workplace rather than political considerations. Where antecedent regimes in the historical cases had not afforded labor-based parties the opportunity to become parliamentary actors (as in Finland in 1906 and France in 1848, as well as Britain in 1884), the protest arena was used more exclusively.

As in these latter cases, the streets were also a more predominant arena of action in patterns of more recent democratization because the antecedent regime defined virtually all social actors as "outs." Here too, then, labor-based parties were excluded from the pre-transition regimes. Compared not only with parties but also with other collective actors, unions were relatively privileged sites of protest and mobilizational activity. Union movements had certain advantages and resources that gave them the potential for playing a leading and coordinating role in mounting protest against authoritarianism. They had a history of collective existence and action, however controlled, state-penetrated, and repressed they had been in some of these countries, and herein lay important resources. In his analysis of social movements, Tarrow (1994:7, 18) emphasizes the political opportunity structure that social movements may seize and expand, yet his formulation remains quite close to the transitions literature in identifying those opportunities first of all with elite splits, regime liberalization, moments of realignment, and the like. I would put more stress on the way a reservoir of resources routinely emphasized by social movement analysts (including Tarrow) gave unions greater possibilities of taking the initiative and *creating* space. These resources include networks (both domestic and international), repertoires and historical memories of collective action, symbolic frames, culture, and, of course, ongoing organization.

In many of these countries, the labor movements had previously been highly developed, with rich traditions and histories of collective action. Some derived significant benefits from international networks, including the ILO, the AFL-CIO, and the international Socialist and Communist organizations. Unions also had a certain advantage in that, although there were many mechanisms to control them, most of the time they remained legal, legitimate organizations even under authoritarianism. Furthermore, they could take advantage of a certain ambiguity owing to their dual role as a sectoral and political actor, or a certain fuzziness between what the government begrudgingly had to consider a legitimate, acceptable, and presumably narrow sphere of industrial relations and a broader more threatening political sphere. Strikes, which formed the cutting edge of labor participation in democratization, often started out with less threatening workplace concerns regarding the terms of employment but then spilled beyond that narrower conception into the more overtly political.[8] As in Brazil, for instance, wage demands could spill over into broader anti-government positions in a context in which the government had a major hand in wage determination; or, as often happened, union rights, starting with more specific sectoral issues concerning the constraints on the organization and activities of unions, became inextricably linked with larger issues of political control and repression, freedom and political rights, in short, with authoritarian rule itself. With these advantages, unions were often able to open political space that otherwise did not exist.

Though predominant, protest was not the only form of labor participation in the recent cases. We should not lose sight of what was mentioned earlier: in several of the recent cases leaders or representatives of labor-based parties and unions won a place in negotiations or discussions regarding the transitions or were members of the constituent assemblies that oversaw the transition and wrote the new charter. In a literature that has placed emphasis on negotiations, the participation of labor organizations in these negotiations has been insufficiently recognized. Needless to say, their relative power in this arena varied, and a careful comparative analysis awaits further research.

THE INSTITUTIONAL CONTENT OF DEMOCRACY

Finally, we come to labor's role in shaping the institutional content of democratization. It is an exaggeration to say that the introduction of manhood suffrage was the historical task of the working class. This was on the whole the historical project of other classes, and in most countries the principle of mass or manhood suffrage was first introduced without

---

8 In this regard, I would go further than Foweraker (1994:221), who has suggested that while initial demands were often about bread-and-butter issues rather than overtly political or pro-democratic, under conditions of authoritarian control "it was making demands at all that mattered." While this point should not be overlooked, these initial demands soon came to be explicitly identified with an anti-authoritarian, pro-democracy stance.

working-class demands. With quite different degrees of influence, working-class organizations participated in the politics of the country's first reform introducing manhood suffrage in only six of the historical cases: Sweden in 1907/9, Finland in 1906, Belgium in 1893, the Netherlands in 1917, Norway in 1898, and Britain in 1918.

Further, in many of the reform episodes in which labor participated, the major thrust of the reform was about something else. In most cases of recent democratization the principle of universal suffrage was already established[9] and larger regime issues were at stake. But something of this sort was also operating in many of the historical cases as well. Indeed, as mentioned, a strong effective labor role was virtually premised on "in" status based on the success of the working class in having elected members of parliament from labor-based parties. Thus, in many episodes when labor organizations participated in the fight for democratic reform it was not so much to extend the right to vote as to bestow greater authority on elected bodies, extend the institutional application of the full suffrage, or to make it equal, and this was particularly true in those cases where the participation of labor organizations was the most decisive – the 1918 reforms in Germany, Belgium, and Sweden. Related but analytically distinct from extending the suffrage per se, these reforms (sometimes in addition to the goal of full suffrage) were aimed at establishing parliamentary sovereignty (most dramatically in Germany in 1918–19, but also in Finland in 1906 and 1919, and Norway in 1898); democratizing the upper house by extending to it the already established principle of manhood suffrage (Denmark in 1915, Sweden in 1918); or achieving greater equality of the vote, by abolishing (Belgium in 1918) or reducing (Britain in 1918) plural voting. While clearly related to increasing working-class political influence, these reforms were aimed not only at a particularistic class interest but, like those for which labor organizations fought in the 1970s and 1980s, at a larger public interest related to the overall structure of the regime.

In the recent cases, in addition to pressing for a more general regime change, labor organizations made particular substantive contributions that have been neglected in theoretical accounts of democratization. In their analysis of labor in the South African transition, Adler and Webster (1995: 76) argue that social movements "can inject more progressive content into democratization and wrest important concessions." While the South African labor movement may have been more successful than many others in this regard, the point has been unduly ignored in other settings. Perhaps

9 The exceptions were Brazil, Peru, and Ecuador, where prior to the military regimes literacy requirements had continued to restrict the suffrage.

for obvious and important reasons, the transitions literature, with a focus on degree of incumbent control, has in some ways been more helpful in accounting for the concessions extracted by the incumbents – for example, the limits in various post-transition constitutional arrangements, the relative continuity of policy, military amnesty, and the ongoing military prerogatives. It has been less helpful in accounting for certain democratic achievements.[10]

Particularly important in this regard is the way in which labor activation expanded the scope of contestation in the new democracies by securing the legalization of labor-based parties, whether of Marxist or populist background. Virtually all these authoritarian regimes were established as transformative regimes with the motivation of excluding precisely these parties from the political arena and from political influence. Yet the authoritarian incumbents were ultimately prevented from realizing their goal to exorcise these parties. That they did not succeed should not be attributed to something inherent in the transition process but rather, in most cases, to labor activation. As a result, in a way that is unprecedented in many of these countries, these parties have been admitted as normal participants to the democratic arena.

Electorally these reactivated (or in the case of Brazil, newly founded) parties have often done surprisingly well in the new democracies. If their working-class constituencies and union movement have lost political influence, it is not because these transformative projects succeeded, but because of the new conjuncture in world historical time, in which Marxism is seen to be defeated and globalized markets are providing a new opportunity structure within which interests are formed, power is realigned, and decisions are made. Indeed it is an ironic moment in world historic time for the triumph of the left or labor-based parties. At the end of the twentieth century the task of governing has put great strains on these parties and exerted enormous pressures to restructure their constituency relations, and the weakness of unions has often in part been advanced by labor-based parties confronting difficult contradictions and dilemmas once they have come to power.

ANALYTIC FRAMEWORKS

On the basis of the present study, we can revisit existing comparative and theoretical accounts of democratization. Three general observations about

10 An interesting attempt to tease out the way social movement activity and labor protest may contribute to securing citizenship rights is the analysis in Foweraker and Landman 1997.

the role of the working class in democratization have emerged from this analysis. First, for those (historical) cases that have become the paradigmatic examples of the claim that labor protest was crucial in achieving democratic reform, another type of labor participation was also important: labor-based parties with close ties to the union movement were already prominent parliamentary actors, engaging, with other parties, in competitive electoral strategies. Second, the role of labor protest in the recent cases is more consistently an important factor than has been suggested in comparative and theoretical accounts. Third, despite the focus on negotiation (rather than protest), these accounts have offered little recognition of the extent to which leaders of labor-based organizations (parties and unions) participated in the negotiation arena, often in central ways. Why have these points largely been missed? For most cases the issue does not concern empirical disagreements: the accounts presented here generally do not depart substantially from standard country monographs and analyses – on which this study has in fact relied – or indeed from those given by Rueschemeyer et al. or the case studies in the *Transitions from Authoritarian Rule* volumes. The discrepancy, rather, is primarily one of interpretation, and relates to the analytic frameworks employed. For both periods, the dominant frameworks have conceptualized the process as pitting the "ins" *versus* the "outs," but, consistent with different views of the politics of democratization, those actors have been identified differently, thereby drawing attention to the working-class role in the historical cases and obscuring it in the recent ones (see Figure 5.2).

HISTORICAL CASES

Certainly, the two periods of democratization consisted of different democratization processes. In most of the earlier cases, democratization was more incremental. We may return to our definition of a democratic regime as one involving constitutional rule, legislative authority, and classical elections with a mass suffrage. In most of the historical cases these components tended to be introduced in a more piecemeal fashion, rather than in a single reform episode of sweeping regime change, which was more characteristic of the late twentieth century cases. Of the historical cases, only Denmark in 1849 and Spain in 1931 (and to some extent Finland in 1906, though parliamentary sovereignty remained notably lacking) could be said to have experienced comparable changes. Among the recent cases, the pre-reform governments were not constrained by a fundamental law or constitution, or a classically elected authoritative legislature; the only component in place in some countries (Brazil, Spain, Portugal) was a voting arena, but with highly constrained contestation.

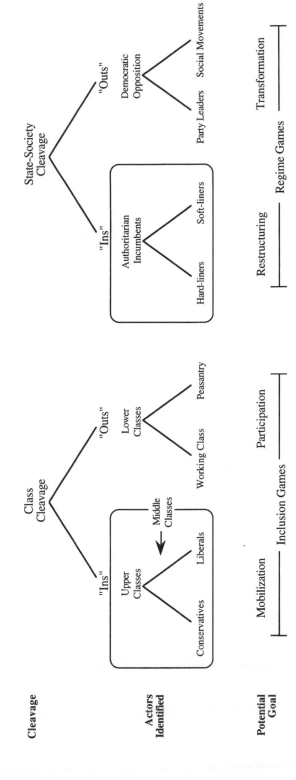

Figure 5.2. *Analytic framing of democratization: Overview of established interpretations*

Thus, prior to the reform episodes on which this analysis has focused the antecedent regimes tended to be quite different in the two historical periods. In the recent period these were authoritarian regimes or autocracies, with few if any democratic components, while in the earlier period some of these components were more likely to be in place. Reflecting the fact that mass suffrage was a component that often came late, the analytical framework used in the historical cases has often presented democratization as a process of inclusion. The framing of the issue of democratization in these cases has tended to be oriented around the implicit assumption that the antecedent regimes were restricted democracies, or what Dahl (1971: 7) has called competitive oligarchies, in which virtually all the components of democracy were in place, with the exception that mass participation was still lacking. Democratization, accordingly, has been seen as the class-defined extension of participation. This image is suggested, for instance, when Rueschemeyer et al. present a model of democratization in which each class fights for its own inclusion.

Accordingly, the actors have typically been conceived of in class terms, with, *grosso modo*, the upper classes distinguished from the lower classes. The former, which prior to the transition were seen as participants in restricted democracies, have often been divided into conservatives and liberals, largely corresponding to political persuasion or to the parties that were the vehicles for their political expression. The latter, in keeping with their political exclusion, have tended to be identified in class rather than political or party terms: working class and peasantry. In other words, where analysts saw democratization as an issue of the political inclusion of the lower classes, the "ins" and the "outs" have been identified in terms of classes, corresponding to upper classes versus lower classes, with the middle classes included according to a distinctive rhythm in each country. This framework focuses on the role of the lower classes playing an inclusion game in which they wrest the concession of their own participation.

There are, however, three problems with this conceptualization, which the foregoing analysis makes clear. First, although the politics of inclusion may take the form of a participation game in which the "outs" sought political rights, political influence, and admittance to the formal political arena, it was not necessarily the lower classes who were the main actors even with regard to their own inclusion. In several cases the middle classes fought for a broad suffrage that essentially by default included the working class. And sometimes working-class organizations fought for a suffrage extension, but in most cases only after the working class had already been at least partly enfranchised, that is, operating partly from an "in" position, when a labor-based party could be seen as both fighting for a principle and mobilizing support.

Second, then, the inclusion game is not necessarily played as a partici-pation game on the part of the "outs": it may also take the form of a mobilization game on the part of the "ins," even nonlabor-affiliated "ins" (which include both "government" and "opposition"), seeking political support often in the context of partisan competition. Indeed, this second possibility is important precisely when the antecedent regime is a restricted democracy – that is, when a competitive arena and political contestation already exist. The competitive arena itself defines a game of elite strategies on the part of the "ins," a game in which support mobilization is impor-tant.

The third problem is that the image of democratization as an inclusion game may itself be overdrawn. Quite often, inclusion was not the demo-cratic component – or not the only democratic component – that was missing. Other issues were often involved as well. In some cases inclusion in the sense of mass enfranchisement did not come as the final step in an incremental process; rather, it may have been addressed relatively early before other components (e.g., before parliamentary sovereignty in Ger-many or France, or before components providing for free and fair elections, as in Argentina). In Belgium and Britain the issue was plural voting, and in Denmark and Sweden the final step concerned the reform of the upper house, which was elected on a more restricted franchise. More often, multiple issues were addressed simultaneously in the final step. In the pattern of Middle-Sector Democratization, inclusion was typically part of a larger package of liberal reforms. Parliamentary sovereignty was a driving issue in Finland and Norway, where it was tied up with the issue of national autonomy. Most of these issues affected not only the working class, but other groups or parties as well. As a result, democratization was a more multifaceted process and less a lower-class or working-class process than suggested by a model of democratization as a process of stepwise inclusion down the social strata.

RECENT CASES

If the analytic framework used for the historical cases has tended to over-emphasize the role of the working class, particularly at the expense of other strategic actors, the transitions framework used for the recent cases has underemphasized it. For the recent democratic transitions, where the an-tecedent regime was an autocracy, a different framework of analysis has been employed. Here the process of democratization has been characterized not as an (incremental) inclusion game, but as a regime change game that potentially affects virtually the entire citizenry. Analysts have accord-ingly tended to identify actors differently, since the politics of "ins" versus "outs" pitted authoritarian incumbents of the state against a repressed civil society. Thus, actors have tended to be identified not by class but in terms closer to a state-society distinction. The main distinction has typically been between the authoritarian (usually military) incumbents of the state and the democratic opposition in society. The former have been differentiated by political strategy into hard-liners and soft-liners, and the latter primarily into party leaders and social movements (or sometimes strategically into moderate and maximalist opposition). With this identification of the actors, the class question is submerged, and the spotlight is put on the negotiations of individual leaders.

The regime change game could also take two different forms. The "ins" could play a restructuring game, by which they sought to change the capacity for collective action of social groups. Different approaches were adopted for systems of interest representation (those more corporative and those more atomized through the market) and for the limitation of contestation through the party system (by restricting the party system, particularly excluding the left). The restructuring game aimed at legitimation and institutionalization, but stopped short of democratization. The "outs" on the other hand could play a transformation game, which, unlike the restructuring game of the "ins," had an explicit goal of democracy.

If a problem with the framework for the historical cases is that it has privileged social classes over strategizing actors, a problem with the transitions perspective used for the recent cases is that it has done the opposite. It has privileged elites as strategic players — strategizing leaders, whose class identities are either left undifferentiated and defined instead on the basis of strategic posture, or, among the "outs" asserted to be "compromising moderates" who eschew class issues in favor of a willingness to reassure skittish incumbents. The overtly comparative or theoretical literature, where this analytic framework has been most explicitly articulated, has captured an important part of the dynamic of recent democratization, but it is not the whole picture. The more empirically based monographic accounts have emphasized the role of labor organizations, but this aspect of recent democratization has not been incorporated systematically into comparative or theoretical accounts.

If analyses of the historical cases have implicitly tended to overstate the degree to which the pre-reform regime was a restricted democracy, lacking only the inclusion of the lower classes, a drawback for present purposes of the transitions literature is that it has underemphasized the extent to which an autocratic regime that politically excludes almost all of civil society may nevertheless have a class coloration. The class content of these regimes comes as no surprise: from their installation they were — and were analyzed as – reactions to working-class mobilization and a Communist or Marxist threat associated with the working class. Yet this issue was not incorporated as a central concern in the dominant framework, which was useful for addressing certain questions but went too far in becoming hegemonized in the transitions literature.

TOWARD COMBINING FRAMEWORKS

At a general level, the two frameworks come from very different analytic traditions. The first continues a long tradition of class analysis that has its roots not only in Marxist analysis but also in historical sociology, particularly as inaugurated by Barrington Moore (1966). The second framework has emphasized strategic interaction and has not engaged structural issues or class analysis. Each has certain advantages but, like all frameworks, is necessarily partial. Each thus adds a useful perspective, and each benefits from the complementarity of the other.

Rueschemeyer et al., explicitly locating their analysis within the Moore tradition, contest his substantive assertion that associates democracy with the bourgeoisie. Yet they in turn are too quick to identify democratization with the working class and to reject it as a liberal project, which it sometimes was. Furthermore, it is important to keep structure (class balance) and agency analytically distinct. The structural argument is that the presence of a rising working class alters the strategic calculations of all actors. This is correct, but it does not necessarily imply working-class agency. Often a growing working class did champion democratic reforms. But equally important was the way it affected the strategies of other class actors and made *them* advocates of democratic reform. Sometimes the working class seemed to present a revolutionary threat, which they answered with a co-optive response. More important was the partisan challenge posed as rising social democratic parties changed the balance of power among parties, causing other parties to adopt coalitional strategies with the social democrats or to promote democratic reforms such as proportional representation systems. Thus, although democracy may be a class project, it is not necessarily the project of a single class. The opposition of democracy as a bourgeois versus a working-class project may be a false one: sometimes it is both.[11]

---

11 The pitfall of ignoring the strategy of other classes and viewing the working class as simply or unproblematically extracting concessions is made clear from the following contrast. Under some circumstances an organized, threatening, and socialist working class with a seeming possibility of forming at least the plurality political force led to

The advantage of this perspective is that it is helpful in framing the question regarding the way democratization should be analyzed in part as a class process; the disadvantage is that it marginalizes the strategic calculations of parties. Rueschemeyer et al. (1992:287), for instance, acknowledge the role of parties, but as "mediating mechanisms" – by which they mean class instruments – not as strategic actors themselves. With this (over)emphasis on class structure, there is, in a certain sense, too much sociology here – or, rather, too little political science. As suggested, this is particularly problematic in a context of an incremental process of democratization with a competitive political arena already in existence and defining a set of electoral rather than class-derived payoffs for parties, which are the main strategic actors in this arena. A strategic interaction approach of the type proffered in the transitions literature is useful here. Its disadvantage, in turn, is the mirror image: too little sociology. Actors are defined strategically – in terms of strategic posture, but without social content. In this framework there is a neglect of classes, and no attention is paid to the social construction of the transition as imbued with class meaning for the working class or, for that matter, other classes. For instance, studies of business pressure have not made their way into the theoretical literature on recent democratization in a sufficient or systematic way.[12] Yet, as the monographic literature makes clear, many class issues were being played out. With respect to the working class, the labor question was central in the origins and repressive practices of these authoritarian regimes, and therefore it was also relevant to their demise.

The present study suggests that it is useful to analyze democratization in at least three interrelated ways. First, it should be seen as a class-based process. This perspective is as appropriate in the recent cases as in the historical cases. A class-based perspective does not imply that in any given instance democratization is the project of a single class. Rather, various classes, pursuing class-based interests, can promote democratic change simultaneously. Among the historical cases, a pattern of multiple class origins was seen particularly among the Joint Projects, and this pattern is even more characteristic among the recent cases. That said, the role of labor organizations has been particularly neglected in the later cases. Yet

democratic strategies on the part of other classes (Joint Project democratization), whereas in others it led to anti-democratic strategies (bureaucratic-authoritarianism).

12 In addition to many other studies that have since appeared, it is interesting that the compendium to which the O'Donnell and Schmitter essay (1986) is the conclusion includes a chapter that analyzes the role of Brazilian entrepreneurs. (It contains no comparable chapter on the labor movement.) Yet class actors are not systematically incorporated into theoretical or comparative analysis in the transitions literature. More recent studies of the role of the private sector include Conaghan and Malloy 1994 and Bartell and Payne 1995.

working-class groups got involved *qua* working-class groups – through unions and labor-based parties, as groups with specifically working-class demands embedded within the larger fight for democracy.

Second, democratization is a politicostrategic process. Quite clear is the attempt of the "outs" to pursue access to power. Beyond that, the transitions literature has been particularly helpful in suggesting the political motivations of the "ins" as they embark on reform and the strategic interaction by which the they come to follow a path to democracy. Further analysis along these lines would be welcome for the historical cases, as the strategy of the "ins" is not simply a concession to the pressure of the "outs." Parties are the key strategic actors in democratization. The "ins" of the Support Mobilization pattern had their own incumbency-enhancing reasons for promoting reform, but so did those in the Joint Projects. These are the situations in which, beyond providing an incentive for co-optation, the presence of the union-affiliated parties changed the strategic situation of parties representing other classes and interests, and many "in" actors (parties with and without working-class constituencies) came to pursue democratic reform.

Third, and relatedly, democratization is a resource-based process that operates in different arenas of action. In the case histories presented here we have encountered the same factors emphasized by the social movements literature – resources such as historical memories, symbolic frames, organization, and power resources. These resources are embedded in historical experience and institutions. Among the historical cases, these factors were important for distinguishing the labor role in northern as opposed to Latin countries, as was the crucial resource of holding parliamentary seats.

The importance of similar kinds of resources is also suggested in the recent cases.[13] Labor unions were particularly well positioned with respect to a number of resources that have been identified: organization, discipline, a well-defined constituency, and mobilizational capacity. They were also often affiliated with parties that were themselves disciplined and well organized – sometimes with parties that had experience with underground activities. In addition, in the negotiating arena, these labor-based parties often had the resources to become crucial interlocutors for authoritarian incumbents and gained a place in the final regime negotiations.

Clearly all of these perspectives must come together to understand democratization. The politics of democratic innovation are both variable across cases and multidimensional within them. As such they are not easily captured by the prevailing frameworks. By their very nature, of course,

---

13 The transitions framework centrally recognizes this general point and, of course, models the labor movement and collective action more generally as a resource for negotiating leaders.

frameworks are particular perspectives that define certain factors or variables as central or peripheral to the analysis. In privileging some factors and ignoring or downplaying others, they are necessarily partial perspectives. Their appropriateness lies in their usefulness for illuminating a particular question or a particular aspect of social processes. From the point of view of inquiring about democratization as a project from above or below and the role of the labor organizations, it is useful to combine the frameworks that have been so prominent. Democratization must be analyzed as both a class and a strategic process, engaged in by those politically included as well as the excluded, acting in both deliberation/negotiation and mobilization/protest arenas.

This book has examined the role of the working class in the process of democratization in two historical epochs across two world regions. As a general rule, democracy has hardly been a "popular victory" in the sense that the lower classes were responsible for bringing it about. Rather, democratization is a multifaceted process with many actors and interests weighing in. In terms of political actors, democratization occurs as a result of the interests and initiatives of political "ins" as well as political "outs," and of upper as well as lower classes. In terms of processes, it involves negotiation, compromise, and the decisions of political leaders as well as collective protest. In the historical cases, for which the working-class hypothesis has been asserted most strongly in the literature, the present analysis demonstrates that elite strategies and upper-class interests or demands were often important. In the recent cases, for which scholarly attention has centered on elite strategies, the analysis shows that union-led protest and the participation, demands, and even a negotiating role of labor-based parties were more central than comparative or theoretical accounts have recognized, though, of course, as for the earlier cases their importance varied from country to country.

This analysis was originally motivated by an effort to understand the political position of the labor movement in the new democracies. These labor movements have been on the defensive in a way that most political analysts did not anticipate. Many analysts had initially hypothesized that unions would have the clout to prevent the new and fragile democracies from implementing marketizing reforms. Yet the record more often reveals the reverse – the incapacity of unions to block such economic reorientation and often to defend their interests through compensatory measures. The dominant framework employed for analyzing recent democratization suggested that the character of the new regimes is shaped by the mode of democratic transition, and it tended to understand these regime transitions primarily in terms of elite strategic games. The question thus arose: does labor's apparently marginal role in the politics of democratic transition explain the weak position of the working class in general and the union movement in particular in the new democracies?

Posing this question took me beyond the set of cases of my initial interest to the historical cases of the nineteenth and early twentieth centuries, which the literature has tended to treat quite differently – as cases where the working class was centrally involved in the process of democratization and where labor interests were generally better represented in the resulting regimes. The analysis of the larger set of cases suggests that the images in much of the literature about the role of the working class during both historical periods are overdrawn or misleading. Because, as a generalization, the labor role was not more salient in the earlier cases, its relatively marginal role in the process of democratic transition cannot explain the weak position of the labor movement in the new democracies. The comparison across historical epochs does not show that, in contrast to the earlier cases, recent democratic transitions were elite affairs with little labor participation. One cannot easily translate the politics of democratic transition into patterns of democratic governance or policy making.

The implication is that one must turn to larger political-economic factors for explanatory leverage. Having often been more active in the transition and more influential in creating space for labor-based parties in the new democracies than many have acknowledged, labor movements subsequently find themselves in a weak position as an outcome not so much of the mode of transition as of the way politics has unfolded under the subsequent democratic regimes. As many have noted, a democratic regime is one of uncertainty in partisan terms, in the sense of which parties will win. Beyond that, democratic regimes are indeterminate in the sense that despite their creation of a currency of majorities or pluralities, they do not determine which interests will be better represented – they do not determine how parties can construct winning coalitions or which social categories get politically aggregated or disaggregated; nor do they even ensure the policy-making salience of the currency of votes. Not democratic transition games but political economy becomes crucially important: the shift of preferences, resources, constraints, and opportunities that resulted from ongoing economic crisis, from the reordering of the world economy, and from the crisis of socialist and statist alternatives. These shifts fundamentally altered the balance of power among class actors. It is not that labor movements were such marginal actors in the politics of democratic transition, but rather that they were subsequently marginalized under the new democratic regimes. The political economy of democratic governance remains a central area of inquiry.

BIBLIOGRAPHY

Abós, Alvaro. 1984. *Las organizaciones sindicales y el poder militar, 1976–1983*. Buenos Aires: Centro Editor de América Latina.

Adler, Glenn, and Eddie Webster. 1995. "Challenging Transition Theory: The Labor Movement, Radical Reform, and Transition to Democracy in South Africa." *Politics and Society* 23, no. 1:75–106.

Alapuro, Risto. 1988. *State and Revolution in Finland*. Berkeley: University of California Press.

   ed. 1985. *Small States in Comparative Perspective: Essays for Erik Allardt*. Oslo: Norwegian University Press.

Allardt, Erik, et al., eds. 1981. *Nordic Democracy: Ideas, Issues, and Institutions in Politics, Economy, Education, Social and Cultural Affairs in Denmark, Finland, Iceland, Norway, and Sweden*. Copenhagen: Det Danske Selskab.

Alonso, Paula. 1996. "Voting in Buenos Aires (Argentina) before 1912." In *Elections before Democracy: The History of Elections in Europe and Latin America*, ed. Eduardo Posada-Carbó, 181–99. New York: St. Martin's Press.

Aminzade, Ronald. 1993. *Ballots and Barricades: Class Formation and Republican Politics in France, 1830–1871*. Princeton: Princeton University Press.

Amsden, Jon. 1972. *Collective Bargaining and Class Conflict in Spain*. London: London School of Economics and Political Science.

Anderson, K. B. 1958. "Political and Cultural Development in 19th Century Denmark." In *Scandinavian Democracy: Development of Democratic Thought and Institutions in Denmark, Norway and Sweden*, ed. J. A. Lauwyers, 150–59. Copenhagen: Danish Institute, Norwegian Office of Cultural Relations, and the Swedish Institute, in cooperation with the American Scandinavian Foundation.

Anderson, R. D. 1977. *France, 1870–1914: Politics and Society*. London: Routledge & Kegan Paul.

Andren, Nils. 1964. *Government and Politics in the Nordic Countries: Denmark, Finland, Iceland, Norway, Sweden*. Stockholm: Alqvist & Wiksell.

1981. "Five Roads to Parliamentary Democracy." In *Nordic Democracy: Ideas, Issues, and Institutions in Politics, Economy, Education, Social and Cultural Affairs in Denmark, Finland, Iceland, Norway, and Sweden*, ed. Erik Allardt et al., 44–52. Copenhagen: Det Danske Selskab.

Andreucci, Franco. 1990. "Italy." In Vol. 1 of *The Formation of Labour Movements, 1870–1914: An International Perspective*, ed. Marcel van der Linden and Jürgen Rojahn, 191–208. Leiden: E. J. Brill.

Angell, Alan. 1996. "International Support for the Chilean Opposition, 1973–1989: Political Parties and the Role of Exiles." In *The International Dimensions of Democratization: Europe and the Americas*, ed. Laurence Whitehead, 175–200. New York: Oxford University Press.

Arriagada Herrera, Genaro. 1986. "The Legal and Institutional Framework of the Armed Forces." In *Military Rule in Chile: Dictatorship and Oppositions,* ed. J. Samuel Valenzuela and Arturo Valenzuela, 118–24. Baltimore: Johns Hopkins University Press.

1991. *Pinochet: The Politics of Power*. Trans. Nancy Morris with Vincent Ercolano and Kristen A. Whitney. Boulder, Colo.: Westview Press.

Arter, David. 1987. *Politics and Policy-Making in Finland*. New York: St. Martin's Press.

Augustinos, Gerasimos. 1977. *Consciousness and History: Nationalist Critics of Greek Society, 1897–1914*. Boulder, Colo.: East European Quarterly.

Balfour, Sebastian. 1989. *Dictatorship, Workers, and the City: Labour in Greater Barcelona since 1939*. Oxford: Clarendon Press.

Baloyra, Enrique A. 1987. "Democratic Transition in Comparative Perspective." *Comparing New Democracies*, ed. Enrique A. Baloyra, 9–52. Boulder, Colo.: Westview Press.

Bandeira, Antonio Rangel. 1976. "The Portuguese Armed Forces Movement: Historical Antecedents, Professional Demands, and Class Conflict." *Politics and Society* 6, no. 1:1–56.

Barrán, José P., and Benjamín Nahum. 1982. *El nacimiento del batllismo*. Montevideo: Ediciones de la Banda Oriental.

Barrera, Manuel, and J. Samuel Valenzuela. 1986. "The Development of Labor Movement Opposition to the Military Regime." In *Military Rule in Chile: Dictatorship and Oppositions*, ed. J. Samuel Valenzuela and Arturo Valenzuela, 230–69. Baltimore: Johns Hopkins University Press.

Bartell, Ernest, and Leigh A. Payne, eds. 1995. *Business and Democracy in Latin America*. Pittsburgh: University of Pittsburgh Press.

Ben-Ami, Shlomo. 1978. *The Origins of the Second Republic in Spain*. Oxford: Oxford University Press.

Bendix, Reinhard. 1964. *Nation-Building and Citizenship*. New York: John Wiley and Sons.

Bermeo, Nancy. 1997. "Myths of Moderation: Confrontation and Conflict during Democratic Transitions," *Comparative Politics* 29, no. 3:305–22.

Bertelsen Repetto, Raúl. 1974. *El Senado en España*. Madrid: Instituto de Estudios Administrativos.

Biagini, Eugenio. 1992. *Liberty, Retrenchment and Reform: Popular Liberalism in the Age of Gladstone, 1860–1880*. Cambridge: Cambridge University Press.

1996. *Citizenship and Community: Liberals, Radicals and Collective Identities in the British Isles, 1865–1931*. Cambridge: Cambridge University Press.

Blackburn, Robert. 1995. *The Electoral System in Britain*. New York: St. Martin's Press.

Blake, Robert. 1967. *Disraeli*. New York: St. Martin's Press.

Blaustein, Albert P., and Jay A. Sigler. 1988. *Constitutions That Made History*. New York: Paragon House.

Blewett, Neal. 1965. "The Franchise in the United Kingdom 1885–1918." *Past and Present* 32:27–56.

Blok, Petrus Johannes. 1912. *History of the People of the Netherlands*. Part V: *Eighteenth and Nineteenth Centuries*. Trans. Oscar A. Bierstadt. New York: G. P. Putnam's Sons, Knickerbocker Press.

Bobbio, Norberto. 1984. *The Future of Democracy: A Defence of the Rules of the Game*. Minneapolis: University of Minnesota Press.

Bogdanor, Vernon, and David Butler, eds. 1983. *Democracy and Elections: Electoral Systems and Their Political Consequences*. Cambridge: Cambridge University Press.

Bonjour, E., H. S. Offler, and G. R. Potter. 1952. *A Short History of Switzerland*. Oxford: Oxford University Press.

Brand, Carl F. 1974. *The British Labour Party: A Short History*. Stanford, Calif.: Hoover Institution Press.

Buchanan, Paul. 1995. *State, Labor, Capital: Democratizing Class Relations in the Southern Cone*. Pittsburgh: University of Pittsburgh Press.

Buiting, Henry. 1989. *Richtingen – en partijstijd in de SDAP: Het ontstaan van de Sociaal-Democratische Partij in Nederland (SDP)*. Amsterdam: Stichting Beheer IISG.

      1990. "The Netherlands." In Vol. 1 of *The Formation of Labour Movements, 1870–1919: An International Perspective*, ed. Marcel van der Linden and Jürgen Rojahn, 57–84. Leiden: E. J. Brill.

Burks, R. V. 1961. *The Dynamics of Communism in Eastern Europe*. Princeton: Princeton University Press.

Burton, Michael, Richard Gunther, and John Higley. 1992a. "Elites and Democratic Consolidation in Latin America and Southern Europe: An Overview." In *Elites and Democratic Consolidation in Latin America and Southern Europe*, ed. John Higley and Richard Gunther, 323–48. Cambridge: Cambridge University Press.

      1992b. "Introduction." In *Elites and Democratic Consolidation in Latin America and Southern Europe*, ed. John Higley and Richard Gunther, 1–37. Cambridge: Cambridge University Press.

Butler, D. E. 1953. *The Electoral System in Britain, 1918–1951*. Oxford: Clarendon Press.

      1963. *The Electoral System in Britain, since 1918*. 2nd ed. Oxford: Clarendon Press.

Caetano, Gerardo. 1992. *La república conservador, 1916–1929*. Vol. 1. Montevideo: Editorial Fin de Siglo.

Caetano, Gerardo, and José Rilla. 1991. *Breve historia de la dictadura (1973–1985)*. Montevideo: CLAEH/Ediciones de la Banda Oriental.

Callesen, Gerd. 1990. "Denmark." In Vol. 1 of *The Formation of Labour Movements, 1870–1914: An International Perspective*, ed. Marcel van der Linden and Jürgen Rojahn, 131–62. Leiden: E. J. Brill.

Campbell, John, and Philip Sherrard. 1968. *Modern Greece*. New York: Praeger.

Campero, Guillermo, and José A. Valenzuela. 1984. *El movimiento sindical en el régimen militar Chileno, 1973–1981*. Santiago, Chile: ILET.

Carey, Jane Perry Clark, and Andrew Galbraith Carey. 1968. *The Web of Modern Greek Politics*. New York: Columbia University Press.

Carnero Arbat, Teresa. 1997. "Democratización limitada y deterioro político en España, 1874–1930." In *Democracia, elecciones y modernización en Europa*, ed. Salvador Forner, 203–40. Madrid: Ediciones Cátedra.

Carr, Raymond. 1980. *Modern Spain, 1875–1980*. Oxford: Oxford University Press.

———. 1987. "Introduction: The Spanish Transition to Democracy in Historical Perspective." In *Spain in the 1980s: The Democratic Transition and a New International Role*, ed. Robert P. Clark and Michael H. Haltzel, 1–14. Cambrige, Mass.: Ballinger.

Carr, Raymond, and Juan Pablo Fusi Aizpurua. 1979. *Spain: Dictatorship to Democracy*. London: George Allen & Unwin.

Carstairs, Andrew McLaren. 1980. *A Short History of Electoral Systems in Western Europe*. London: George Allen & Unwin.

Carton de Wiart, Henry. 1948. *Souvenirs politiques*. Vol. 1: *1878–1918*. Bruges: Desclee, de Brouwer.

Castillo, Santiago. 1990. "Spain." In Vol. 1 of *The Formation of Labour Movements, 1870–1914: An International Perspective*, ed. Marcel van der Linden and Jürgen Rojahn, 209–42. Leiden: E. J. Brill.

Cavarozzi, Marcelo. 1992. "Patterns of Elite Negotiation and Confrontation in Argentina and Chile." In *Elites and Democratic Consolidation*, ed. John Higley and Richard Gunther, 208–36. Cambridge: Cambridge University Press.

Chagas, Jorge, and Mario Tonarelli. 1989. *El sindicalismo uruguayo bajo la dictadura, 1973–1984*. Montevideo: Ediciones del Nuevo Mundo.

Chile, Oficina Central de Estadística en Santiago. 1875, 1885, 1920, and 1930. *Censo Jeneral de la Población de Chile*, Valparaiso: Imprenta de "La Patria."

Christensen, Jens. 1983. *Rural Denmark, 1750–1980*. Trans. Else Buchwald Christensen. Copenhagen: Central Co-operative Committee of Denmark.

Christiansen, Niels Finn. 1988. "The Role of Labor Movement in the Process of Democratisation in Denmark, 1848–1901." In *Democratisation in Scandinavia in Comparison*, ed. Bo Strath, 12–20. Gothenburg: Gothenburg University.

Clark, G. Kitson. 1965. *The Making of Victorian England*. London: Methuen.

Clark, Robert P., and Michael H. Haltzel, eds. 1987. *Spain in the 1980s: The Democratic Transition and a New International Role*. Cambridge, Mass.: Ballinger.

Clegg, Hugh Armstrong. 1985. *A History of British Trade Unions since 1889*. Vol. 2: *1911–1933*. Oxford: Clarendon Press.

Clogg, Richard. 1986. *A Short History of Greece*. 2nd ed. Cambridge: Cambridge University Press.

1992. *A Concise History of Greece*. Cambridge: Cambridge University Press.

Cole, G. D. H. 1941. *British Working-Class Politics, 1832–1914*. London: George Routledge & Sons.

1948. *A Short History of the British Working-Class Movement, 1789–1947*. London: George Allen & Unwin.

Collier, David, and Steven Levitsky. 1997. "Democracy with Adjectives: Conceptual Innovation in Comparative Research." *World Politics* 49, no. 3:430–51.

Collier, Ruth Berins. 1999. "The Transformation of Labor-Based One-Partyism at the End of the 20th Century: The Case of Mexico." In *The Awkward Embrace: One-Party Domination and Democracy*, ed. Hermann Giliomee and Charles Simkins. 219–44. London: Harwood.

Collier, Ruth Berins, and David Collier. 1991. *Shaping the Political Arena*. Princeton: Princeton University Press.

Collier, Ruth Berins, and James Mahoney. 1997. "Adding Collective Actors to Collective Outcomes: Labor and Recent Democratization in South America and Southern Europe." *Comparative Politics* 29, no. 3:285–303.

Colombo, Ariel, and V. Palermo. 1985. *Participación política y pluralismo en la Argentina contemporánea*. Buenos Aires: Centro Editor de América Latina.

Conaghan, Catherine M. 1987. "Party Politics and Democratization in Ecuador." In *Authoritarians and Democrats: Regime Transition in Latin America*, ed. James M. Malloy and Mitchell A. Seligson, 145–63. Pittsburgh: University of Pittsburgh Press.

1992. "Capitalists, Technocrats, and Politicians: Economic Policy Making and Democracy in the Central Andes." In *Issues in Democratic Consolidation: The New South American Democracies in Comparative Perspective*, ed. Scott Mainwaring, Guillermo O'Donnell, and J. Samuel Valenzuela, 199–242. Notre Dame, Ind.: University of Notre Dame Press.

Conaghan, Catherine M., and Rosario Espinal. 1990. "Unlikely Transitions to Uncertain Regimes? Democracy without Compromise in the Dominican Republic and Ecuador." *Journal of Latin American Studies* 22:553–74.

Conaghan, Catherine M., and James M. Malloy. 1994. *Unsettling Statecraft: Democracy and Neoliberalism in the Central Andes*. Pittsburgh: Univeristy of Pittsburgh Press.

Corkill, David, and David Cubitt. 1988. *Ecuador: Fragile Democracy*. London: Latin America Bureau.

Costa Bonino, Luis. 1995. *La crisis del sistema político uruguayo*. Montevideo: Fundación de Cultura Universitaria.

Cotler, Julio. 1986. "Military Interventions and 'Transfer of Power to Civilians' in Peru." In *Transitions from Authoritarian Rule: Latin America*, ed. Guillermo O'Donnell, Philippe C. Schmitter, and Laurence Whitehead, 148–72. Baltimore: Johns Hopkins University Press.

Cowling, Maurice. 1967. *Disraeli, Gladstone and Revolution: The Passing of the Second Reform Bill*. Cambridge: Cambridge University Press.

Craig, Gordon. 1978. *Germany, 1866–1945*. New York: Oxford University Press.

1988. *The Triumph of Liberalism: Zurich in the Golden Age, 1830–1869*. New York: Scribner.

Cronin, James E. 1989. "Strikes and Power in Britain, 1870–1920." In *Strikes, Wars and Revolutions in an International Perspective: Strike Waves in the Late*

Nineteenth and Early Twentieth Centuries, ed. Leopold H. Haimson and Charles Tilly, 79–100. Cambridge: Cambridge University Press.

Cuadrado, Miguel M. 1969. *Elecciones y partidos políticos de España (1868–1931)*. Madrid: Taurus Ediciones.

Cudell, Guy. 1960. *Histoire du mouvement ouvrier belge*. Brussels: Service d'edition de la Federation Nationale des Jeunes Gardes Socialistes.

Daalder, Hans. 1987. *Party Systems in Denmark, Austria, Switzerland, the Netherlands, and Belgium*. New York: St. Martin's Press.

Dahl, Robert. 1971. *Polyarchy: Participation and Opposition*. New Haven: Yale University Press.

Dändliker, Karl. 1899. *A Short History of Switzerland*. New York: Macmillan Company.

Danopoulis, Constantine P. 1989. "Democratic Undercurrents in Praetorian Regimes: The Greek Military and the 1973 Plebiscite." *Journal of Strategic Studies* 12, no. 3:349–68.

Derry, T. K. 1973. *A History of Modern Norway, 1814–1972*. Oxford: Clarendon Press.

De Schryver, Reginald. 1981. "The Belgian Revolution and the Emergence of G's Biculturalism." In *Conflict and Coexistence in Belgium: The Dynamics of a Culturally Divided Society*, ed. Arend Lijphart, 13–33. Institute of International Studies, Research Series no. 46. Berkeley: University of California.

de Schweinitz, Karl. 1964. *Industrialization and Democracy: Economic Necessities and Political Possibilities*. New York: Free Press.

De Sierra, Gerónimo. 1992. *El Uruguay post-dictadura: Estado-política-actores*. Montevideo: Facultad de Ciencias Sociales, Universidad de la República.

Devreese, Daisy E. 1990. "Belgium." In Vol. 1 of *The Formation of Labour Movements, 1870–1914: An International Perspective*, ed. Marcel van der Linden and Jürgen Rojahn, 25–56. Leiden: E. J. Brill.

Diamandouros, P. Nikiforos. 1983. "Greek Political Culture in Transition: Historical Origins, Evolution, Current Trends." In *Greece in the 1980s*, ed. Richard Clogg, 43–70. London: Macmillan.

———. 1986. "Regime Change and the Prospects for Democracy in Greece: 1974–1983." In *Transitions from Authoritarian Rule: Southern Europe*, ed. Guillermo O'Donnell, Philippe C. Schmitter, and Laurence Whitehead, 138–64. Baltimore: Johns Hopkins University Press.

Dietz, Henry. 1992. "Elites in an Unconsolidated Democracy: Peru during the 1980s." In *Elites and Democratic Consolidation*, ed. John Higley and Richard Gunther, 237–81. Cambridge: Cambridge University Press.

Di Palma, Giuseppe. 1990. *To Craft Democracies: An Essay on Democratic Transitions*. Berkeley: University of California Press.

Downs, Charles. 1989. *Revolution at the Grassroots: Community Organizations in the Portuguese Revolution*. Albany: State University of New York Press.

Drake, Paul W. 1996. *Labor Movements and Dictatorships: The Southern Cone in Comparative Perspective*. Baltimore: Johns Hopkins University Press.

Drake, Paul W., and Ivan Jaksic. 1991. "Introduction: Transformation and Transition in Chile, 1982–1990." In *The Struggle for Democracy in Chile, 1982–*

1990, ed. Paul W. Drake and Ivan Jaksic, 1–20. Lincoln: University of Nebraska Press.

Dunkerley, James. 1984. *Rebellion in the Veins: Political Struggle in Bolivia, 1952– 1982*. London: Verso.

Dybdahl, Vagn. 1969. "Summary and Conclusions." In Vol. 2 of *Partier og Erhverv: Studier i Partiorganisation og Byerhvervenes Politiske Aktivitet ca. 1880–ca. 1913*, 5–27. Udgivet af Erhvervsarkivet: Universitersforlaaget i Aarhus.

Elster, Jon. 1996. "The Constitution-Making Process." In *Current Issues in Public Choice*, ed. José Cases Pardo and Friedrich Schneider, 93–114. Brookfield, Vt.: Edward Elgar.

Elwitt, Sanford. 1975. *The Making of the Third Republic: Class and Politics in France, 1866–1884*. Baton Rouge: Louisiana State University Press.

Epstein, Edward C. 1989. "Labor Populism and Hegemonic Crisis in Argentina." In *Labor Autonomy and the State in Latin America*, ed. Edward C. Epstein, 13–38. Boston: Unwin Hyman.

Ertman, Thomas. 1998. "Parties, Nationbuilding and Democratization in Western Europe from the French Revolution to the Second World War." Cambridge, Mass. Unpublished manuscript.

Fahrni, Dieter. 1987. *An Outline History of Switzerland*. Zurich: Pro Helvetia.

Falabella, Gonazalo. 1990. "La diversidad en el movimiento sindical chileno bajo el régimen militar." In *Sindicatos bajo regímenes militares: Argentina, Brasil, Chile*, ed. Manuel Barrera and Gonzalo Falabella, 223–81. Santiago: CES.

Falabella, Gonzalo, and Guillermo Campero. 1991. "Los sindicatos en la transición a la democrácia chilena." In Vol. 1 of *El sindicalismo latinoamericano en los 90*, ed. Guillermo Campero and Alberto Cuevas, 133–64. Santiago: CLACSO/Planeta.

Farelo Lopes, Fernando. 1994. *Poder política e caciquismo na primeira república portuguesa*. Lisbon: Editorial Estampa.

Feldman, Gerald. 1966. *Army, Industry, and Labor in Germany, 1914–1918*. Princeton: Princeton University Press.

Fernández, Arturo. 1985. *Las prácticas sociales del sindicalismo, 1976–1982*. Buenos Aires: Centro Editor de América Latina.

Finn, Margot C. 1993. *After Chartism: Class and Nation in English Radical Politics, 1848–1874*. Cambridge: Cambridge University Press.

Fishman, Robert M. 1990a. *Working-Class Organization and the Return to Democracy in Spain*. Ithaca, N.Y.: Cornell University Press.

1990b. "State and Regime: Southern Europe's Transition to Democracy." *World Politics* 42, no. 3:422–40.

Fitzmaurice, John. 1981. *Politics in Denmark*. London: C. Hurst.

Flora, Peter, et al. 1983. *State, Economy, and Society in Western Europe, 1815–1975: A Data Handbook in Two Volumes*. Chicago: St. James Press.

Fontana, Andres. 1984. *Fuerzas armadas, partidos políticos y transición a la democrácia en Argentina*. Buenos Aires: Estudios CEDES.

Foweraker, Joe. 1987. "The Role of Labor Organizations in the Transition to Democracy in Spain." In *Spain in the 1980s: The Democratic Transition and a New International Role*, ed. Robert P. Clark and Michael H. Haltzel, 97– 122. Cambridge, Mass.: Ballinger.

1989. *Making Democracy in Spain: Grass-roots Struggle in the South, 1955–1975.* Cambridge: Cambridge University Press.

1994. "Popular Political Organization and Democratization: A Comparison of Spain and Mexico." In *Developing Democracy*, ed. Ian Budge and David McKay, 218–31. London: Sage Publications.

Foweraker, Joe, and Todd Landman. 1997. *Citizenship Rights and Social Movements: A Comparative and Statistical Analysis.* Oxford: Oxford Univesity Press.

Fox, Alan. 1985. *History and Heritage.* London: George Allen & Unwin.

Friedman, David. 1943. "Political Parties." In *The Netherlands*, ed. Bartholomew Landheer, 107–31. Berkeley: University of California Press.

Fulbrook, Mary. 1990. *A Concise History of Germany.* Cambridge: Cambridge University Press.

1992. *The Divided Nation: A History of Germany, 1918–1990.* New York: Oxford University Press.

Galdames, Luis. 1941. *A History of Chile.* Trans. and ed. Isaac Joslin Cox. Chapel Hill: University of North Carolina Press.

Gallagher, Tom. 1983. "From Hegemony to Opposition: The Ultra Right before and after 1974." In *In Search of Modern Portugal: The Revolution and Its Consequences*, ed. Lawrence S. Graham and Douglas L. Wheeler, 81–104. Madison: University of Wisconsin Press.

Gargiulo, Martin. 1989. "The Uruguayan Labor Movement in the Post-Authoritarian Period." In *Labor Autonomy and the State in Latin America*, ed. Edward C. Epstein, 219–46. Boston: Unwin Hyman.

Garretón, Manuel Antonio. 1989a. *The Chilean Political Process.* Trans. Sharon Kellum in collaboration with Gilbert W. Merkx. Boston: Unwin Hyman.

1989b. "Popular Mobilization and the Military Regime in Chile: The Complexities of the Invisible Transition." In *Power and Popular Protest*, ed. Susan Eckstein, 259–77. Berkeley: University of California Press.

Gerard-Libois, Jules, and Xavier Mabille. 1981. "Belgian Electoral Politics." In *Conflict and Coexistence in Belgium: The Dynamics of a Culturally Divided Society*, ed. Arend Lijphart, 127–38. Institute of International Studies, Research Series no. 46. Berkeley: University of California.

Gillard, Charles. 1955. *A History of Switzerland.* Trans. D. L. B. Hartley. London: George Allen & Unwin.

Gillespie, Charles Guy. 1991. *Negotiating Democracy: Politicians and Generals in Uruguay.* Cambridge: Cambridge University Press.

Gillespie, Richard. 1989. *The Spanish Socialist Party: A History of Factionalism.* Oxford: Clarendon Press.

Gilmour, David. 1985. *The Transformation of Spain.* London: Quartet Books.

Gitermann, Valentin. 1941. *Geschichte der Schweiz.* Thayngen-Schaffhausen: Augustin-Verlag.

Gómez, Xavier Tusell. 1976. "The Functioning of the Cacique System in Andalusia, 1890–1931." In *Politics and Society in Twentieth-Century Spain*, ed. Stanley G. Payne, 1–28. New York: New Viewpoints.

González, Luis E. 1991. *Political Structures and Democracy in Uruguay.* Notre Dame, Ind.: University of Notre Dame Press.

Gould, Andrew C. Forthcoming. *Origins of Liberal Dominance: State, Church, and*

Party in Nineteenth Century Europe. Ann Arbor: University of Michigan Press.

Graham, Carol. 1992. *Peru's APRA: Parties, Politics, and the Elusive Quest for Democracy*. Boulder, Colo.: Lynne Rienner.

Graham, Lawrence S. 1993. *The Portuguese Military and the State: Rethinking Transitions in Europe and Latin America*. Boulder, Colo.: Westview Press.

Greece. 1971. *Statistical Yearbook of Greece*. Athens: National Statistical Service.

Greenfield, Gerald Michael, and Sheldon L. Maram. 1987. *Latin American Labor Organizations*. New York: Greenwood Press.

Gunther, Richard. 1987. "Democratization and Party Building: The Role of Party Elites in the Spanish Transition." In *Spain in the 1980s: The Democratic Transition and a New International Role*, ed. Robert P. Clark and Michael H. Haltzel, 35–66. Cambridge, Mass.: Ballinger.

——— 1992. "Spain: The Very Model of the Modern Elite Settlement." In *Elites and Democratic Consolidation in Latin America and Southern Europe*, ed. John Higley and Richard Gunther, 1–37. Cambridge: Cambridge University Press.

Gunther, Richard, P. Nikiforos Diamandouros, and Hans-Jürgen Puhle, eds. 1995. *The Politics of Democratic Consolidation: Southern Europe in Comparative Perspective*. Baltimore: Johns Hopkins University Press.

Guttsman, W. L. 1981. *The German Social Democratic Party, 1875–1933*. London: George Allen & Unwin.

Hand, Geoffrey, Jacques Georgel, and Christoph Sasse, eds. 1979. *European Electoral Systems Handbook*. London: Butterworths.

Harrison, Royden. 1965. *Before the Socialists: Studies in Labour and Politics, 1861–1881*. London: Routledge & Kegan Paul.

Harsgor, Michael. 1976. *Portugal in Revolution*. The Washington Papers 3, no. 32. Beverly Hills: Sage Publications.

Hartung, Frits. 1950. *Deutsche Verfassungsgeschichte: Vom 15. Jahrhundert bis zur Gegenwart 5*. Stuttgart: Auflage, K. F. Koehler Verlag.

Haworth, Nigel. 1983. "The Peruvian Working Class, 1968–1979." In *Military Reformism and Social Classes: The Peruvian Experience, 1968–1980*, ed. David Booth and Bernardo Sorj, 94–116. London: Macmillan.

——— 1989. "Political Transition and the Peruvian Labor Movement." In *Labor Autonomy and the State in Latin America*, ed. Edward C. Epstein, 195–218. Boston: Unwin Hyman.

Held, David. 1996. *Models of Democracy*. Stanford, Calif,: Stanford University Press.

Hermet, Guy. 1978. "State-Controlled Elections: A Framework." In *Elections without Choice*, ed. Guy Hermet, Richard Rose, and Alain Rouquié, 1–18. New York: John Wiley.

Higley, John, and Richard Gunther, eds. 1992. *Elites and Democratic Consolidation in Latin America and Southern Europe*. Cambridge: Cambridge University Press.

Himmelfarb, Gertrude. 1966. "The Politics of Democracy: The English Reform Act of 1867." *Journal of British Studies* 6, no. 1:97–138.

Hindess, Barry. 1980. "Marxism and Parliamentary Democracy." In *Marxism and Democracy*, ed. Alan Hunt, 21–54. Atlantic Highlands, N.J.: Humanities Press.

Hinton, James. 1983. *Labour and Socialism: A History of the British Labour Movement, 1867–1974*. Amherst, Mass.: University of Massachussetts Press.

Hovde, B. J. 1943. *The Scandinavian Countries, 1720–1865: The Rise of the Middle Classes*. Vol. 2. Boston: Chapman and Grimes.

Huard, Raymond. 1991. *Le suffrage universel en France, 1848–1946*. Paris: Aubier.

Humphrey, A. W. 1912. *A History of Labour Representation*. London: Constable and Company.

Hunt, Alan. 1980. "Introduction: Taking Democracy Seriously," in *Marxism and Democracy*, ed. Alan Hunt, 7–19. Atlantic Highlands, N.J.: Humanities Press.

Hunt, Christ. 1976. *Portuguese Revolution, 1974–1976*. Ed. Lester A. Sobel. New York: Facts On File.

Hunt, E. H. 1981. *British Labour History, 1815–1914*. Atlantic Highlands, N.J.: Humanities Press.

Huntington, Samuel P. 1968. *Political Order in Changing Societies*. New Haven: Yale University Press.

———. 1991. *The Third Wave: Democratization in the Late Twentieth Century*. Norman: University of Oklahoma Press.

Huyse, Luc. 1981. "Political Conflict in Bicultural Belgium." In *Conflict and Coexistence in Belgium: The Dynamics of a Culturally Divided Society*, ed. Arend Lijphart, 107–26. Institute of International Studies, Research Series no. 46. Berkeley: University of California.

Ifantis, Konstantinos. 1995. "From Factionalism to Autocracy: PASOK's De-Radicalization during the Regime Transition of the 1970s." In *Factional Politics and Democratization*, ed. R. Gillespie, M. Waller, and L. Nieto, 77–89. London: Frank Cass.

ILO. 1990. *Year Book of Labour Statistics: Retrospective Edition on Population Censuses*. Geneva: ILO.

Isaacs, Anita. 1993. *Military Rule and Transition in Ecuador, 1972–92*. Pittsburgh: University of Pittsburgh Press.

Jessop, Bob. 1978. "Capitalism and Democracy: The Best Possible Political Shell?" In *Power and the State*, ed. Gary Littlejohn et al., 10–51. New York: St. Martin's Press.

———. 1980. "The Political Indeterminacy of Democracy." In *Marxism and Democracy*, ed. Alan Hunt, 55–80. Atlantic Highlands, N.J.: Humanities Press.

Jones, Andrew. 1972. *The Politics of Reform, 1884*. Cambridge: Cambridge University Press.

Jones, W. Glyn. 1986. *Denmark: A Modern History*. London: Croom Helm.

Jost, Hans Ulrich. 1990. "Switzerland." In Vol. 1 of *The Formation of Labor Movements, 1870–1914: An International Perspective*, ed. Marcel van der Linden and Jürgen Rojahn, 271–92. Leiden: E. J. Brill.

Judge, David. 1984. "Why Reform? Parliamentary Reform since 1832: An Interpretation." In *The Politics of Parliamentary Reform*, ed. David Judge, 9–36. Rutherford, N.J.: Fairleigh Dickinson University Press.

Karl, Terry Lynn. 1990. "Dilemmas of Democratization in Latin America." *Comparative Politics* 23, no. 1:1–21.

Karl, Terry Lynn, and Philippe Schmitter. 1991. "Modes of Transition in Latin America, Southern and Eastern Europe." *International Social Science Journal* no. 128:269–84.

Katsanevas, Theodore K. 1984. *Trade Unions in Greece*. Athens: National Center of Social Research.

Katznelson, Ira. 1986. "Working-Class Formation: Constructing Cases and Comparisons." In *Working-Class Formation: Nineteenth-Century Patterns in Western Europe and the United States*, ed. Ira Katznelson and Aristide R. Zolberg, 3–44. Princeton: Princeton University Press.

Katznelson, Ira, and Aristide R. Zolberg, eds. 1986. *Working-Class Formation: Nineteenth-Century Patterns in Western Europe and the United States*. Princeton: Princeton University Press.

Keck, Margaret E. 1989. *The Workers' Party and Democratization in Brazil*. New Haven: Yale University Press.

KEPE (Center of Planning and Economic Research). 1976. *Report on Human Resources*. Athens: KEPE.

Kern, Robert W. 1974. *Liberals, Reformers and Caciques in Restoration Spain, 1875–1909*. Albuquerque: University of New Mexico Press.

Kirby, David. 1990. "Finland." In Vol. 2 of *The Formation of Labour Movements, 1870–1914: An International Perspective*, ed. Marcel van der Linden and Jürgen Rojahn, 523–42. New York: E. J. Brill.

Kocka, Jürgen. 1986. "Problems of Working-Class Formation in Germany: The Early Years, 1800–1875." In *Working-Class Formation: Nineteenth-Century Patterns in Western Europe and the United States*, ed. Ira Katznelson and Aristide R. Zolberg, 279–351. Princeton: Princeton University Press.

Kohn, Hans. 1956. *Nationalism and Liberty: The Swiss Example*. London: George Allen & Unwin.

Korpi, Walter. 1981. "Labor Movements and Industrial Relations." In *Nordic Democracy: Ideas, Issues, and Institutions in Politics, Economy, Education, Social and Cultural Affairs of Denmark, Finland, Iceland, Norway, and Sweden*, ed. Erik Allardt et al., 308–23. Copenhagen: Det Danske Selskab.

Kucinski, Bernardo. 1982. *Abertura: Historia de Uma Crise*. São Paulo: Brasil Debates.

Ladman, Jerry. 1982. "The Failure to Redemocratize." In *Modern-Day Bolivia: Legacy of the Revolution and Prospects for the Future*, ed. J. Ladman, 345–70. Tempe: Center for Latin American Studies, Arizona State University.

Landauer, Carl. 1959. *European Socialism: A History of Ideas and Movements*. Vol. 1. Berkeley: University of California Press.

Lazarte, Jorge. 1989. *Movimiento obrero y procesos políticos en Bolivia. Historia de la C.O.B. 1952–1987*. La Paz: ILDIS.

Lee, Stephen J. 1994. *Aspects of British Political History, 1815–1914*. London: Routledge.

Legg, Keith R. 1969. *Politics in Modern Greece*. Stanford, Calif.: Stanford University Press.

Lijphart, Arend. 1975. *The Politics of Accommodation: Pluralism and Democracy in the Netherlands*. Berkeley: University of California Press.

——— ed. 1981. *Conflict and Coexistence in Belgium: The Dynamics of a Culturally Divided Society*. Institute of International Studies, Research Series no. 46. Berkeley: University of California.

Linden, Herman Vander. 1920. *Belgium: The Making of a Nation*. Trans. Sybil Jane. Oxford: Clarendon Press.

Linden, Marcel van der, and Jürgen Rojahn, eds. 1990. *The Formation of Labour*

Movements, 1870–1914: An International Perspective. 2 vols. Leiden: E. J. Brill.

Linz, Juan J. 1978. *Crisis, Breakdown and Reequilibration.* Vol. 1 of *The Breakdown of Democratic Regimes: Latin America,* ed. Juan J. Linz and Alfred Stepan, 3–124. Baltimore: Johns Hopkins University Press.

———. 1981. "Some Comparative Thoughts on the Transition to Democracy in Portugal and Spain." In *Portugal since the Revolution: Economic and Political Perspectives,* ed. Jorge Braga de Macedo and Simon Serfaty, 25–46. Boulder, Colo.: Westview Press.

Linz, Juan J., and Alfred Stepan. 1996. *Problems of Democratic Transition and Consolidation: Southern Europe, South America and Post-Communist Europe.* Baltimore: Johns Hopkins University Press.

Linz, Juan J., Alfred Stepan, and Richard Gunther. 1995. "Democratic Transition and Consolidation in Southern Europe, with Reflections on Latin America and Eastern Europe." In *The Politics of Democratic Consolidation: Southern Europe in Comparative Perspective,* ed. Richard Gunther, P. Nikiforos Diamandouros, and Hans-Jürgen Puhle, 77–123. Baltimore: Johns Hopkins University Press.

Livermore, H. V. 1976. *A New History of Portugal.* 2nd ed. Cambridge: Cambridge University Press.

Logan, John R. 1983. "Worker Mobilization and Party Politics: Revolutionary Portugal in Perspective." In *In Search of Modern Portugal: The Revolution and Its Consequences,* ed. Lawrence S. Graham and Douglas L. Wheeler, 135–48. Madison: University of Wisconsin Press.

Lomax, Bill. 1983. "Ideology and Illusion in the Portuguese Revolution: The Role of the Left." In *In Search of Modern Portugal: The Revolution and Its Consequences,* ed. Lawrence S. Graham and Douglas L. Wheeler, 105–34. Madison: University of Wisconsin Press.

Longley, Lawrence D., and David M. Olson, eds. 1991. *Two into One: The Politics and Processes of National Legislative Cameral Change.* Boulder, Colo.: Westview Press.

Lowden, Pamela. 1996. *Moral Opposition to Authoritarian Rule in Chile, 1973–1990.* New York: St. Martin's Press.

Lowenthal, Abraham F. 1975. *The Peruvian Experiment.* Princeton: Princeton University Press.

Luebbert, Gregory M. 1991. *Liberalism, Fascism, or Social Democracy: Social Classes and the Political Origins of Regimes in Interwar Europe.* New York: Oxford University Press.

Mabille, Xavier. 1986. *Histoire politique de la Belgique.* Brussels: CRISP.

Mackie, Thomas, and Richard Rose. 1991. *The International Almanac of Electoral History.* 3rd ed. Washington, D.C.: Congressional Quarterly.

Maddison, Angus. 1989. *The World Economy in the 20th Century.* Paris: Development Centre of the Organisation for Economic Co-operation and Development.

———. 1995. *Monitoring the World Economy.* Paris: Development Centre of the Organisation for Economic Co-operation and Development.

Mainwaring, Scott, Guillermo O'Donnell, and J. Samuel Valenzuela, eds. 1992. *Issues in Democratic Consolidation: The New South American Democracies in Comparative Perspective.* Notre Dame, Ind.: University of Notre Dame Press.

Malloy, James M., and Eduardo Gamarra. 1987. "The Transition to Democracy in Bolivia." In *Authoritarians and Democrats: Regime Transition in Latin America*, ed. James M. Malloy and Mitchell A. Seligson, 93–120. Pittsburgh: University of Pittsburgh Press.

Malloy, James M., and Mitchell A. Seligson, eds. 1987. *Authoritarians and Democrats: Regime Transition in Latin America*. Pittsburgh: University of Pittsburgh Press.

Mann, Michael. 1993. *The Rise of Classes and Nation-States, 1760–1914*. Vol. 2: *The Sources of Social Power*. Cambridge: Cambridge University Press.

——— 1995. "Sources of Variation in Working-Class Movements in Twentieth Century Europe." *New Left Review* 212: 14–54.

Maravall, José. 1978. *Dictatorship and Dissent*. London: Tavistock Publications.

——— 1982. *The Transition to Democracy in Spain*. London: Croom Helm.

Markoff, John. 1995. *The Great Wave of Democracy in Historical Perspective*. Western Studies Occasional Paper no. 34. Ithaca, N.Y.: Cornell University.

——— 1996. *Waves of Democracy: Social Movements and Political Change*. Thousand Oaks, Calif.: Pine Forge Press.

——— 1997. "Really Existing Democracy: Learning from Latin America in the Late 1990s." *New Left Review* 223:48–68.

Marques, A. H. de Oliveira. 1970. *A primeira república portuguesa*. Lisbon: Livros Horizonte.

——— 1972. Vol. 2: *History of Portugal. From Empire to Corporate State*. New York: Columbia University Press.

Martín Najera, Aurelio. 1991. *Fuentes para la historia del Partido Socialista Obrero Español y de las Juventudes Socialistas de España*. Madrid: Editorial Pablo Iglesias.

Martz, John D. 1980. "The Quest for Popular Democracy in Ecuador," *Current History* 78, no. 454:66–70.

Matheson, David K. 1979. *Ideology, Political Action and the Finnish Working Class: A Survey Study of Political Behavior*. Helsinki: Societas Scientiarum Fennica.

Matthew, H. C. G., R. I. McKibbin, and J. A. Key. 1976. "The Franchise Factor in the Rise of the Labour Party." *English Historical Review* 91, no. 361: 723–52.

Maxwell, Kenneth. 1986. "Regime Overthrow and the Prospects for Democratic Transition in Portugal." In *Transitions from Authoritarian Rule: Southern Europe*, ed. Guillermo O'Donnell, Philippe C. Schmitter, and Laurence Whitehead, 109–37. Baltimore: Johns Hopkins University Press.

——— 1995. *The Making of Portuguese Democracy*. Cambridge: Cambridge University Press.

Mayorga, René Antonio. 1990. "¿Bolivia: Democrácia como Gobernabilidad?" In *Estrategias para el desarrollo de la democrácia en Perú y América Latina*, ed. Julio Cotler, 159–94. Lima: Instituto de Estudios Peruanos.

McClintock, Cynthia. 1989. "Peru: Precarious Regimes, Authoritarian and Democratic." In *Democracy in Developing Countries: Latin America*, ed. Larry Diamond, Juan Linz, and Seymour Martin Lipset, 335–85. Boulder, Colo.: Lynne Rienner.

McClintock, Cynthia, and Abraham F. Lowenthal, eds. 1981. *The Peruvian Experience Reconsidered*. Princeton: Princeton University Press.

McCrackan, W. D. 1901. *The Rise of the Swiss Republic*. New York: Henry Holt.

McGuire, James W. 1995. "Interim Government and Democratic Consolidation: Argentina in Comparative Perspective." In *Between States: Interim Governments and Transitions to Democracy*, ed. Yossi Shain and Juan Linz, 179–210. Cambridge: Cambridge University Press.

McKibbin, Ross. 1974. *The Evolution of the Labour Party, 1910–1924*. Oxford: Oxford University Press.

Meaker, Gerald H. 1974. *The Revolutionary Left In Spain, 1914–1923*. Stanford, Calif.: Stanford University Press.

———. 1976. "Anarchists versus Syndicalists: Conflict within the Confederación Nacional del Trabajo, 1917–1923." In *Politics and Society in Twentieth-Century Spain*, ed. Stanley G. Payne, 29–72. New York: New Viewpoints.

Medhurst, Kenneth. 1984. "Spain's Evolutionary Pathway from Dictatorship to Democracy." In *The New Mediterranean Democracies: Regime Transition in Spain, Greece, and Portugal*, ed. Geoffrey Pridham, 30–49. Totowa, N.J.: Frank Cass.

Metcalf, Michael F., ed. 1987. *The Riksdag: A History of the Swedish Parliament*. New York: St. Martin's Press.

Middlemas, Keith. 1979. *Politics of Industrial Society: The Experience of the British System since 1911*. London: Andre Deutsch.

Middleton, A. 1982. "Division and Cohesion in the Working Class: Artisans and Wage Laborers in Ecuador." *Journal of Latin American Studies* 14:177ff.

Miller, Kenneth E. 1968. *Government and Politics in Denmark*. Boston: Houghton Mifflin.

Ministry for Coordination. 1976. *National Accounts of Greece*. Athens: Ministry for Coordination.

Mitchell, B. R. 1980. *European Historical Statistics, 1750–1975*. New York: Facts on File.

———. 1983. *International Historical Statistics: The Americas and Australasia*. Detroit: Gale Research Company.

Moisés, José Alvaro. 1990. "La estrategia del nuevo sindicalismo." in *Sindicatos bajo regímenes militares: Argentina, Brasil, Chile*, ed. Manuel Barrera and Gonzalo Falabella, 91–131. Santiago: CES.

Moncayo, Patricio. 1982. *¿Reforma o democrácia? alternativas del sistema político ecuatoriano*. Quito, Ecuador: Editorial El Conejo.

Moore, Barrington. 1966. *The Social Origins of Dictatorship and Democracy*. Boston: Beacon Press.

Moore, Roger. 1978. *The Emergence of the Labour Party, 1880–1924*. London: Hodder and Stoughton.

———. 1978. *Injustice: The Social Bases of Obedience and Revolt*. White Plains, N.Y.: M. E. Sharpe.

Moreira Alves, Maria Helena. 1985. *State and Opposition in Military Brazil*. Austin: University of Texas Press.

———. 1989. "Trade Unions in Brazil: A Search for Autonomy and Organization." In *Labor Autonomy and the State in Latin America*, ed. Edward C. Epstein, 39–72. Boston: Unwin Hyman.

Mourre, Michel, ed. 1978. *Dictionnaire encyclopedique d'histoire*. Paris: Bordas.

Mouzelis, Nicos P. 1978. *Modern Greece: Facets of Underdevelopment*. London: Macmillan.

1985. *Politics in the Semi-Periphery: Early Parliamentarism and Late Industriali-zation in the Balkans and Latin America.* New York: St. Martin's Press.

1986. *Politics in the Semi-Periphery: Early Parliamentarism and Late Industriali-zation in the Balkans and Latin America.* London: Macmillan.

Munck, Gerardo L. 1990. "State Power and Labor Politics in the Context of Military Rule: Organized Labor, Peronism and the Armed Forces in Argentina, 1976–1983." Ph.D. dissertation, University of California, San Diego.

1993. "Explaining Variations in Transitions from Authoritarian Rule: Chile in Comparative Perspective." University of Illinois, Urbana-Champaign. Unpublished manuscript.

1998. *Soldiers and Workers in Argentina, 1976–83.* University Park: Pennsyl-vania State University Press.

Munck, Ronaldo. 1981. "The Labor Movement and the Crisis of the Dictatorship in Brazil." In *Authoritarian Capitalism: Brazil's Contemporary Economic and Political Development,* ed. Thomas C. Bruneau and Philippe Faucher, 219–38. Boulder, Colo.: Westview Press.

1987. *Argentina: From Anarchism to Peronism.* London: Zed Books.

1989. *Latin America: The Transition to Democracy.* London: Zed Books.

Mylly, Juhani, and R. Michael Berry, eds. 1984. *Political Parties in Finland: Essays in History and Politics.* Turku, Finland: University of Turku.

Nahum, Benjamín. 1977. *La época batllista, 1905–1929.* Montevideo: Ediciones de la Banda Oriental.

1995. *Manual de historia del Uruguay 1903–1990.* 2 vols. Montevideo: Edi-ciones de la Banda Oriental.

Nataf, Daniel, and Elizabeth Sammis. 1990. "Classes, Hegemony, and Portuguese Democratization." In *Transitions from Dictatorship to Democracy: Compara-tive Studies of Spain, Portugal, and Greece,* by Ronald Chilcote et al., 73–130. New York: Crane Russak.

Newton, Gerald. 1978. *The Netherlands: An Historical and Cultural Survey, 1795–1977.* London: E. Benn; Boulder, Colo.: Westview Press.

Nipperdey, Thomas. 1990. *Deutsche Geschichte, 1866–1918.* Vol. 2. Munich: C. H. Beck.

Nolan, Dieter. 1993. *Enciclopedia electoral latinoamericana y del caribe.* 2 vols. San José, Costa Rica: Instituto de Derechos Humanos.

Noronha, Eduardo G. 1992. "Greves na transição brasileira." Vols. 1 and 2. Dissertação de mestrado, University of São Paulo, Brazil.

1994. "Greves e estratégias sindicais no Brasil." In *O mundo do trabalho: Crise e mudança no final do século,* ed. Carlos Alonso de Oliveira et al., 323–57. São Paulo: Página Aberta.

North, Liisa L. 1983. "Ideological Orientations of Peru's Military Rulers." in *The Peruvian Experiment Reconsidered,* ed. Cynthia McClintock and Abraham E. Lowenthal, 245–74. Princeton: Princeton University Press.

Nousiainen, Jaakko. 1971. *The Finnish Political System.* Cambridge, Mass: Harvard University Press.

Noutsos, Panagiotis. 1990. "Greece." In Vol. 1 of *The Formation of Labour Move-ments, 1870–1914: An International Perspective,* ed. Marcel van der Linden and Jürgen Rojahn, 439–50. Leiden: E. J. Brill.

Núñez, Jorge. 1992. "La democrácia en Ecuador: Actualidad y perspectiva," In *La democrácia en América Latina: Actualidad y perspectiva*, ed. Pablo González and Marcos Roitman Rosenmann, 253–86. Madrid: Editorial Complutense.

Oakley, Stewart. 1972. *A Short History of Denmark*. New York: Praeger.

O'Brien, Philip, and Paul Cammack, eds. 1985. *Generals in Retreat*. Manchester: Manchester University Press.

O'Donnell, Guillermo. 1979. "Tensions in the Bureaucratic-Authoritarian State and the Question of Democracy." In *The New Authoritarianism in Latin America*, ed. David Collier, 285–318. Princeton: Princeton University Press.

O'Donnell, Guillermo, and Philippe C. Schmitter. 1986. *Transitions from Authoritarian Rule: Tentative Conclusions about Uncertain Democracies*. Baltimore: Johns Hopkins University Press.

Oppenheim, Lois Hecht. 1993. *Politics in Chile: Democracy, Authoritarianism, and the Search for Development*. Boulder, Colo.: Westview Press.

Ortiz Villacis, Marcelo. 1984. *El control del poder, Ecuador 1966–1984*. Quito: Gráficas San Pablo.

Paavolainen, Jaako. 1971. *Vankileirit Suomessa 1918*. Helsinki: Tammi.

Pabón, Jesös. 1941–45. *La revolución portuguesa*. 2 vols. Madrid: Espasa-Calpe.

Palmer, David Scott. 1980. *Peru: The Authoritarian Tradition*. New York: Praeger.

Paso, Leonardo. 1983. *Historia de los partidos políticos en la Argentina, 1900–1930*. Buenos Aires: Ediciones Directa.

Payne, Stanley G. 1993. *Spain's First Democracy: The Second Republic, 1931–1936*. Madison: University of Wisconsin Press.

Pease García, Henry. 1978. *Los caminos del poder: Tres años de crisis en la escena política*. Lima: DESCO.

———. 1979. *El ocaso del poder oligárquico: Lucha política en la escena oficial 1968–75*. Lima: DESCO.

Pelling, Henry. 1963. *A History of British Trade Unionism*. London: Macmillan.

Pérez-Díaz, Victor M. 1993. *The Return of Civil Society: The Emergence of Democratic Spain*. Cambridge, Mass.: Harvard University Press.

Pérez-Llorca, José. 1987. "The Beginning of the Transition Process." In *Spain in the 1980s: The Democratic Transition and a New International Role*, ed. Robert P. Clark and Michael H. Haltzel, 15–24. Cambridge, Mass.: Ballinger.

Pérez Sainz, Juan Pablo. 1985. *Clase obrera y democrácia en Ecuador*. Quito, Ecuador: Editorial el Conejo.

Pimlott, Ben, and Jean Seaton. 1983. "Political Power and the Portuguese Media." In *In Search of Modern Portugal: The Revolution and Its Consequences*, ed. Lawrence S. Graham and Douglas L. Wheeler, 43–60. Madison: University of Wisconsin Press.

Pinto, Antonio Costa. 1995. *Salazar's Dictatorship and European Fascism: Problems of Interpretation*. Boulder, Colo.: Social Science Monographs.

Pinto, Antonio Costa, and Pedro Tavares de Almeida. Forthcoming. "On Liberalism and the Emergence of Civil Society in Portugal." In *Civil Society before Democracy: Lessons from Nineteenth Century Europe*, ed. Nancy Bermeo and Philip Nord. Boulder, Colo.: Rowman and Littlefield.

Portuguese Revolution, 1974–1976. 1976. New York: Facts on File.

Pounds, N. J. G. 1990. *An Historical Geography of Europe.* Cambridge: Cambridge University Press.

Powell, David. 1992. *British Politics and the Labour Question, 1868–1990.* New York: St. Martin's Press.

Pozzi, Pablo. 1988. *Oposición obrera a la dictadura, 1976–1982.* Buenos Aires: Editorial Contrapunto.

Preston, Paul. 1978. *The Coming of the Spanish Civil War: Reform, Reaction and Revolution in the Second Republic, 1931–1936.* New York: Harper and Row.

——— 1986. *The Triumph of Democracy in Spain.* London: Methuen.

Price, Richard. 1990. "Britain." In Vol. 1 of *The Formation of Labour Movements, 1870–1914: An International Perspective,* ed. Marcel van der Linden and Jürgen Rojahn, 3–24. Leiden: E. J. Brill.

Price, Roger. 1972. *The French Second Republic: A Social History.* Ithaca, N.Y.: Cornell University Press.

——— 1975. *1848 in France.* Ithaca, N.Y.: Cornell University Press.

Przeworski, Adam, and Fernando Limongi. 1997. "Modernization: Theories and Facts." *World Politics* 49:155–83.

Przeworksi, Adam, and John Sprague. 1986. *Paper Stones: A History of Electoral Socialism.* Chicago: University of Chicago Press.

Pugh, Martin. 1978. *Electoral Reform in War and Peace, 1906–1918.* London: Routledge and Kegan Paul.

——— 1982. *The Making of Modern British Politics, 1867–1939.* New York: St. Martin's Press.

——— 1996. "The Limits of Liberalism: Liberals and Women's Suffrage, 1867–1914." In *Citizenship and Community: Liberals, Radicals and Collective Identities in the British Isles, 1865–1931,* ed. Eugenio F. Biagini, 45–65. Cambridge: Cambridge University Press.

Pulzer, Peter. 1983. "Germany." In *Democracy and Elections: Electoral Systems and Their Political Consequences,* ed. Vernon Bogdanor and David Butler, 84–109. Cambridge: Cambridge University Press.

Raby, David L. 1983. "Populism and the Portuguese Left: From Delgado to Otelo." In *In Search of Modern Portugal: The Revolution and Its Consequences,* ed. Lawrence S. Graham and Douglas L. Wheeler, 61–80. Madison: University of Wisconsin Press.

——— 1988. *Fascism and Resistance in Portugal: Communists, Liberals and Military Dissidents in the Opposition to Salazar, 1941–1974.* Manchester: Manchester Univeristy Press.

Reid, Michael. 1985. *Peru: Paths to Poverty.* London: Latin American Bureau.

Remmer, Karen. 1984. *Party Competition in Argentina and Chile: Political Recruitment and Public Policy, 1890–1930.* Lincoln: University of Nebraska Press.

——— 1989. "Neopatrimonialism: The Politics of Military Rule in Chile, 1973–1987." *Comparative Politics* 21, no. 2:149–70.

Reyes Abadie, Washington, and Andrés Vázquez Romero. n.d. *Crónica general del Uruguay: El Uruguay del siglo XX,* nos. 57, 72–74. Montevideo: Ediciones de la Banda Oriental.

Rial, Juan. 1980. *Estadísticas históricas de Uruguay 1850–1930.* Montevideo: CIESU.

1984. *Partidos políticos, democrácia y autoritarismo*. 2 vols. Montevideo: CIESU/ Ediciones de la Banda Oriental.

Ritter, Gerhard A. 1976. *Arbeiterbewegung, Parteien, und Parlamentarismus: Aufsätze zur Deutschen Sozial- und Verfassungsgeschichte des 19. und 20. jahrhunderts*. Göttingen: Vandenhöck.

Roberts, J. M., and G. A. Homes. 1976. "The Franchise Factor in the Rise of the Labour Party." *English Historical Review* 91, no. 361:723–52.

Roberts, Kenneth. 1995. "From the Barricades to the Ballot Box: Redemocratization and Political Realignment in the Chilean Left." *Politics and Society* 23 no. 4:495–519.

Robinson, R. A. H. 1979. *Contemporary Portugal: A History*. London: George Allen & Unwin.

Rock, David. 1975. *Politics in Argentina, 1890–1930: The Rise and Fall of Radicalism*. Cambridge: Cambridge University Press.

1985. *Argentina 1516–1982: From Spanish Colonization to the Falklands War*. Berkeley: University of California Press.

Rodrigues, Iram J. 1993. *Trabalhadores, sindicalismo e democracia: A CUT*. São Paulo: Tese de doutouramento, University of São Paulo.

Rokkan, Stein. 1966. "Norway: Numerical Democracy and Corporate Pluralism." in *Political Oppositions in Western Democracies*, ed. Robert A. Dahl, 70–115. New Haven: Yale University Press.

1970. *Citizens, Elections, Parties*. New York: David McKay.

1981. "The Growth and Structuring of Mass Politics." In *Nordic Democracy: Ideas, Issues, and Institutions in Politics, Economy, Education, Social and Cultural Affairs of Denmark, Finland, Iceland, Norway, and Sweden*, ed. Erik Allardt et al., 53–79. Copenhagen: Det Danske Selskab.

Rokkan, Stein, and Jean Meyriat, eds. 1969. *International Guide to Electoral Statistics*. The Hague: Mouton.

Roth, Guenter. 1963. *The Social Democrats in Imperial Germany: A Study in Working-Class Isolation and National Integration*. Totowa, N.J.: Bedminster Press.

Rueschemeyer, Dietrich, Evelyne Huber Stephens, and John D. Stephens. 1992. *Capitalist Development and Democracy*. Chicago: University of Chicago Press.

Ruíz-Tagle, Jaime. 1989. "Trade Unionism and the State under the Chilean Military Regime." In *Labor Autonomy and the State in Latin America*, ed. Edward C. Epstein, 73–100. Boston: Unwin Hyman.

Rustow, Dankwart A. 1955. *The Politics of Compromise*. Princeton: Princeton University Press.

1970. "Transitions to Democracy: Toward a Dynamic Model." *Comparative Politics* 2 no. 3:337–63.

1971. "Sweden's Transition to Democracy: Some Notes toward a Genetic Theory." *Scandinavian Political Studies*, ser. 1, 6:9–26.

Salomone, A. William. 1945. *Italy in the Giolittian Era: Italian Democracy in the Making, 1900–1914*. Philadelphia: University of Pennsylvania.

Salvemini, Gaetano. 1945. "Introductory Essay." In *Italy in the Giolittian Era: Italian Democracy in the Making, 1900–1914*, by A. William Salomane, xiii–xxii. Philadelphia: University of Pennsylvania.

Schattschneider, E. E. 1942. *Party Government*. New York: Holt, Rinehart, and Winston.

Schmitter, Philippe C. 1975. "Liberation by *Golpe*: Retrospecitve Thoughts on the Demise of Authoritarian Rule in Portugal." *Armed Forces and Society* 2, no. 1:5–33.

———. 1986. "An Introduction to Southern European Transitions from Authoritarian Rule: Italy, Greece, Portugal, Spain, and Turkey." In *Transitions from Authoritarian Rule: Southern Europe*, ed. Guillermo O'Donnell, Philippe C. Schmitter, and Laurence Whitehead, 3–10. Baltimore: Johns Hopkins University Press.

Schurmann Pacheco, Mauricio, and María Luisa Coolighan Sanguinetti. 1965. *Historia del Uruguay*. Montevideo: Palacio del Libro.

Scotland, Nigel. 1996. "The National Agricultural Labourers' Union and the Demand for a Stake in the Soil, 1872–1896." In *Citizenship and Community: Liberals, Radicals and Collective Identities in the British Isles, 1865–1931*, ed. Eugenio Biagini, 151–67. Cambridge: Cambridge University Press.

Searle, G. R. 1993. *Entrepreneurial Politics in Mid-Victorian Britain*. Oxford: Oxford University Press.

Seidman, Gay W. 1994. *Manufacturing Militance: Workers' Movements in Brazil and South Africa, 1970–1985*. Berkeley: University of California Press.

Senen González, Santiago. 1984. *Diez años de sindicalismo argentino: de Perón al Proceso*. Buenos Aires: Corregidor.

Serrão, Joel. 1982. "Du Socialisme libertaire al Anarchisme." In *Utopie et socialisme au Portugal au XIXe siecle, Actes du colloque, Paris, 10–13 janvier 1979*, 331–68. Paris: Centre Culturel Portuguais.

Seton-Watson, Christopher. 1967. *Italy from Liberalism to Fascism*. London: Methuen.

Sewell, William H., Jr. 1986. "Artisans, Factory Workers, and the Formation of the French Working Class, 1789–1848." In *Working-Class Formation. Nineteenth-Century Patterns in Western Europe and the United States*, ed. Ira Katznelson and Aristide R. Zolberg, 45–70. Princeton: Princeton University Press.

Seymour, Charles, and Donald Paige Frary. 1918. *How the World Votes: The Story of Democratic Development in Elections*. 2 vols. Springfield, Mass.: C. A. Nichols.

Shain, Yossi, and Juan J. Linz, eds. 1995. *Between States: Interim Governments and Transitions to Democracy*. Cambridge: Cambridge University Press.

Share, Donald. 1986. *The Making of Spanish Democracy*. New York: Praeger.

Share, Donald, and Scott Mainwaring. 1986. "Transitions through Transaction: Democratization in Brazil and Spain." In *Political Liberalization in Brazil: Dynamics, Dilemmas and Future Prospects*, ed. Wayne A. Selcher, 175–216. Boulder, Colo.: Westview Press.

Sheehan, James. 1978. *German Liberalism in the 19th Century*. Chicago: Chicago University Press.

———. 1989. *German History, 1770–1866*. New York: Oxford University Press.

Silva, Patricio. 1993. "Social Democracy, Neoliberalism and Ideological Change in the Chilean Socialist Movement, 1973–1992." *Nordic Journal of Latin American Studies* 23, nos. 1–2; 92–115.

Simonson, Birger. 1990. "Sweden." In Vol. 1 of *The Formation of Labour Movements, 1870–1914: An International Perspective*, ed. Marcel van der Linden and Jürgen Rojahn, 85–102. Leiden: E. J. Brill.

Skidmore, Thomas. 1988. *The Politics of Military Rule in Brazil, 1964–1985.* New York: Oxford University Press.

Smith, C. Jay, Jr. 1958. *Finland and the Russian Revolution, 1917–1922.* Athens: University of Georgia Press.

Smith, Paul. 1967. *Disraelian Conservatism and Social Reform.* London: Routledge and Kegan Paul.

Smith, Peter H. 1974. *Argentina and the Failure of Democracy: Conflict among Political Elites, 1904–1955.* Madison: University of Wisconsin Press.

——— 1978. "The Breakdown of Democracy in Argentina, 1916–1930." In *The Breakdown of Democratic Regimes: Latin America*, ed. Juan J. Linz and Alfred Stepan, 3–27 (Part 3). Baltimore: Johns Hopkins University Press.

Smith, William C. 1987. "The Political Transition in Brazil: From Authoritarian Liberalization to Democratization." In *Comparing New Democracies: Transition and Consolidation in Mediterranean Europe and the Southern Cone*, ed. Enrique A. Baloyra, 179–240. Boulder, Colo.: Westview Press.

——— 1989. *Authoritarianism and the Crisis of the Argentine Political Economy.* Stanford, Calif.: Stanford University Press.

Soikkanen, Hannu. 1984. "Revisionism, Reformism and the Finnish Labour Movement before the First World War." In *Political Parties in Finland: Essays in History and Politics*, ed. Juhani Mylly and R. Michael Berry, 121–36. Turku, Finland: University of Turku.

Soikkanen, Timo. 1984a. "Changing Bourgeois Parties in Changing Finnish Society." In *Political Parties in Finland: Essays in History and Politics*, ed. Juhani Mylly and R. Michael Berry, 58–97. Turku, Finland: University of Turku.

——— 1984b. "The Development of Political Parties: An Introduction and Overview." In *Political Parties in Finland: Essays in History and Politics*, ed. Juhani Mylly and R. Michael Berry, 28–34. Turku, Finland: University of Turku.

Steinberg, Jonathan. 1976. *Why Switzerland?* Cambridge: Cambridge University Press.

Stepan, Alfred C. 1978. *The State and Society: Peru in Comparative Perspective.* Princeton: Princeton University Press.

——— 1986. "Paths Toward Redemocratization." In *Transitions from Authoritarian Rule: Comparative Perspectives*, ed. Guillermo O'Donnell, Philippe C. Schmitter, and Laurence Whitehead, 64–84. Baltimore: Johns Hopkins University Press.

——— ed. 1989. *Democratizing Brazil: Problems of Transition and Consolidation.* New York: Oxford University Press.

Stephens, Evelyne Huber. 1980. *The Politics of Worker's Participation: The Peruvian Approach in Comparative Perspective.* New York: Academic Press.

Stoleroff, Alan. 1988. "Labor and Democratization in Portugal: Problems of the Union-Party Relationship." Paper prepared for the Conference on Labor

Movements and the Transition to Democracy, University of Notre Dame, Kellogg Institute, South Bend, Indiana.

Sulmont, Denis. 1980. *El movimiento obrero peruano (1989–1980): Reseña histórico.* Lima: Tarea.

Svensson, Palle. 1993. "The Development of Danish Polyarchy: Or How Liberalization also Preceded Inclusiveness in Denmark." In *Party Systems, Party Behavior, and Democracy*, ed., Tom Brydes, 169–89. Copenhagen: Political Studies Press.

Sztejnberg, Maurice. 1963. "La fondation du Parti Ouvrier Belge et le ralliement de la classe ouvrière à la politique." *International Review of Social History* 8:198–215.

Tanner, Duncan. 1990. *Political Change and the Labour Party, 1900–1918.* Cambridge: Cambridge University Press.

Tarrow, Sidney. 1994. *Power in Movement: Social Movements, Collective Action and Politics.* Cambridge: Cambridge University Press.

——— 1995. "Mass Mobilization and Regime Change: Pacts, Reform, and Popular Power in Italy (1918–1922) and Spain (1975–1978)." In *The Politics of Democratic Consolidation: Southern Europe in Comparative Perspective*, ed. Richard Gunther, P. Nikiforos Diamandouros, and Hans-Jürgen Puhle, 204–30. Baltimore: Johns Hopkins University Press.

Tavares de Almeida, Maria Hermínia. 1992. "Difícil caminho: Sindicatos e política na construção da democracia." in *A democracia no Brasil: Dilemas e perspectivas*, ed. F. W. Reis and Guillermo O'Donnell, 327–67. São Paulo: Vertice.

Tavares de Almeida, Pedro. 1991. *Eleições e caciquismo no Portugal oitocentista (1868–1890).* Lisbon: DIFEL.

Taylor, Philip B., Jr. 1960. *Government and Politics of Uruguay.* New Orleans: Tulane University Press.

Terjesen, Einar A. 1990. "Norway." In Vol. 1 of *The Formation of Labour Movements, 1870–1914: An International Perspective*, ed. Marcel van der Linden and Jürgen Rojahn, 103–30. Leiden: E. J. Brill.

Terlinden, Charles. 1928–30. "Historie politique interne: Formation et évolution des partis." In *Histoire de la Belgique contemporaine, 1830–1914*, 2: 7–239. Brussels: A. Dewit.

Therborn, Göran. 1977. "The Rule of Capital and the Rise of Democracy." *New Left Review* 103: 3–41.

——— 1979. "The Travail of Latin American Democracy." *New Left Review* 113–14 (January – April): 71–109.

Thomas, Neville Penry. 1956. *A History of British Politics from the Year 1900.* London: Herbert Jenkins.

Thomson, David. 1964. *Democracy in France since 1870.* London: Oxford University Press.

Thürer, Georg. 1971. *Free and Swiss.* Coral Gables, Fla.: University of Miami Press.

Tilton, Timothy. 1974. "Social Origins of Liberal Democracy: The Swedish Case." *American Political Science Review* 68, no. 2:561–71.

Tokmakoff, George. 1981. *P. A. Stolypin and the Third Duma: An Appraisal of the Three Major Issues.* Washington D.C.: University Press of America.

Tornudd, Klaus. 1968. *The Electoral System of Finland*. London: Hugh Evelyn.
Tsoucales, Constantine. 1970. *The Greek Tragedy*. Baltimore: Penguin Books.
    1981. *Social Development and the State: The Formation of the Public Sphere in Greece*. Athens: Themelio.
UN/ECLAC. 1997. *Statistical Yearbook for Latin America and the Caribbean*. Chile: UN/ECLAC.
Upton, A. F. 1973. *The Communist Parties of Scandinavia and Finland*. London: Weidendelf and Nicolson.
    1980. *The Finnish Revolution, 1917–1918*. Minneapolis: University of Minnesota Press.
Uruguay, Dirección Jeneral de Estadística. 1911. *Censo jeneral de la República en 1908*. Montevideo: Juan J. Dornleche.
Urzöa Valenzuela, Germán. 1979. *Diccionario político institucional de Chile*. Santiago: Editorial Ariete.
    1992. *Historia política de Chile y su evolución electoral*. Santiago: Editorial Jurídica de Chile.
Valenzuela, Arturo. 1977. *Political Brokers in Chile: Local Government in a Centralized Polity*. Durham, N.C.: Duke University Press.
    1983. "The Origins of Democracy: Theoretical Reflections on the Chilean Case." Working Paper no. 129. Washington, D.C.: Latin America Program, Wilson Center.
    1991. "The Military in Power: The Consolidation of One-Man Rule." In *The Struggle for Democracy in Chile, 1982–1990*, ed. Paul Drake and Ivan Jaksic, 21–72. Lincoln: University of Nebraska Press.
Valenzuela, J. Samuel. 1979. "Labor Movement Formation and Politics: Chilean and French Cases in Comparative Perspective." Ph.D. dissertation, Columbia University.
    1985. *Democratización vía reforma: La expansión del sufragio en Chile*. Buenos Aires: IDES.
    1989. "Labor Movements in Transitions to Democracy: A Framework for Analysis." *Comparative Politics* 21, no. 4:445–72.
    1992. "Democratic Consolidation in Post-Transitional Settings: Notion, Process, and Facilitating Conditions." In *Issues in Democratic Consolidation: The New South American Democracies in Comparative Perspective*, ed. Scott Mainwaring, Guillermo O'Donnell, and J. Samuel Valenzuela, 57–104. Notre Dame, Ind.: University of Notre Dame Press.
    1996. "Building Aspects of Democracy before Democracy: Electoral Practices in Nineteenth Century Chile." In *Elections before Democracy: The History of Elections in Europe and Latin America*, ed. Eduardo Posada-Carbó, 223–58. New York: St. Martin's Press.
Vanger, Milton I. 1980. *The Model Country: José Batlle y Ordóñez of Uruguay, 1907–1915*. Hanover, N.H.: University Press of New England.
Varela Ortega, José. 1997. "De los orígenes de la democracia en España, 1845–1923." In *Democracia, elecciones y modernización en Europa*, ed. Salvador Forner, 129–202. Madrid: Ediciones Cátedra.
Vergara, Pilar. 1985. *Auge y caída del neoliberalismo en Chile*. Santiago de Chile: FLACSO.

Verney, Douglas. 1957. *Parliamentary Reform in Sweden, 1866–1921*. Oxford: Clarendon Press.

Villarreal, Juan. 1987. "Changes in Argentine Society: The Heritage of the Dictatorship." In *From Military Rule to Liberal Democracy in Argentina*, ed. Monica Peralta-Ramos and Carlos Waisman, 69–96. Boulder, Colo.: Westview Press.

Webster, R. A. 1975. *Industrial Imperialism in Italy, 1908–1915*. Berkeley: University of California Press.

Wehler, Hans-Ulrich. 1985. *The German Empire, 1871–1918*. Trans. Kim Traynor. Dover, N.H.: Berg Publishers.

Wellhofer, E. Spencer. 1996. *Democracy, Capitalism and Empire in Late Victorian Britain, 1885–1910*. New York: St. Martin's Press.

Wheeler, Douglas L. 1978. *Republican Portugal: A Political History, 1910–1926*. Madison: University of Wisconsin Press.

Whitehead, Laurence. 1986. "Bolivia's Failed Democratization, 1977–1980." In *Transitions from Authoritarian Rule: Latin America*, ed. Guillermo O'Donnell, Philippe C. Schmitter, and Laurence Whitehead, 49–71. Baltimore: Johns Hopkins University Press.

Wilhelm, Mommsen. 1952. *Deutsche Parteiprogramme: Eine Auswahl vom Vormaerz bis zur Gegenwart*. Munich: Isar Verlag.

Windmuller, John P. 1969. *Labor Relations in the Netherlands*. Ithaca, N.Y.: Cornell University Press.

Witney, Fred. 1965. *Labor Policy and Practices in Spain: A Study of Employer-Employee Relations under the Franco Regime*. New York: Frederick A. Praeger.

Woodhouse, C. M. 1968. *The Story of Modern Greece*. London: Faber.

1985. *The Rise and Fall of the Greek Colonels*. London: Granada Press.

1986. *Modern Greece: A Short History*. London: Faber & Faber.

World Bank. 1983. *World Tables*. Vol. 2. Baltimore: Johns Hopkins University Press.

Wright, D. G. 1970. *Democracy and Reform: 1815–1885*. London: Longman.

Wright, Gordon. 1995. *France in Modern Times*. 5th ed. New York: Norton.

Young, Kenneth. 1969. *The Greek Passion*. London: J. M. Dent & Sons.

Zolberg, Aristide R. 1978. "Belgium." In *Crises of Political Development in Europe and the United States*, ed. Raymond Grew, 99–138. Princeton: Princeton University Press.

Zubillaga, Carlos. 1985. "El Batllismo: Una Experiencia Populista." In *El primer batllismo*, 11–45. Montevideo: Ediciones de la Banda Oriental.

INDEX

Abós, Alvaro, 122, 125
actors: in demonstrations, 166–71; in dimensions and patterns of democratization, 19–22, 166–71; elites, 17–19; working class, 15–17
ADAV, Germany, 103
Adler, Glenn, 186
Alapuro, Risto, 86, 87, 88
Aminzade, Ronald, 41, 42, 43
anarchosyndicalism, 35; Argentina, 45; Italy, 69; Portugal, 49; Spain, 51–54; Uruguay, 75
Andreucci, Franco, 69
Angell, Alan, 152, 153
antecedent regime, 12–14, 18, 22, 53, 170, 171, 173, 175–77, 179, 180–81, 183–84, 190–91
Anti-Revolutionary Party, Netherlands, 94–96
ANWV, Netherlands, 94
APRA, Peru, 115, 118–19
arenas of action, 19–22, 166, 168–69f, 170, 195–96; Electoral Mobilization pattern, 171; Joint Projects pattern, 77, 108, 171, 183–84; Middle-Sector Democratization pattern, 36, 75, 171; recent democratization, 110, 177, 183–84
Argentina: CNT, 122; constitutions, 44, 125; CUTA, 122; democratization in nineteenth century, 44–46; Destabilization/Extrication pattern (1970s–1980s), 113t, 114, 119–26, 170, 182–

83; elites, 46; General Labor Confederation (CGT), 123–25; labor movement, 45–46, 114–15, 120–26, 179; Malvinas invasion, 119, 120, 124–25; Middle-Sector pattern in early twentieth century, 28t, 34–35, 35t, 44–46, 73, 75, 178t; Multipartidaria, 126; political strike, 121, 124; Radical Civic Union, 45, 75; suffrage, 44; working class, 35, 45–46
Armed Forces Movement (MFA), Portugal, 161, 163–64
Arriagada Herrera, Genaro, 151
Arter, David, 85
Augustinos, G., 40

Baloyra, Enrique A., 162
Banner Suárez, Hugo (Bolivia), 144–45
Barrán José, 74
Barrera, Manuel, 151, 152, 153, 154
Batlle y Ordóñez, José (Uruguay), 73–74
Belgium: Catholic Party, 89–92; Joint Projects pattern in nineteenth and twentieth centuries, 35t, 78–80, 89–93; Liberal Party, 90–92; parliamentary sovereignty, 89; political strike, 90; Progressive Liberal Party, 91–92; Socialist Labor Party, 89; suffrage, 90–91; working class, 77–78, 89–90, 92
Ben-Ami, Shlomo, 54
Bendix, Reinhard, 4
Bermeo, Nancy, 183
Bertelsen Repetto, Paul, 52